The Novels of
CLAUDE SIMON

The Novels of
CLAUDE SIMON

by J. A. E. LOUBÈRE

Cornell University Press | ITHACA AND LONDON

To my familiar spirits
Leo, Paul-Louis, and Philip

Contents

Acknowledgments

Grateful acknowledgment is made to the following: Claude Simon and his wife, Réa Axelos, for the information and insight they have so generously provided; Thomas E. Connolly, Department of English, State University of New York at Buffalo, for his willing helpfulness; Eleanor Kleinschmidt of the Western New York Library Resources Council and Miriam Goldeen for their constant aid and encouragement; members of the editorial staff of Cornell University Press for their patient assistance; the editors of *Entretiens* and the Editions Subervie, Rodez, France; the libraries at Cornell University and at the State University of New York at Buffalo; J. H. Matthews, Department of Romance Languages, Syracuse University, and Syracuse University Press, for permission to publish the chapter on *Le Palace* which originally appeared in similar form in *Symposium,* XXVII (Spring 1973), under the title "Claude Simon's *Le Palace:* A Paradigm of Otherness."

J. A. E. Loubère

Buffalo, New York

The Novels of
CLAUDE SIMON

Introduction

At the beginning of the twentieth century critics were already prepared to address disturbing questions to the novelist. After two hundred years of prolific and outstanding production, was the novel as a genre played out? Could the novelist still justify his activity and foresee a future for it that was not based on needless repetition? These questions have since been earnestly debated at length, but nowhere more than in France, where the custom of publishing literary manifestos and *enquêtes* (questionnaires answered by authors) serves to keep the subject before the public.[1] And the answer has come with the most positive assurance from France, where a segment of the generation of novelists that appeared after World War II—the generation to which the writer we are about to study belongs—has clearly demonstrated its conviction that the novel is as rich in possibilities, as prodigal of surprises as ever before.

How do we recognize a literary generation? In her penetrating *Histoire du roman français depuis 1918* Claude-Edmonde Magny[2] suggests that a generation should be defined as a

---

1. See, for example, *Problèmes du roman,* ed. Jean Prevost (Lyon, Confluences, 1943), or the questionnaires noted in P. Astier, *Encyclopédie du Nouveau Roman* (Paris, Debresse, 1969), and the large number of interviews in periodicals such as *Les Nouvelles littéraires, L'Express, Les Lettres françaises, La Revue de Paris, Le Figaro littéraire.*
2. Paris, Editions du Seuil, 1950.

group of writers sharing essentially the same patrimony and the same attitudes toward their art (though not necessarily the same birthdate or social background), whose activity covers a period of approximately thirty-three years. Since, in her view, a new century takes about fifteen years to get started, the first generation of twentieth-century writers dates from the beginning of the First World War and ends after the Second, roughly around 1940, when Magny's study is interrupted. At that time a new generation, as distinct from a transitional group, was due to appear. If we accept this convenient definition, we may add that it is no accident that world events so neatly punctuate these divisions. In France, a postwar euphoria pervaded the novel until the thirties; a boding sense of disaster crept in before the forties and the world that was beginning to put itself together again after 1945 was to put together a new approach to fiction as well. Then, in fact, the literary generation with which we are now concerned began to manifest itself in a series of conflicts that sharply separated the writers who preferred continuity and traditional values from those who thought that the time had come for renewal.

Magny severely criticizes the post World War I writers, in spite of their abundant production and the often brilliant roster of names—Radiguet, Chardonne, Martin du Gard, Romains, Mauriac, Giraudoux—for their attachment to formulas and structures inherited from the nineteenth century and for their inability to discover a new form to match the outlook and events of a different time. She could not yet know, since her study was published in 1950, that this very criticism was to be the basis for the revolt of the second generation (many of whom were her faithful readers), nor could she see that the glimmerings of unorthodoxy and rejection that she discerns were suddenly, in the space of a few years, to burst into vigorous flame. A transitional group, which included the existentialist writers, novelists "committed" to humanist causes, and later writers influenced by surrealist trends, was less concerned with renewing novelistic form than with transmitting a changed vision of mankind. The idea that such a change might also entail a complete revision of the means of transmission made headway only very slowly before 1950. Despite the experiments of eccentric and little-known writers like Raymond Roussel,[3] novelists were lagging seriously behind poets, painters, and adepts of a new art, the cinema, in technical innovation.

The revolt—if it may be called that, for the old order was by no means upset—or rather the "turning-away" took place, as it so often does, in the name of realism. Alain Robbe-Grillet, one of the leading practitioners of what has come to be known as the "New Novel"[4] remarks: "Realism is the ideology which each one of us brandishes in the face of his neighbor."[5] The tenets of realism in other words, are as variable as those who hold them. The mighty novel of the nineteenth century seems to confirm a happy moment of equilibrium between the theories concerning the outside world and the sense perceptions through which man constructs these theories. In a novel by Balzac or Dickens the outer shell of reality—a house, a body, a piece of clothing—faithfully represents an inner truth. But the pact between sense, thought, and matter was of

3. Raymond Roussel (1877–1933) produced strange works in which he experimented with the auditory and visual characteristics of language. He was admired by the Surrealists. His best-known work, *Impressions d'Afrique* (1910), has been translated by Lindy Foord and Rayner Heppenstall as *Impressions of Africa* (Berkeley, University of California Press, 1967). His *Oeuvres complètes* were published in Paris by J.-J. Pauvert in 1964.

4. Richard Howard, in the preface to his translation of Michel Butor's *Inventory*, explains that this term was first used by Henry James.

5. "From Realism to Reality," in *For a New Novel*, trans. Richard Howard (New York, Grove Press, 1965), p. 157.

very short duration. The equilibrium was at best precarious, and the drive toward further discovery that intensified throughout the century made this equilibrium impossible to maintain. Still the hope of seizing, codifying, and eventually knowing the real world was not abandoned.

As the twentieth century progressed, reality became less and less manageable. It is a commonplace to say that our increasing scientific knowledge and power have made the "real" world steadily more incomprehensible to the lay mind. Technical, political, and economic upheavals have changed our outlook to such an extent that not the world that we see, nor the way we see it, nor the language in which we describe our experience within it has remained what it was at the beginning of the century.

Writers belonging to the new group of realists that appeared in the 1950s were heirs to decades of constant disorder and turbulence and were aware that a kind of subterranean shifting was moving all the old landmarks from their foundations. They asserted, loudly and clearly, that conventions designed for rendering reality as conceived by positive materialism, simple sensationalist and mechanistic philosophies, were no longer valid. The well-structured novel with its plot, subplots, realistic dialogue, refined character study, setting, and descriptions was not destined to produce an "objective" study of the outer and inner worlds of man, but rather a formalistic deformation of them. The three best-known and most combative of these authors, Nathalie Sarraute, Alain Robbe-Grillet, and Michel Butor, put forward this thesis with considerable *brio* in the fifties, in a number of essays that first appeared separately and afterward were collected in volumes that have become classics. In her aptly named "Ere du soupçon," published in *Les Temps modernes* in 1950, Sarraute attacks traditional procedures: "The sense of life to which, in the long run, all art harks back . . . has deserted these erstwhile promising forms and betaken itself elsewhere. By virtue of the ceaseless movement which tends to bring it ever nearer to the mobile point where, at a given moment, experiment and the peak of effort meet, it has broken through the earlier novel form and forsaken, one by one, all the old, useless accessories."[6]

In 1956, Robbe-Grillet, offering "Une Voie pour le roman futur" (a title which, like Sarraute's, was later absorbed in a collection of essays on the novel), points out that the old tired conventions now stand between the reader and the world, causing him to interpret what he sees according to prearranged patterns of meaning (or lack of meaning), instead of revealing present reality:

But the world is neither significant nor absurd. It *is*, quite simply. That, in any case, is the most remarkable thing about it. And suddenly the obviousness of this strikes us with irresistible force. All at once, the whole splendid construction collapses; opening our eyes unexpectedly, we have experienced, once too often, the shock of this stubborn reality we were pretending to have mastered. Around us, defying the noisy pack of our animistic or protective adjectives, things *are there*. Their surfaces are distinct and smooth, *intact*, neither suspiciously brilliant nor transparent. All our literature has not yet succeeded in eroding their smallest corner, in flattening their slightest curve.[7]

If we could escape formalist literature with its meanings and its symbols, we should begin to see reality with the pure, unbiased eye of the movie camera, which registers objects as they are.

Butor, in an important essay from *Répertoire,* entitled "Le Roman comme recherche" and written in 1955, states the argument concisely:

6. *The Age of Suspicion,* trans. Maria Jolas (New York, George Braziller, 1963), p. 60.
7. Robbe-Grillet, p. 19.

Different forms of narrative correspond to different realities. Now, it is clear that the world in which we live is being transformed with great rapidity. Traditional narrative techniques are incapable of integrating all the new relations thus created. There results a perpetual uneasiness; it is impossible for our consciousness to organize all the information which assails it, because it lacks adequate tools.

The search for new novelistic forms with a greater power of integration thus plays a triple role in relation to our consciousness of reality: unmasking, exploration, and adaptation. The novelist who refuses to accept this task, never discarding old habits, never demanding any particular effort of his reader, never obliging him to confront himself, to question attitudes long since taken for granted, will certainly enjoy a readier success, but he becomes the accomplice of that profound uneasiness, that darkness, in which we are groping for our way. He stiffens the reflexes of our consciousness even more, making any awakening more difficult; he contributes to its suffocation, so that even if his intentions are generous, his work is in the last analysis a poison.

Formal invention in the novel, far from being opposed to realism as shortsighted critics often assume, is the *sine qua non* of a greater realism.[8]

In search of greater realism, the founders of the New Novel, as it quickly came to be known, agreed on this general point: techniques must be developed to reveal present reality, cure the reader of his idle habits, and force him to view the world as it is, now.

Preceding generations had certainly been aware of the nature of twentieth-century changes. During the menacing thirties and the disastrous forties, as Magny says, "the *reality* of the moment they are living is such that it will force writers, each in turn and according to his own style, to take a stand with respect to it, to refuse it or to accept it, to wager on the dead past or the unknown future. . . . The question is

8. *Inventory*, trans. Richard Howard (New York, Simon & Schuster, 1968), p. 28.

whether literature will help man to live within truth, either critically, by attacking former ideas of what is good, or constructively, by becoming conscious of what this new truth in its bond with the world, and of what man may be."[9] However, the writers of that time generally saw the changes in terms of political beliefs or of philosophy to be propagated or combated *through* literature, a literature in itself essentially unchanged, respecting traditional norms of exposition and argument. The "roman engagé" and the existentialist novel in France, even when dealing with the disturbed and often desperate condition of man, made merely superficial attempts to reproduce that disturbance in the modes of writing. This is why Sarraute criticizes Camus for pretending, in *L'Etranger,* to dispense with the old, well-known psychological resources, when in reality the effect of the book depends largely on the emotion aroused in the reader. Robbe-Grillet condemns him even more severely for introducing the old pathetic fallacy into the landscape with every adjective he uses, instead of maintaining a true "innocence" in his relationship with the world. Sartre also, says Robbe-Grillet, has a "strictly visceral" outlook and propagates in *La Nausée* the "humanist affirmation" by infusing some essence of the human into the objects that fascinate him so much. The reality communicated by the novels of this period, which deal with metaphysical and social problems, depends for expression on traditional patterns of logic and language, with little change in rhetoric, even when the maximum effort is made to introduce strangeness into matter and organization. Meursault and Roquentin are still subject to laws of causality, progression, and syntax, and their discourse is expository and sequential. These philosophical novels assume that man's vision of the world, however tragic

9. Magny, p. 57. My translation.

or absurd either may be, can still be formulated in traditional terms. No faltering in that vision passes into the writing itself.

It is true that a number of writers had hoped to revolutionize man's modes of being in such a way as to "transform the world" and "change life" as commanded by Marx and Rimbaud. The history of the Surrealist movement is well known. Claiming to change man's vision of the world through as many unorthodox methods as can be imagined (dreams, madness, drugs, *spiritisme,* chance, games, psychic disorders), the Surrealists sought unexplored ways of expression (automatic writing, collage, psychoanalysis, cinema), to communicate the discovery of "super-reality"; that is, they sought to redefine reality as including all possible actual and potential states of being. Although for a period they were allied to the Communist Party, their explorations were unwelcome to orthodox political revolutionaries who had no taste for the unusual. The Surrealists were a highly unstable group; under the stormy leadership of André Breton it numbered among its members, at different times, such celebrities as Eluard, Aragon, Dali, Buñuel, Artaud, and others whose attitude toward established art forms was iconoclastic. Their new methods of recording experience were introduced with less public furor into the novel than into painting, the plastic arts, and the cinema, where they were of primordial importance and were to exercise, through visual effect, a new influence upon writing. The mark they left was deep, and even if the Surrealists did not change the world, according to Marx's dictum, they contributed largely to transforming our contemporary approach to it.

The Surrealists believed that language is one of the ways in which super-reality can be brought to us. Super-reality, however, interested the new realists less than the reassessment of what occurs at the juncture of language as writing and reality in any form. They preferred, therefore, to distinguish as their models and predecessors those authors whose genius had illuminated this particular relationship. Thus they were able to include in their ascendancy Flaubert, who (Sartre notwithstanding) demonstrates the attempts of consciousness to transform into a new object—the book[10]—the worlds of myth and matter that impinge upon it. They also include Dostoievsky, who, taking the opposite approach to Flaubert's, brings into the light indistinct states of awareness in constant flux, an "incessant swirl, similar to the movement of atoms,"[11] which swells and overflows into the outer world, creating its own indisputable reality.

These two divergent trends meet in the art of Proust, who proclaims in *Le Temps Retrouvé:* "The grandeur of real art . . . is to rediscover, grasp again and lay before us that reality from which we have become more and more separated as the formal knowledge which we substitute for it grows in thickness and imperviousness—that reality which there is grave danger we might die without ever having known and yet which is simply our life, life as it really is, life disclosed at last and made clear."[12] Proust, however great a monument he may have become, is, we realize, a figure to whom all twentieth-century innovators must pay homage as they humbly rediscover his experience, his patient investigation of subjective time, memory, and the metamorphoses of consciousness stimulated by various forms of desire, his delicate understanding of the reciprocal action of one form of sensitivity on another, his modulations of points of view, his molding of lan-

10. See, for example, Jean Ricardou, "DE NATURA ficTIONis," in *Pour une théorie du Nouveau Roman* (Paris, Editions du Seuil, 1971), pp. 33–38.

11. Sarraute, p. 30.

12. *The Past Recaptured,* trans. Frederick A. Blossom (New York, Random House, 1934), p. 224.

guage to follow the sinuous line of thought, his revelation of the productive power of language itself.

In a wasteland that is almost the negative of Proust's world lies that of Kafka. (Jean Carrive, one of Kafka's Surrealist translators, insists on the importance of forgetting in Kafka, as opposed to remembering in Proust.)[13] Kafka, like Proust, interrogates the baffling signs that surround him, and his use of the questioning that provides no answers, and of the search that by its very nature destroys or modifies its own purpose, has influenced the techniques of many New Novelists. Whatever the debate may be concerning the metaphysics of Kafka's work, the place he occupies between the obvious, everyday world and the hinterlands of metamorphosis is one to be increasingly explored.

Here, it is important to consider the contribution of someone who was neither novelist nor philosopher, but who has been recognized by Magny, Ricardou, and others as being one of the prompters of the revolution in the novel. Paul Valéry first published *La Soirée avec Monsieur Teste* in 1896, but it became better known after its republication by Gallimard in 1919, and through its subsequent amplifications. This short text was Valéry's first and last attempt at a "novel"—"the life of a theory," he calls it in his correspondence with Gide. While composing it, he learned many things, among others the difficulty of inventing for his hero a "psychology," simulated speech, action, and so became convinced of the gratuitousness of the anecdote and the arbitrariness of all description. As the first drafts of *Monsieur Teste* show,[14] Valéry came to these conclusions through experimentation. Having reached

13. Preface, *Les Recherches d'un chien* (Lyon, *L'Arbalète*, 10, 1945).

14. See Jean Levaillant, "Genèse et signification de *La Soirée avec Monsieur Teste*," Thèse complémentaire de lettres, Université de Paris, 1966.

them, he produced the extraordinary personage who was to have been (but is not quite) all anonymous intelligence, a personage stripped of personality, appearance, and history, but possessing a *"moi,"* the remaining element when all idiosyncrasies, all variations in life, all features subject to change have been eliminated—a kernel of pure intellect, which observes and judges its own activity in a language strictly adapted to its own needs.

This novel of essences was of necessity extremely brief and unrepeatable, even though Valéry throughout his life was constantly drawn back to his hero by the desire to communicate the incommunicable, like the solitary hermit in *Mon Faust*. From this strange experiment, he retained the conviction that the "reality" of the traditional novel was both thin and fraudulent, at the mercy of any whim of the skeptical reader. In one well-known passage he remarks that when reading a novel he cannot prevent himself from replacing the printed sentences by others that would serve the author's purposes just as well as those in the original text.[15]

Paradoxically, Valéry's skepticism concerning the undefined and open fictional form, compared with the closed and perfected poetic form, and his refusal to believe in the creatures "without entrails" who perform actions dependent on an arbitrary causality invented by their creator, had the effect of challenging some novelists eager to create prose structures as lasting as poetry and as inexhaustible as the scene that Valéry himself discovered unfolding before the intellect. Besides being the negative novelist, the skeptical commentator, and the poet, Valéry was also the patient, scrupulous annotator of the unending spectacle of the inner world of the mind. The observations of a lifetime, carefully recorded in the famous *Ca-*

15. See *Oeuvres complètes* (Paris, Bibliothèque de la Pléiade, 1957), I, 1468.

hiers, made Valéry the great familiar of that inward variable scene, from which he tried to deduce invariable rules of mental functioning. He did not succeed, but the observations are of incomparable value.

Valéry retained a nineteenth-century faith in the practical efficacy of science and in the possibility of an intellectual domination of the Self. His investigations, however, led him to recognize the distance between perception and effective knowledge, and between both of these and the density of the real world. Reality was, for him, something that could always disconcert our predictions.[16] It did not occur to him, however, that these very distances and miscalculations could be the foundation of a narrative as fascinating as any account of human social behavior, even though he himself, in *La Soirée,* had made the beginning of such a narrative. His acid criticism and his intransigent research provided a stimulus for those determined to present phenomena in a new form.

Credit should also be given to Valéry's friend and correspondent André Gide, who helped to focus attention on form in the novel. Stimulated, no doubt, by their early exchanges, Gide restlessly investigated the relationship of the writer with the practice of writing, with the work created, and with the reader. He experimented with various kinds of freedom in the text, now attempting to bestow autonomy on his characters, now using them as pawns in his argument, now intervening in the action in his own name or as commentator or double. He discovered, particularly through the form of the *sotie* (in which his creatures often discuss at length their own significance or indulge in gratuitous activities which he pretends to admire as though they were not part of himself), the vital importance of "point of view" (which Henry James and Vir-

16. *Oeuvres complètes,* II (1960), 734.

ginia Woolf had revealed in other ways to English readers).
The angle and distance from which attention is directed to
the scenes described and the identification of the director become the central matter of *Les Faux-Monnayeurs* and its accompanying *Journal*. Here, one of the fictional characters in
the novel, a writer, comments on the progress of his own work,
discusses the characters he is inventing, and observes to what
extent they apparently take on an autonomous existence and
become opaque to him. On the other hand, the writer is aware
that the real anecdote embedded in his narrative becomes
transformed as the plot develops almost without his intervention.

Gide, the real author, looks on at these pirouettes and occasionally comments in his turn on his own fiction, thus creating
the famous *mise en abyme,* or reproduction within the text of
the whole novel's larger theme. As he says in the *Journal des
Faux-Monnayeurs,* we must recognize "on one side, the event,
the fact, the external datum; on the other side, the very effort
of the novelist to make a book out of it all. The latter is the
main subject, the new focus that throws the plot off center
and leads it toward the imaginative."[17] Through this technique he adds to the novel (as Butor says elsewhere, speaking
of Faulkner) two new real characters who can no longer be
ignored: the author and the reader, who is constantly being
called on to observe and evaluate the author's decisions. While
these characters may be added, as Gide declares, *"pour la
majeure irritation du lecteur,"* they contribute to the reader's
maximum awareness that the novel may no longer be a simulated "slice of life," for which the author mysteriously claims
all the credit and none of the responsibility.

The greatest stimulus for research into new techniques has

17. *Journal of "The Counterfeiters,"* trans. Justin O'Brien (New
York, Alfred A. Knopf, 1952), p. 392.

come from two English-language writers: Joyce the Irishman and Faulkner the American. Of the enormous contribution of Joyce one cannot speak adequately in a restricted space; rather his work should be considered as a vast treasury into which, at various times and places, lesser writers dip and emerge enriched. But the better-known innovations can be briefly recalled. Joyce had been made known to the French not only by the scandal with which the Anglo-American world surrounded his name, but more seriously by a host of translators, among them Valéry Larbaud, Auguste Morel, and Ludmila Savitsky, not to mention such Surrealist associates as Ivan Goll, Philippe Soupault, and Samuel Beckett. Joyce rapidly became famous, even to those who never read his work, for the use (if not the invention) of the "stream-of-consciousness," which reveals the frequencies and rhythms of the thoughts and images passing incessantly through the mind, creating a "grammar of consciousness" that gradually and implacably defines the monologuist.

No less well known are the games that Joyce plays with language, explosively mixing native with foreign, ancient with modern, common with erudite, vulgar with precious. Section VII of *Ulysses*, the Eolus passage, contains, we are told, as many as ninety-six figures of speech; Section XI, the Sirens, is a fugue, *per canonem;* Section XIV, the Oxen of the Sun, is a panorama of the English language from Anglo-Saxon to American slang.[18] It is as though a vital, tremendous freedom had been suddenly conferred upon all the syllables ever invented by man, to mate and mix in strangely fertile combinations. Yet—and this third point is even more impressive to serious students of Joyce—neither the apparently ungoverned flowing of consciousness nor the wild dance of the syllables

18. *Ulysses* (New York, Random House, 1961), pp. 116–150, 256–291, 383–428.

leads to chaos. Instead, a cosmic structure is held together by an infinite number of intricate internal links of sound and sense, in which myth and reality, the instant and the eternal, the commonplace and the ideal are tightly bound by every possible technique of composition.

In *Finnegans Wake,* at least four levels of interpretation are possible, the legendary, the actual, the prophetic, and the symbolic, not to mention the purely linguistic. All are inexhaustible. What most impresses writers in search of a new, indestructible form for the novel is the fact that Joyce cannot be simply read. He must be constantly reread and can never be "finished," dispensed with. This point is made by Butor in two lucid essays on Joyce, "Petite croisière préliminaire à une reconnaissance de l'Archipel Joyce" and "Esquisse d'un seuil pour Finnegan": "It is part of the very essence of this work that it can only be read and understood gradually. It has a chaotic appearance, and each of us may enter into its organization in his own way. In such and such a passage, it is not necessarily the same literal meaning which each of us perceives at first. . . . Its dimensions and difficulties are such that it is impossible ever to exhaust it in detail."[19]

Into this work of unparalleled richness, a work displaying an architectural complexity that even Valéry could not undo, Joyce introduces legends and myths from all times and places, mingled with the most common forms of daily life. His excursions into verbal fantasia surpass any dreamed of even by that prescient eccentric, Raymond Roussel. His virtuosity molds language as if its relationship with rational thought were but one of the multitudinous bonds linking it to reality. Joyce's accomplishment has been a constant lesson and temptation to later writers.

19. *Répertoire,* I (Paris, Editions de Minuit, 1960), 210. My translation.

His impact is reinforced by that of Faulkner. The first translations of *Sanctuary* (1933), *As I Lay Dying* (1934), and *Light in August* (1935) aroused attention chiefly through the remarkable prefaces by Larbaud and Malraux. A study by Maurice Le Breton in *Etudes anglaises* (1937) emphasized the links between time and psychology in Faulkner's work, the insistence on sequences of contrasted images, the suppression of commentary and transition, the substitution of suggestion for direct expression. *Sartoris,* translated in 1937, drew Sartre's fire for its use of gesture and action to conceal instead of to reveal human truth. But it is indisputably *The Sound and the Fury,* translated in 1938, that left a lasting impression on the French literary world. Less inclined than the American reader to be distracted by the Southern legend, less able, despite the admirable efforts of translators, to appreciate the remarkable tonality of the language, French readers were immediately sensitive to the structural peculiarities of the work and to the apparent puzzle it represented for the reader to decipher. While disapproving the metaphysical implications of the novel, Sartre clearly defined those features which make it so disturbing: the narrative devices through which time oscillates, never really advancing but turning back upon itself and congealing into an eternal past-in-present, the ambiguity of the actors, the strangely modern sense of detachment and dislocation which Sartre recognizes when he compares Faulkner's vision of the world to a static landscape perceived by a man speeding along, looking backwards from the seat of an open car. Faulkner's monologues, Sartre suggests, are like airplane trips punctuated by plunges into airpockets, each time that consciousness drops into the past.[20]

Other writers were to be impressed not only with the role

20. *Situations,* I (Paris, Gallimard, 1947), 73–74.

of subjective time and the monologue in *The Sound and the Fury*, but by various techniques that reinforce the hallucinatory effect of a static, nonchronological past continually invading and corrupting the present: the descriptions of consciousness obsessed with an ever-repeating series of images; the fragmentary, obscure dialogues, embedded in the prevailing monologue, emerging at the call of sense or sound; the return of certain symbols, such as the honeysuckle, the bones in the ditch, the flowing water, the meaningless striking of clocks; intentional confusion in the naming of characters; the doubling or "folding over" of certain events, such as Quentin's two fights with Dalton Ames and with Bland; the general refusal to explain, thrusting on the reader himself the role of the idiot who sees but only imperfectly comprehends. The reader is with the Faulknerian character, feels with him, gets under his skin, but is never invited to understand him. He is conscious of him without knowing him.

Faulkner's techniques for transcribing the restructured reality of his world have been of primary importance in the evolution of the novel. In attempting to record the flickering, memory-haunted nature of perception, he complemented Joyce's all-embracing awareness with a reminder of the obscurity, the sensual and intellectual confusion that also fills our lives. Both writers attacked so boldly the conventional forms of the narrative and the very foundations of language that after them the novelist could no longer, in good faith, remain secure in the stronghold of tradition.

Revolutionary techniques of writing were confirmed and illustrated by similar developments in the cinema. We noted earlier that Robbe-Grillet thought the camera's unbiased eye might record reality more faithfully than the human one. Those, like him, who chose to catalogue in infinite detail the visible world, as though from the far side of an apparently impersonal lens, were generally grouped as the *école du regard*, believers in the purifying power of sight. However debatable this categorization may be, it is certain that procedures such as crosscutting, flashbacks, inserts, close-ups, panning, and montage correspond so well to the literary effects obtained by memory sequences, parallel constructions, sudden jumps in time, dreams, and minutely detailed descriptions, that it is not surprising to find the writer becoming a movie-maker (the most famous case is Robbe-Grillet, whose first film, *L'Année dernière à Marienbad*, was produced with Alain Resnais in 1961). Or, more frequently, the movie camera has invaded the novel, either indirectly in the "filming" of various scenes, or even directly as a visible participator in the action.

If we accept Magny's specification of a literary generation as one which reacts in a definable fashion, at a given moment, to certain more-or-less-known factors, then we can say that the New Novelists are those who, in varying degrees, respond to the lesson of these predecessors and contemporaries, and attempt to go beyond them in their own writings. The group is close-knit, not because of age or individual origin, but because of the nature of French intellectual life. This life is centered in Paris on publishing houses and periodicals that carry out exhaustive inquiries into the activities of "their" writers and on the institutions of learning that encourage workshops, meetings, and symposiums, or *décades,* called to study progress in all levels of research. Many members of the group have come to be labeled the "midnight" writers, because their work is published by one house, Les Editions de Minuit. Many have come to be connected with periodicals such as *Tel Quel* or *Critique,* where such critical theorists as Ricardou and the celebrated Roland Barthes comment on their work. This close association with learning and publishing also favors the spread and utilization of ideas put forward by original thinkers and critics, disciples of Husserl and Heidegger, for example, and others famous in special fields, such as Claude Lévi-Strauss in anthropology, Michel Foucault in epistemology, Jacques Lacan in psychology, Jacques Derrida in "grammatology," all of whom have colored the writings of the new realists in one way or another.

All members of the group agree, theoretically, that the results of their efforts should be shared and freely discussed; for example, in the famous meetings at Cerisy-la-Salle, writers defend and attack, not without acrimony, each other's views. Their general intent was summarized in 1961 by Robbe-Grillet in an essay "Nouveau Roman, homme nouveau" (included in *Pour un Nouveau Roman*). The New Novel, he assures us, (1) is not a theory, but an act of research, (2) continues the constant evolution of the novelistic genre, (3) has as its main interest man and his situation in the world, (4) has as its only aim total subjectivity, (5) addresses itself to all sincere readers, (6) does not propose any ready-made meaning, (7) is based on the belief that the only possible commitment for the writer is literature.

This last point is the most important of all, for it turns attention to the text itself. No longer subordinate to other ends, to be fashioned into argument or ornament, the recital of the emergence of consciousness from existence *is* the novel, at the same time that it *is* reality. Narration is not the art of a writer who selects and organizes words like separate, maneuverable objects according to a preconceived plan in order to represent an autonomous universe. It is the voice of things as experienced; it recreates consciousness and forges between the word and the experience a unique and unrepeatable bond. By recording this voice, these authors hope to capture the new reality, a reality of confusion, illusion, faulty perception, and imperfect memory, in a continuum free from the rationalist concepts of space, time, cause, and effect. Here, the illogical structures are perfectly feasible, and opposites meet and merge, such encounters being inherent in language.

Yet their work is no flight into Surrealism, art-for-art's sake, or unleashed fantasy. Theirs is a mental world closely dependent on outside phenomena and continually nourished by them, a mental world increasingly studied not only by psychologists, but also by philosophers and linguists. Those who follow most conscientiously the phenomenological definition set forth by Merleau-Ponty, uniting "extreme subjectivism and extreme objectivism in one idea of the world,"[21] do not offer any "solution" for the universe. There are no explanations. These authors merely note what is, in that strange domain of representation that is constantly forming and re-forming itself.

The writers who attempt to incorporate existential fluidity into their art do so, of course, in vastly different ways. No sooner has a "school" been discerned than its component parts are found to be of uncertain compatibility. Each writer finds his reality through completely personal research. Is the new realism to be restricted to exhaustive description of the "distinct . . . smooth, intact" surfaces of objects, as first postulated by Robbe-Grillet—a process to be known as *chosisme,* that is, a concentration on the signs that reveal to us the presence of the outside world—or should it be rather the effort to discover how our consciousness receives and relates these signs? There is little agreement, even about the scope of various productions. Robbe-Grillet, for example, is seen diversely as a practitioner of pure phenomenology, an adherent of classical materialism, and an interpreter of Freud.[22] Sarraute dissects

21. *Phénoménologie de la perception* (Paris, Gallimard, 1945), "Avant-propos," p. xv. My translation.
22. Compare the assessments of Olga Bernal in *Alain Robbe-Grillet: Le Roman de l'absence* (Paris, Gallimard, 1964), Stephen Heath in *The*

visceral, prereflective reactions among anonymous characters. Butor distinguishes himself in analyzing the plurality of mental structures. Beckett, regarded by some rather as a precursor, pursues the myth of self and the "ablation of desire." Philippe Sollers concentrates on the text itself, and others, like Claude Ollier, Robert Pinget, and Claude Mauriac, explore aspects of fictional structure and the proliferation of the fable.[23]

Not all have come full-fledged to the New Novel. One who came gradually, through step-by-step experiment, and who is now recognized as among the most challenging, adventurous, and richly suggestive of these writers is Claude Simon. Although his works have been translated into English almost immediately upon publication, they are still less well known to the American reader than those of some of the authors mentioned above. His reputation among connoisseurs of the novel increases, however, with every new work.

Born in Madagascar in 1913, Simon began writing in the 1940s. He has lived through most of the social, cultural and literary adventures of his time; he was in Spain during the Civil War and became acquainted there with leftist and revolutionary doctrines. Captured while serving in the French army during World War II, he escaped from a German prison camp. He trained originally as a painter and began writing during one of the blackest periods of French history, in a style that experimented with the current realist, existen-

---

Nouveau Roman: A Study in the Practice of Writing (Philadelphia, Temple University Press, 1972), and Bruce Morrissette in *The Novels of Robbe-Grillet* (Ithaca, N.Y., Cornell University Press, 1975; original ed. Paris, 1963).

23. Jean Ricardou distinguishes between the work of the New Novelists who practice *auto-representation* and that of the *Tel Quel* group, which includes Sollers and which engages in *anti-representation*. For clarification, see *Pour une théorie du Nouveau Roman*, p. 32.

tialist, and stream-of-consciousness techniques. He owns a vineyard in the Roussillon, in the south of France. To discover how an artist, a landowner, a thinker with such an activist background has come to distinguish himself among those who believe that writing is a way of joining the world is an adventure in itself.

"Claude Simon has not attracted the patient attention or the critical argument which his dense and manly novels deserve," states the excellent critic John Sturrock in his study *The French New Novel*.[24] Fortunately, this statement is no longer entirely true. The most advanced guard of French criticism, taking up the analysis of Simon's work that Merleau-Ponty left unfinished at the time of his death in 1962, has found it rich in examples of new techniques and complex linguistic structures. Ludovic Janvier, Ricardou, and Michel Deguy have eagerly undertaken to discover the treasures lying beneath the surface of Simon's highly concentrated work and to demonstrate that, in fact, its density is far greater than any first reading could suggest.

The critics' patient exegesis, however, has been limited principally to the later works, and most particularly to the last most innovative and difficult novels. No doubt the reader about to plunge into *La Bataille de Pharsale, Les Corps conducteurs,* or *Triptyque* needs the brilliantly illuminating commentary of Ricardou or Janvier to accompany his own efforts. Should he begin his acquaintance with Claude Simon with these last novels, he would, very probably, be disoriented in the undertaking, and perhaps be discouraged unless he were sustained by some initial indoctrination.

These commentaries themselves demand a knowledge of lit-

24. London, Oxford University Press, 1969.

erary criticism, phenomenology, and linguistics that may be lacking in the general reader. When recommending critical studies, therefore, we run headlong into the question that insistently plagues today's writer, and especially disturbs the novelist, whatever the measure of his desire to be read. Is the reader, enemy and brother, to be considered an active or a passive participator in the text? Can he be something besides the author's double, or rather, can he be made to become the author's double? To what extent is such an assumption fatal to "readibility"? Valéry's Monsieur Teste dreamed of someone who would be both friend and enemy, all-knowing and implacable in judgement, the only reader the unforgiving intelligence of Valéry could tolerate.[25] Simon, who carries the mark of Valéry into all his work, declared early in his career: "I think that the worst dishonesty and the worst contempt that the writer, painter, or speaker can show toward others consists in painting, writing, or speaking in terms of what the public wants, instead of what he has to say."[26]

Such purity is admirable. But what of the reader who is willing, but does not know how, to enter a world of communication that critics assure him contains immense but deeply buried wealth? This question is not entirely foolish. Claude Simon's work is accessible to readers who are not necessarily trained in the subtleties of French criticism. It has been translated into many languages; in the United States, for example, the remarkable translations of Richard Howard make it available to those who do not read French fluently. What a pity if any reader, for lack of a proper introduction, should be excluded from a work so greatly admired by connoisseurs!

Fortunately Simon himself provides many stepping stones to early appreciation. In his novels the rich sensuality and lux-

25. *Oeuvres complètes,* II, 45.
26. *La Corde raide* (Paris, Editions du Sagittaire, 1947), p. 70.

uriance of physical detail, the delicate arrangement of mass
and shadow, the melancholy but often sumptuous appraisal
of man's fleeting destiny turn the passageways of what might
seem arid research into stretches of pure enjoyment. Those
who know the windy and vivid landscape of the Roussillon
cannot fail to respond to the sight, sound, and scent of it as
described in the pages of *Le Vent, L'Horbo*, or *Histoire*. But
even those who have never seen the region where Claude
Simon is known chiefly as a grower of grapes must savor such
passages as this:

They stayed there until it was completely dark . . . until they
could no longer see each others' faces, their eyes hidden in the
thick green darkness beneath the motionless branches . . . until
no more sounds came from the bamboo thicket that was black
now—neither chirping, nor beating of wings, nor murmurs, nor
even rustling—everything, around them, completely motionless or
concealed now, that is, the world (things, animals, people) not
stopping, interrupting its life, but pursuing its complicated,
disturbing, and incomprehensible existence beneath this reassuring and deceptive form of apparent motionlessness. Like the cat,
shortly before: it did not make off, crouching instead on top of
the crumbling wall, staring at her, its legs drawn together, perfectly motionless (merely a spot, a tiger-striped form among the
brilliant jumble of the garden's conflicting shadows, there where
a second before there had been that reddish spring, the lightning-
like materialization not of a body, an animal, but of the very
idea of movement, in the tearing across of the sun, then nothing
more), as if it could pass with no transition from movement to
immobility, or rather as if immobility were somehow the prolongation of movement or, better still, movement eternalized:
probably capable of that (transforming speed into its motionless
representation) at any moment: in the middle of a leap, of a
fall, in mid-air, resting on nothing but time somehow solidified,
the solidified summer afternoon in which the fierce, exuberant
vegetation of briars and sunflowers bathed as in a kind of developing fluid, and the cat too, fierce, cold, circumspect, frozen ir

that same attitude like a sudden condensation of speed (just as a stick of dynamite contains a million times its volume of noise and destruction), petrified, staring at her, spying on her through those two narrow vertical slits, those lentil-shaped pupils cats have, piercing and keen as if they were some sort of weapon, extra claws, razor-sharp and probably capable of tearing and lacerating too, but which, for the moment, were content to spy on her, the circumspect, cruel, vigilant and craven stare not wavering.[27]

Those who are drawn by sheer pleasure into Simon's orbit may facilitate their next steps by reading the author's own comments about his work, although these texts are less readily available. Simon's nonfictional work, *La Corde raide*, is a very useful repertory of themes and explanations of their importance in his life. A number of interviews and articles, dealing with the writer's attitude toward his own activity, show the gradual clarification of his ideas about art. By far the most significant, as we shall see later, is the short treatise *Orion aveugle* (1970), which sums up Simon's conclusions to this date; to this must be added the development of these conclusions in the interview between the author and Ludovic Janvier, in *Entretiens*, No. 31, edited by Marcel Séguier.

Finally, there is a less haphazard method of entry into Claude Simon's world, one that is almost embarrassingly simple but that demands the utmost good faith on the part of the reader. It consists of studying the novels together as a group, and, in an even more elementary fashion, chronologically. In Simon's particular case, this method produces some quite illuminating results. In the first place, the earlier novels, being the most conventional in form, offer fewer difficulties, if less interest to the newcomer than the later works. The earliest of

27. *L'Herbe* (Paris, Editions de Minuit, 1958), translated by Richard Howard as *The Grass* (New York, George Braziller; London, Jonathan Cape, 1960), pp. 16–17. All quotations are from this edition.

all have not been translated and may be discussed as a group, in order to determine their importance for later developments. The reader who begins with *Le Vent,* the first novel to indicate clearly the direction Simon will take, can find footholds of understanding while he accustoms himself to new techniques and perspectives; so that then the later works will open up more easily to a practiced approach. A far less superficial matter than mere familiarization is at stake here. For Simon's work, to a greater degree than that of many modern authors, reveals a clear and purposeful line of development and an ever-progressing research.

This research does not center on any philosophical or metaphysical view of mankind and the universe; in this respect, as Sturrock correctly observes, there is little difference between the early and the late novels. The research is concerned entirely with the rhetorical means of committing to paper what the author has to say. This activity may eventually imply a philosophy, or at least a point of view, and the means finally preferred may also imply a modification of that point of view. Sturrock does, in fact, study Simon's "mercantilist" interpretation of the universe and its relationship to his rhetoric, but, it appears, he follows the assumption that this rhetoric is shaped and molded in a constant effort to communicate this interpretation. The assumption is probably true at the outset. Yet the questions ceaselessly propounded by Simon, at first almost unknowingly and soon with greater and greater conviction and emphasis, are: what is the purpose of novelistic rhetoric, what can it communicate to us, in short, what can the novel possibly *be?*

No question has been asked so often as this last one, nor has any received so many, often belligerent, answers. To the historian of the novel it sometimes appears that more ink has been used defining and defending the genre than has gone into the production of masterpieces. But certainly during the last twenty-five years there has been more investigation into possible solutions than at any other period, accompanied by a determination at all times to put theory to the test. As Jacques Guicharnaud reminds us:

According to Aragon . . . the proliferation of novels in recent years can be described as "a gigantic enterprise comparable to Science." In other words the modern novel is essentially experimental . . . and the experiments are not suspended in a vacuum. While unique in themselves, they are directed as a whole towards the discovery or invention of *the* Novel, just as the specialized work of various scientists contributes, as a whole, to the development of Science. Aragon sees the enterprise as carried along by evolution, "a principle of constant acceleration," comparable to that of scientific research and discovery, and as such, inevitable.[28]

Claude Simon, with amazing persistence and logic, combines definition and production into a single act. Step by step, from his first novel, *Le Tricheur,* which retains many conventional aspects, to his latest, *Triptyque,* which has almost none, he explores the territory of the novelist and tests the tools he must use. Each new novel undertakes a further testing, and each establishes for Simon a truth from which he will not depart. So, little by little, rejecting far more than he retains, he arrives at certain invariables of which the sum is indeed a New Novel.

The reasons exposed by Simon for his rejections and acceptances are not necessarily pleasing to all comers. But within the framework of the writer's own thought they are sequential and closely knit. Each novel is therefore an experimental demonstration of the truth that the author is testing. And since each succeeding novel deals with fundamental aspects of novel

28. "Remembrance of Things Passing: Claude Simon," *Yale French Studies,* No. 24 (Summer 1959), 101–108.

writing, the series offers writer, reader, and critic a challenging summary of the problems and solutions that each has to evaluate. For this reason, if not for this reason alone, the total of Simon's work has a unique value.

Simon makes no effort to deny his debt to Proust—a debt that, indeed, increases as he continues writing. Students of Simon's prose should make a careful study of the classic pages in *Le Temps retrouvé,* in which Proust discusses his discovery of the meaning of art and the need for the artist to read the signs with which the external world is filled. Simon recognizes as well the profound effect that Faulkner's *The Sound and the Fury* had on him and the important influence of Joyce, Dostoievsky, and Flaubert. Conrad and Chekov, and, among contemporaries, Beckett also have his great admiration.[29] On the other hand, he proclaims himself an enemy of the Stendhalian "psychological" novel. Constantly interested in the experiments of his contemporaries, he does not hesitate to adopt techniques employed by fellow authors, as he is convinced, along with many of them, that the voice that speaks our language within us refers to the anonymous and the general at the very moment when it is most intimate.

In the space between *Le Tricheur* and *Triptyque* we observe the progressive widening of this reference to impersonal signs to include, as counterpoint to personal images and memories, the vastness of dictionaries and encyclopedias and the apparent objectivity of learned texts. Simon's demonstration of the developing relationship between a writer and his rhetoric, especially as explained in *Orion aveugle,* should provide innumerable fascinating studies by linguists, grammatologists,

29. These statements are based on conversations and correspondence with the writer and may be verified by consulting the various interviews listed in the bibliography.

and philosophers of language who are interested in such varied approaches as generative semantics, deep structures, or "deconstruction" and *"différance"* (as understood, for example, by the disciples of Jacques Derrida).

The present study is not undertaken from any theoretical point of view. However, the act of writing leads Simon and his reader ever deeper into the controversial thickets surrounding the written word; despite Simon's own disclaimers, it is inevitable that linguists and philosophers, sooner or later, will find exciting material in his work, the former in the new freedom accorded the word, the latter in the metaphysics emerging from that freedom. At present, however, we are interested in Simon as an experimental novelist, one who is not seeking out new ways for the sake of novelty but because of an insuperable urge to discover what the writer's act may be. Simon is an explorer-adventurer, like those so often described in his works, fighting his way through the jungle that springs up around him tenaciously with every thought and every word that gives body to that thought. By his own admission, he is not an inventor; he seeks only to mark a path in the disorder, before things close in on him again, irrevocably. Originality, for such a writer, lies in finding what is already there, not in merely describing it. Representation of reality actually becomes less and less important to him, or rather, appears less and less feasible, as he himself attests:

As far as my own relationships with my work while I am writing (or was writing) are concerned, if by that you mean my motivation, they have naturally greatly changed during all these years. Roughly, if they are to be enumerated in order of priority, this way, for example: (1) Writing because of a need to *do* something; (2) Writing in order to represent; (3) Writing for communication; (4) Writing to find out, discover; I would say that starting with the order 1, 2, 3, 4 thirty years ago, I have little by little arrived at the order 1, 4, 3, No. 2 appearing more and more dubious to me.[30]

This progression is what interests us here. The reader, fascinated by the precision of passages like the one previously quoted from *L'Herbe,* will discover that the careful picture of the outside world the writing appears to offer is the result of a process that cannot be defined as straightforward realistic description. This discovery is of paramount importance for the writer. After long attempts to enmesh reality in words, then to define the slippery nature of the reality that refuses to be enmeshed, Simon realizes that "if description is incapable of reproducing things and always speaks of objects other than the objects that we perceive around us, words on the other hand possess the prodigious capacity of drawing together into confrontation things that, without them, would remain apart."[31]

He himself prefers to be considered as a *"fabricant"*—a maker or manufacturer concerned with the visible structure and web of discourse, led by the meshing of words around the fixed points of reference he has chosen, as the weaver follows the pattern he has set up on his loom. As he said at Cerisy-la-Salle in 1971,[32] it was a chapter in a mathematics course entitled "Arrangements, Permutations, Combinations" that stimulated his interest in the essential structures of writing—they are, he feels, very different from those of everyday speech. (In this he differs from a writer like Queneau, for example.) The idea of constant rearrangement leads to that of repetition with variables, or *"reprise."* In a radio interview with Francine Mallet on August 23, 1971, Simon observed that writing and reading should be like rehearsals in music in which the plea-

30. *Entretiens,* No. 31 (1972), p. 16. My translation.
31. *Orion aveugle* (Geneva, Editions Albert Skira, 1970), Preface, n. p.
32. *Entretiens,* p. 67.

sure lies, as Casals says, in the repeating and perfecting of a theme or passage. The word, like the theme in music, can—by delicate modulations or by deliberate deformation (as in the pun)—lead the mind through a gamut of thought before returning to the dominant note.[33]

To Simon's ideas of combination, repetition, and variation must be added one of structural relationship. Because he was trained as a painter, Simon is acutely conscious of plastic form and organization, and particularly of the fact that in the appreciation of the visual arts, the eye is not constrained to follow any one single linear progression but can return again and again, along different paths, to the same points, to rediscover the relationship of each element with the whole. So important are the ideas of structure, fabrication, repetition, and relationship to Simon that each of his later novels corresponds to a visible graphic pattern. The constant retracing of paths toward a defined point is given pictorial representation in the great painting by Poussin, *Paysage avec Orion aveugle,* in which we see the giant demigod, bearing a small guide on his shoulder near his listening ear and being led through the half-light along an obscure path toward the dawn. Simon has chosen this painting to illustrate his own aesthetic theory, to show how he himself—the writer (but also the reader)—advances under guidance along the difficult winding road to the receding horizon. If the traveler progresses through a strange landscape, knowing only the direction in which he is going but not where his next step may fall, the steps themselves become of paramount importance and require total attention. So Claude Simon, not only in the novel built around Orion—*Les Corps conducteurs*—but in his entire adventure as a writer, advances step by step, intent rather on the surprises and diversions of

33. These statements are based on notes taken by this writer while listening to the broadcast.

the journey than on any proposed end, finally making the steps themselves the purpose of the journey.

His transition from dealing with the ultimate reality of things to examining the present reality of the written word becomes a poetic process that does not go as far as the symbolist one in restoring to words a tremendous occult power over things. But he realizes that the power of the writer lies only in the unexplored resources at his disposal. While searching for these resources, Simon provides ample evidence for each stage in his reasoning in the form of works that are one long inquiry into the use of the written word. This inquiry goes beyond the mere investigation of the novel as a genre; it embraces man's relationship to the universe of his perceptions. The results of this investigation, however, are always "novels" in that they show man's efforts, through fiction, to give a voice to that relationship, "discovering the world gropingly in and through writing."[34]

Whatever may be the inclinations of the reader-critic, the works of Simon will stimulate in him a desire to understand more clearly the conditions of the craft and to re-evaluate his own assumptions on the subject. Many basic problems are touched upon: anecdote, intrigue, adventure, realism, objectivity, involvement, commentary, time, chronology, causality, distance, and interpretation, to name the most evident, are questioned and are tested in action. The questions themselves —of which the most troublesome is undoubtedly that of fabulation and mental truth—have been and still are being treated elsewhere. Here, in the novels of Simon, we meet them immediately, illustrated in works where the beauty, complexity, drama, and mystery of things are matched with, but not identified with, the beauty, complexity, drama, and mystery of

34. *Orion aveugle,* Preface.

words, as though a double bonus of pleasure and reflection were constantly being granted to the conscientious reader.

All the themes that bind together Simon's work in a remarkably coherent whole—and they are the major themes of human existence, as Janvier shows us in *Une Parole exigeante*,[35] the echoing themes of the endless cycles of life, death, war, love, growth, hope, danger, deceit and decay—are restructured by consciousness and by language during the act of writing. Out of the incoherent mass these themes constitute in reality, the word fashions recognizable and connected shapes that impose their presence through features not essentially inherent—organization, design, consonance, and inexhaustible reference. The transforming power of the word can become even more impressive and absorbing than the substance upon which it acts; concentrating on it, the writer discovers, finally, what it is to write.

The earnest hope of any critic should be to send his reader eagerly back to the writer under scrutiny. Far from exhausting the details of Simon's craft, this book is intended to erect the signposts to a new treasure hunt and to suggest that, however much ground has been covered, many paths still remain untried.

35. *Une Parole exigeante: Le Nouveau Roman* (Paris, Editions de Minuit, 1964).

1 ⚜ The First Novels

The critic has a delicate and difficult task when he speaks of the first works of any novelist after studying the later productions. An element of falseness creeps into all comments, whichever way the commentator confronts his undertaking: either the total effort of the writer is turned topsy-turvy, and the earlier works benefit too freely from hindsight, or an uncomfortable make-believe innocence is assumed. The fine line of relevant criticism must lie somewhere in between.

The first three novels of Simon (*Le Tricheur, Gulliver,* and *Le Sacre du Printemps*)[1] attract notice today mainly because of the subsequent development of his art; nevertheless, they possess considerable interest for those in search of object-lessons in experimentation. They clearly illustrate the difficulties in the forties and fifties of the novelist who was trying out his capabilities in the uncertain postwar world where Sartre, Camus, Faulkner, and Hemingway shared the limelight, and who was testing himself by changing direction constantly, even within the framework of each separate novel. Often a discon-

1. Paris, Editions du Sagittaire, 1945; Paris, Calmann-Lévy, 1952; Paris, Calmann-Lévy, 1954. None has been translated into English. *Gulliver* has recently been reissued in French. The passages quoted are in my translation. The points of suspension in quotations from these and other works that appear in the original are closely spaced in the French manner. My own points of suspension are printed in the customary manner.

certing shift of method and perspective results, for the author generally presents his numerous characters through the stream-of-consciousness monologue, situating himself among the thoughts of each, yet making little attempt to provide passage from one series of reflections to the next. If the lesson of the novels is, as it seems to be, the impossibility of human communication and the uselessness of action, a clear delineation of the field of vision in which this impossibility becomes apparent is often difficult to establish.

The obvious defects and problems discovered in each one of these early novels raise, however, extraordinarily fertile questions for discussion. The writer himself, wrestling with the material he has chosen, soon isolates a number of points vital for the novelist, and proceeds, even as he writes, to reflect upon them. By the time he reaches the third novel, as a brief examination will show, these reflections dominate the narrative instinct and irresistibly turn the writer in the direction he should go.

Le Tricheur (written in 1941 and published in 1946), a story with an existentialist savor, is particularly unsettling in its changes of perspective. The chief character, Louis, has run off with a thirteen-year-old girl, but his main preoccupation is a profound discontent with life and the feeling of being manipulated by people and events. His suffering during an unhappy childhood in a religious school, a period when his rigidly devout mother was slowly dying, occupies his thoughts, and he is still filled with resentment against his brutish companions, against the good fathers who sought to fool him, against the uncle who stole his inheritance, and above all against the military father whose example is thrust down his throat. To his resentment is added the envious recollection of a later companion who had the means and the will to be free. These reflections are followed in turn by the meditations of

Catherine, the mother of the runaway girl and the unhappy wife of Gauthier, an unsuccessful painter. Then come those of Gauthier himself, which take off into considerations of death, immortality, war, women, and politics, and which are interrupted by a sudden fall from a bicycle, as though into reality. Finally we have the thoughts of Belle, the young girl; they are a confused mixture of dreams and memories of equivocal relationships with her father.

In a last section, however, a number of new characters appear in the city where the lovers have taken refuge: Ephraim Rosenblaum, the Jew who is attracted to Belle, provides a version of the story as seen by the uninformed outsider; a friend of Louis, Armand, with his family composed of Thérèse, his sick wife, Lydie, her sister (who tries to seduce Louis), and their father, furnish scenes from everyday popular life, down-to-earth conversations, "atmosphere," and "flavor." Finally, in another monologue by Louis, we learn that he is obsessed by a recent meeting with a priest, whose serene belief has re-awakened all the anger of the young man who considers himself mocked by an unjust God and a heartless world. Louis dreams of killing his eternal enemy, embodied in the shape of the man of God. After borrowing a revolver from Armand, he finally uses a brick to commit the murder. But his act does not liberate him from his obsession. Back in his room, he reflects on his enslavement: "And then only I recall the weighted form of my will, forgotten, useless and ridiculous, in my pocket. A brick . . . When day comes, I know what it will show, the same as yesterday, the same as every day, as far as I can see, over the roofs, all around, before and behind these walls" (p. 250).

The isolation of the individual among those he loves or hates, the uselessness of human action, the impossibility of any exchange are common themes repeated in the meditations of each character. In this novel where each maintains his solitude, the author seems to be trying on the skins of the participants one after the other, dressing in temporary disguises. And though the themes are always the same, the paths by which they enter experience are difficult to follow: we pass from the world of Louis to that of Gauthier without being convinced of their authenticity by their apparent parallelism. As for the action, however violent it may be—abduction, family disaster, murder—it is smothered in words, and the general effect is one of frustration and paralysis. No doubt, the reference to Empedocles, the philosopher-magician who transformed the world, is ironic, that is, if it concerns Louis. But if it concerns Gauthier, the artist for whom action is painting, it has a very serious meaning. The heart of the novel lies in the passages of striking intensity that offer a concentrated vision of physical and mental experience. Gauthier rides through the countryside, with the consciousness that comes from an artist's sensitivity to sight, sound, and smell. At the same time, he is able to combine in his thoughts his own practical difficulties, his emotional ties to his wife and daughter, his desires and ambitions, his yearning for freedom stirred by the sight of some gypsies, together with more transcendental speculations about the strange prolongation of man's destiny in his children. As his bicycle gathers speed on the down hill slope, his physical exhilaration grows, and for a brief moment—before the crash sends him, stunned, to the ground—all human activities seem to have found a meeting place in him: perception, memory, reflection, imagination, and exciting bodily involvement with the mechanism of the world. Gauthier, cyclist and painter, far more than the doomed Louis, opens the way to Simon's future inquiry into the transformation of life through art.

In *Gulliver* (1952) Simon attempts the novel of action that *Le Tricheur* did not turn out to be. In the gloomy and brutal environment of postwar France, a provincial family reveals its decadence. Twin brothers, Jo and Loulou de Chavannes, have fought in the war as adversaries, one as a pilot in the Free Forces, the other as a collaborator with the Germans. But, in fact, one is indistinguishable from the other. Their sister, Eliane, has had a child by Max, a rich and enigmatic young man who collects around him all the dubious, sporting society of the town. The grandmother Chavannes continues to live as though the family had been in no way disgraced. Loulou exploits an old Jew, Herzog, pretending that he can locate the Jew's wife and daughter who have disappeared during the Occupation. Everyone is under the surveillance of Bert, an ambitious journalist who is in love with Eliane. During a banquet at a country inn, Bobby, a perverted youth loved by Max, but who has left him for female company, is accidentally killed by Loulou. Eliane, who has been hopelessly following Max, ends by uniting with Tom, a member of Max's band, who has managed, even though he is poor, to live an independent life. Bert tries desperately to pin the blame for Bobby's death on Max—who kills himself—and is ridiculously unsuccessful. Herzog never finds his family and is subjected to insult and cruelty even from his cleaning-woman, who happens to be Bobby's mother.

In such a synopsis, this long and tangled novel seems absurdly melodramatic. Simon himself observes, "Disconcerted by the critical reception of *Le Tricheur,* uncertain of myself, I then tried to prove—a ridiculous undertaking!—that I could write a novel in the traditional form. An excellent and fertile error, incidentally. The result was edifying: I could not!"[2] The book contains, however, at least one character whose thought and actions provide the connecting thread of

2. *Entretiens,* p. 17. My translation.

the story and pose the essential questions: Max Verdier, unhappy king of this wasted kingdom, Gulliver in both his forms.
Son of a rich local manufacturer, Max runs away to join the
army while still very young. Then, wounded and disillusioned,
he returns to Paris to work as a mechanic, refusing all help
from his family until the death of his father. At that time he
comes back to take care of his estate, spending his money ex-
travagantly, often scandalously. The question of commitment
posed by his strange and unsuccessful life forms the basis of the
novel. Max had launched himself into a life of action, believing, perhaps, that he would accomplish something; he returns
from the war, filled with indifference toward the world around
him. The central sections of the novel show him lying motionless on his bed in a wretched room in Paris, reduced to being
a mere spectator of what goes on. Later, he lives impassively
among the provincial people who gossip about his behavior. A
woman has killed herself because of him. Eliane loves him but
will not marry him to save him from himself. Bobby leaves
him and ridicules him. He dies without finding any answers
about his destiny. Everything in this book occurs without explanation; things happen as though beings acted independently of all reasoning. In the end, Max, who had begun by
protesting against his life, knows that he will be its victim:
"The instinct which was warning him, letting him feel that
what was threatening him was something both terrible and
devastating, something that would seal up his solitude forever,
would shut him away, in his indifference, from the crowd"
(p. 291).

From this work full of furious activity, written in sometimes
as vigorous a style as any work by Vailland, emerges once more
the sense that action is useless and human beings are powerless.
Some highlights in the writing are notable: the description of
the chaos in the old Jew's apartment which is filled with

heterogeneous objects, like the debris of a war-wasted country; the anxious searching of the journalist, determined to create his own truth; the frantic struggle of young Bobby against his own pain-wracked body. All are, if one wishes to see them this way, indications of things to come in later novels; they are certainly passages to be admired for their precise detail.

In the third novel, *Le Sacre du printemps* (1954), we see a transformation. The action is still based on what seem to be melodramatic, and sometimes awkward, situations. A change has taken place in the presentation, however. As in *Le Tricheur*, the novel starts off with the young hero's interior monologue, which provides us with the essential data of his story: his anger against his mother who has remarried, against the stepfather with the disillusioned smile, against society and his own sulky adolescence. He expresses his thirst for independence, order, and the ideal. Here an anonymous narrator intervenes to explain young Bernard's adventure. Bernard has volunteered to sell a ring stolen by the sister of a boy he is tutoring from her own mother. Through a school friend he makes the acquaintance of a shady couple, who promise to help him get rid of it. He goes to meet them but finds only the woman, who soon beguiles him into her bed; after this, he discovers that the ring is missing. Humiliated, he decides to sell his precious motor-bike, then learns that the girl he is trying to help, and whom he has idealized, is pregnant. To crown his distress, he is led to believe that his stepfather is responsible for her pregnancy. The crisis ends when the girl is knocked down by a car and miscarries, freeing all the characters from their burden, leaving stepfather and stepson face to face in the act of reconciliation in the hospital waiting room, where the lost ring, miraculously, reappears.

The narrator's story is, however, cut in two by another, the tale of the stepfather, who relates an occurrence in his own life that goes back sixteen years to the Spanish Civil War. As an idealistic student, accompanied by two mutually hostile gun-runners, Ceccaldi the Italian, and Suñer the Spaniard, he was involved in trying to pass arms to the Spanish Republican Army. He observed the sordid maneuvers, the disputes, the hatreds, and the greed dishonoring the cause that had seemed so noble to him. Aware that he was observing the reactions of people really involved "he began to wonder if he had not made a mistake, if the others . . . were not right and if he himself, with his willingness, his zeal, his principles, his ideas learned from the history books, had not been the dupe" (p. 150). When Ceccaldi is assassinated, and the affair reported in the local press in a story filled with suppositions and errors, as though it had been a miserable underworld shoot-out, the student (that is, the stepfather) finally admits that in trying to be a revolutionary for others, he is only engaging in a traffic of ideas, as sordid as any traffic in arms:

A man can traffic in anything, I finally realized that, even to the extent of selling himself to himself for lack of other dupes, or rather, as to a choice client, one for whom the best merchandise is put aside, his own ideas, his own worn, adulterated, faked and falsified feelings; and that, without even the excuse of hunger, without the slightest valid excuse beyond the congenital incapacity of mankind to live, to bear being alive without asserting a belief in something or other, without some certainty, even though it may be obviously the most empty, the most artificial one, just so long as everything is not like a Dostoievsky novel, like *The House of the Dead* . . . [p. 260]

Through this gloomy reasoning, the stepfather draws closer to the youth, who in turn perceives that his own misadventures are like those of the older man, that his Boy-Scout attempts at rescue have been as necessary, as inevitable, as the disillusionment that had to follow. The two stories present a single experience, that of the passage from youth to maturity, though they tell of events distant in time and space. The importance of repetition becomes clear as we realize that the boy is employed as a *"répétiteur,"* the stepfather as a *"revendeur,"* and that their emblem is the ring.

The paradoxical result of this telescoping, however, is a sharper consciousness of time and of the relationship between consciousness and time. The idea of recurrence necessarily raises the question of durability and distance. That which remains in the memory becomes fixed little by little like a viscous substance slowly congealing ("he could plunge into that transparent, gelatinous time, going back through that something without dimension or perspective" [p. 202]). But going back through time and seizing portions of it "without dimension or perspective," and juxtaposing them in a different order according to the needs of the present, can profoundly shock the consciousness attempting to put order into phenomena and therefore trying to hold fast to the soothing principles of chronology and causality. The "diurnal creature accustomed to considering time as a duration cut up into slices alternately devoted, without any possible interpenetration, some to wakefulness and action, others . . . to repose, to sleep" struggles, in his own story, "trying . . . or pretending, or demanding to see only a series of reflex episodes resulting one from the other with an exactness comforting for the mind that prefers to accuse and curse itself rather than be obliged to accuse and curse, that is, to recognize, the proliferating, anarchic and impetuous disorder of life" (p. 241).

Shaken in its habits, consciousness is led to consider its own role in events, and, in so doing, to duplicate itself. This results in a separation, a distance appearing between consciousness and its double. In moments of crisis, the adolescent hero of *Le Sacre* feels as if he is watching someone else. He has "the sensation of being someone half-awakened"; he hears "that something saying "Aah, Aaah, Aaaah... inside himself" (p. 224), and when he has to act, it is only after "his brain . . . had been obliged several times to address to his prostrate body, first insistently, then angrily, then almost despairingly, the order to move" (p. 228). This deeply separated consciousness tries to provide its own surprised being with a rational explanation of its nonrational behavior:

> It was as if another, a double, had suddenly made its appearance in him and was striving, with arrogant joy, to achieve a kind of revenge, to dilapidate, to ridicule—and with the same passion, the same fanaticism, the same furious determination—the hard-earned money, the work, the convictions, the rigidly ambitious puritanical theories: "What a fool! he said (he spoke now as though he were telling the adventures of that other, that second personality, that enemy, with the same vengeful cruelty, the same pitying scorn, the same destructive rage) . . ." [p. 244]

Seen by himself as another, the character stands aside from his double, the better to see and condemn him. But as he does this, he realizes that the very fact of perceiving and speaking about what is perceived fatally changes what has been. "But I am not telling the truth, he thought, without ceasing to speak, without being able to stop speaking, and he knows it. Why am I obliged to tell him, to tell us, what I know he knows is false" (p. 244). Just as the newspaper deforms the news that it gives, the talkative mind changes through language the dimensions and the relationships of everything it encounters.

Is there any way of escaping from this universal treachery, from the plasticity of events, from the elasticity of time that compresses into the space of a minute all the lost years and stretches to infinity the shame of a second? There are only two ways of defending oneself: by recognizing the uselessness of all protest and by accepting the fateful progress of the machine. The stepfather says, "So it's like a kind of mechanism in which no single cog can move without setting all the others in motion, and if we think we are going to escape by going faster or slower, all the rest of the caboodle goes faster or slower as though synchronized" (p. 245). Besides, one must realize at last that all the games with time end with death, and that this death is terribly near. The hospital where the two men are waiting is

one of those places where man, face to face with his fragility, his insignificance, and his solitude sees time, that aberrant illusion of his senses (or of his carelessness, or of his cleverness, or rather of his absurd pride saying, making him say: "I have the time, I've plenty of time, I've all the time in the world!") appear to him no longer in the shape of a soft mass without consistency, disposable, elastic, and malleable as he pleases, but as the uncontrollable, continual hemorrhage of a commodity, or rather of a capital, or rather of a carefully allocated, measured, reckoned-in-cash stock, while in the silence, in the prostration of the mind and the senses takes shape the Mane Theckel Phares of every human adventure. [p. 238]

In these three novels consciousness in every character tends inevitably toward the same pessimistic view, one which sees human will as powerless in the face of the implacable mechanism of the universe. But while the characters in *Le Tricheur* and *Gulliver* struggle against their memories and their premonitions and try to find salvation in action, those in *Le Sacre* end by analyzing and judging their memories and attempts at action, in an effort to prevail, through intelligence, over the nameless thing that is crushing them. Thanks to this effort, they find themselves face to face with great issues, such as Time, Fatality, Death, and they begin to perceive that all beings, however different they may seem, however original or heroic their lives may be, play, with respect to these absolutes, the same monotonous and despairing role. It matters little, then, whether one is oneself or another. Time and Memory multiply us only in order to reduce us all to the same image, and to make us all repeat indefinitely the same story.

The verbalization of these ideas in *Le Sacre* leads to an important modification in form. We now hear only three voices, those of the two men—the self and the other—and the one of the narrator. Since all three offer the same message, we suspect the possibility of a still more radical reduction. The chaotic perceptions that we found in the first two novels are also reduced, and closer relationships are established among them. The parallel adventures of the two men contain many corresponding details: in both we find bars, prostitutes, political discussions, bargaining, violence, and always the fundamental errors of history (Ceccaldi is not Ceccaldi, he is not a Communist, the arms have not been shipped out, Bernard did not lose the ring, he was not robbed, the stepfather was not guilty, and so forth). Thus the texture of the novel is denser and its structure stronger. Above all, the author organizes his story in a way that makes it impossible for the reader to ignore the questions he asks. What can we know of the phenomena of the outside world? How does the mind register them? What relationship is there between the registering mind and the activity that surrounds it? How does the mind deal with the apparent disorder of things? What is the relationship between the mind and the multiplicity of minds? How does the mind perceive itself? How can all of this be expressed by language without essential falsification?

Behind the sometimes melodramatic disorder of these novels the perplexity of the writer becomes apparent, the writer who is led by the very act of writing to ask himself some of the fundamental questions troubling twentieth-century philosophers. We say "by the very act of writing," for the will toward realistic depiction of the outside world, especially in *Gulliver*, is initially very strong. This will is overcome each time, however, by reflection, where the contemplation of the act immobilizes the action. Simon's early heroes combine the need to act, often in a violent way, with the inextinguishable desire to hear their own voices repeat tirelessly the memories, the motives, the reasonings that accompany the process of being. Often they react with violence to escape from that voice, but it will not be stilled, except by death. This voice finally dominates even the most activist of the novels.

The human condition, as perceived by the novelist, is that of the novelist himself. He *is* that voice which betrays action by speaking of it. As he seeks conscientiously to produce realism, in the minute descriptions of place, the scrupulous imitations of language, the faithful detailing of gestures, the writer discovers that all of this realism is nothing but a reflection in the mind, a re-presentation of something already past. Thus he is led to seek things in their original milieu: the minds of his characters. But here also he discovers another form of betrayal. Nothing is left but the mind of the writer. So he tries one voice after another, from the "I" of the monologue, to the "he" of the narrator. But *"faire vrai"* and to tell a story are much more difficult than the novice may think. Whose truth shall it be and whose story? After three novels, Simon still has no answer to these questions, but they persistently emerge from everything he writes.

No doubt, the pessimistic vision of the world that we receive from these writings is that of the author himself, who concludes that order is an illusion, that movement is a characteristic of the unchanging, that thought is futile, that ideals are deceptive and language treacherous—but the desire remains to transmute these dismal conclusions into novelistic form. The author has ascertained that it is not sufficient to distribute opinions and feelings among "characters" who soon turn out to be variously disguised bearers of the same message. Nor is it enough to reproduce a "real" world, which is only as real as an image in the mind transcribed in language; nor to connect persons and language in a "story" that can only be a fabrication ("Why do I have to tell him, to tell us, what I know he knows is false?"). How, then, and what can a writer write?

In these first novels Claude Simon succeeds in defining the nature of the research that will keep him absorbed for the next twenty years, a research that will eventually transform his own art, and perhaps the art of the novel. His last novels differ greatly from the early ones. But without these early experiments, Simon could not clear his path of the obstacles offered by the traditional forms of the art, or even discover that for him they are obstacles. From our weaknesses come our strengths. The inability that Simon recognizes in his judgement of *Gulliver* to tell the story of individual human activities in a realistic manner has forced the writer to examine the refusals embedded in that inability and to discover in such refusals a tale more fascinating than the first. Through the revelation of such difficulties *Le Tricheur, Gulliver,* and *Le Sacre du printemps* have driven Simon in a direction so absolutely opposed to, and yet so closely dependent on, his initial efforts. From this point on, we shall see how the writer's monologue, at first tending outward in an attempt to reproduce the confused and wavering shapes of the alien world, gradually concentrates upon itself, drawing the world with it.

2 ❧ Le Vent

An unusual little book published by Simon in 1947, one year after the first novel, is entitled *La Corde raide* (the tightrope).[1] It resembles an essay or artist's journal, where memories of the veteran of the Spanish Civil War and World War II are combined with the ideas of the writer and artist that Simon wanted to be. Precise description of past experience alternates with anxious interrogation of the present; the book is obviously the quarry from which Simon will extract the raw material for most of his future work. We shall recognize the scenes from the Civil War, the World War, and the prisoners' camps over and over again. The descriptions of the stifling, moribund city of Barcelona will reappear particularly in *Le Palace,* while those of the 1940 defeat, the death of the commander, the misery of the prisoner-of-war camp are most evident in *La Route des Flandres.* Traces of all these themes are to be found in almost every novel.

Very important are the pages where these memories begin to contaminate each other, where one sign or incident draws one scene after another, without logical or temporal sequence, and leads the writer back to the present, to the persistent questioning of his identity and the nature of his own reality.

I look at my face in the mirror, and I see the tree with its foliage of hair, I see the bark, and I wonder what there is under

1. See my Introduction, n. 26.

the bark, which is not me, which is the fellow who brought me this far, or rather who brought himself, because I had nothing to do with it, and the proof is that he has done exactly the opposite of what I clearly see I should have done. . . .

As though I were somebody. Then who is this somebody with various names in various mouths and all the names in my hearing and all the people with the same name in the frames and the still photos at the bottom of drawers. Not even my hand. Hands keep absolutely nothing of what they have grasped. Frustrated hands, forever tirelessly clutching at vanishing realities. [pp. 173–174]

The passages about painting are revealing, especially those that defend Cézanne in his confrontation with official art:

Any being which expresses itself is only giving a form to what is formless, illuminating a little of that blur without language, words, or vocabulary, giving it a visible and communicable aspect. That is all he can do, that and nothing else. . . . No truth can stand disguise. . . . I think that the worst dishonesty and the worst contempt that the writer, painter, or speaker can show toward others consists in painting, writing, or speaking in terms of what the public wants, instead of what he has to say. [p. 70]

This demand for honesty is accompanied by the confession that, apart from the immediate view of things, Simon could see "nothing, nothing but an incoherent, disconnected muddle, without consistency, no thicker than a layer of varnish over something made up of darkness and viscosity, unfathomable . . ." (p. 105). At best, the determined artist can try "to explain with awkward words what he had discovered—not trees, faces, houses, bottles, or fruit, but that 'something else' without reason or the assumption of reason that is trees, faces, houses, bottles, fruit, and what there is between them, justified only by their existence—and expressed by means of colors and lines" (p. 113). Thus he sees the universe of Cézanne "stripped for the first time of signposts" (p. 117), a place where "the same forms can change, inflated with their own substance and with the substance absorbed through ceaseless osmosis from their near and distant neighbors, a perpetual obscure gestation, blind and ardent . . . the multiple infinity of realities, all equally possible, all equally true, driving upwards, their presence an erection . . ." (p. 122).

Stated here are decisive positions that Claude Simon will take. As yet he has not succeeded in passing from the universe of the painter to that of the writer. Unlike Cézanne, who was often sullen and uncommunicative, he will tell us of his attempts to discover how the forms of objects, the multiple aspects of reality, can become part of the interminable monologue of the mind. The first three novels have served to point out the pitfalls along the road. It remains for Simon to discover in which direction a move should be made. He took the first tentative step with *Le Vent*.[2]

The subtitle of the novel deserves some reflection. "Tentative de restitution d'un retable baroque," warns us to expect first of all a *tentative,* that is, an attempt, an unfinished endeavor, a by no means definitive work, and second, a *restitution,* that is, nothing original but a return to something that once existed and that can be recovered only by piecing together the fragments that remain. As for the baroque *retable,* we can assume that we shall be offered something suggesting both ceremony and mystery, combined with complexity or exaggerated richness of design. We may expect a restoration, then, one that implies effort, ingeniousness, and intelligence, before we can glimpse the outlines of the complete picture. In *Le Vent,* the wind has a relationship with the picture that becomes apparent as the book progresses. A constant, tormented,

2. Paris, Éditions de Minuit, 1957, translated by Richard Howard as *The Wind* (New York, George Braziller, 1959). All passages quoted are from this translation.

physical presence, the wind is also the final master of the fragmentary order that man has imposed on life, sweeping both man and fragments into oblivion, like the scraps of paper on a city street.

The novel has a "story." In a southern French town worn down by sun and wind, a man arrives—a species of Idiot or Innocent[3]—characterized by his old raincoat, his beret, his camera, and the fascination he exercises over the weak, particularly women and children. He has come to claim the estate of his dead father, whom he never knew, his mother having left the man even before the birth of their son. The newcomer is immediately embroiled in litigation with the bailiff of the estate and is forced to settle down in a third-class hotel, where his attraction for all who are lost and oppressed brings him into sympathetic relationship with a poor servant, the mother, by a flamboyant and thieving gypsy, of two little girls. The curious attraction of the Innocent works also upon a young cousin on the prosperous side of the family, an impertinent and spoiled girl who throws over her fiancé and writes the newcomer a letter that compromises her completely. The charm turns out to be fatal for everybody. The servant is killed by her lover when he discovers that she has entrusted some stolen jewelry to the stranger, and the gypsy in turn is killed by the police. The two little girls end up in an orphanage, where the Innocent can do nothing for them. A shady commercial traveler, pretending friendship, steals the young cousin's compromising letter and attempts to blackmail the family; the girl, in a rage, then gives herself to her former fiancé before dismissing him. The stranger loses his lawsuit and is forced to sell his estate and leave. Nothing remains to mark his passage.

3. On Claude Simon's admission, *Le Vent* is a "remake" of Dostoievsky's *The Idiot*.

The novel is therefore constructed in the traditional manner around a basic plot supported by subsidiary actions, which contribute to the climax. In many other ways also the book uses traditional forms of the novel: the characters are clearly defined and described at length, their relationships are carefully examined and identified by visible, significant details; landscape and background are vividly rendered, with strong symbolic references to the action and fate of the actors; conversations reveal character and modes of thought; skillful expressions of feeling involve the reader directly in the tragedy; and above all there are events which take place and move the story along to its inevitable culmination.

In spite of this conventional structure, we note in the novel something that results in a blurring of the perspective. The narration is entrusted to a character who plays no part in the drama, who merely runs into the protagonist by accident and who tries to put the whole story together some time after it has happened, basing it on the confused evidence he has gathered or recalled after the moment of crisis. Since he becomes the confidant of Montès, the Innocent, he is aware of many intimate details that anyone else would not have been able to discover, without this rather uncharacteristic unveiling of Montès' hidden thoughts. For under all other circumstances, Montès appears almost inarticulate. After the departure of the Innocent, the narrator fills in the gaps in the story by consulting the notary who took care of the lawsuit and who also belongs to the same social class as Montès' wealthy relatives. This notary provides the details concerning the property and the behavior of the cousins, details that enable the researcher to construct a logical, connected, and closed history of the whole series of events.

But this does not happen. The continuity of the narrative is broken because of a perpetual vacillation in the mind of the narrator. Sometimes he sees the person of Montès through the eyes of the notary, who, in turn, is perceived and characterized by his listener. Sometimes during the speech of the notary other characters come to life and speak and act on their own account, so that we apparently have access to a new level of consciousness. Often the narrator has recourse to his imagination—"So I seemed to see him sitting here" (p. 12)—or to creative organization: listening to the notary who is "a sort of ancient chorus" (p. 114), he hears the background voices of the whole town, "they said, she had said—or let it be understood, or permitted it to be supposed, or imagined—to the friend who had told it to other friends who had confided it to each other at the top of their lungs . . ." (pp. 121–123)—commenting and disclosing the most secret occurrences. Sometimes the narrator reports directly his own recollections of Montès: "Later on he was to tell me about that period of his life" (p. 86), "And I could see him that way, just as he described it to me . . ." (p. 87). But such recollections have all the fuzziness of a snapshot of a moving object, since we encounter them first in the words of Montès himself, then through the narrator's account, so that all we perceive are "uncertain silhouettes, hastily glimpsed, incomplete . . . looming vaguely in a time of equally uncertain extent" (p. 87). These uncertain images appear doubly and triply blurred because they are grasped by an inattentive mind and then reconstituted through a thickening layer of time that deforms them still further. Montès is depicted as "seeing, registering without being quite conscious of it all, so that the account he gave me was probably somewhat false, artificial, as any account of events is bound to be false after the fact, since by the very act of being described even the most insignificant events assume a formal, consequential aspect they didn't have at the time of their occurrence" (p. 51).

The images are welded together in the memory of the narrator, this existence guaranteed by nothing beyond the fact
that he remembers them. Yet this narrator identifies himself
only late in the book, in the seventh chapter, although we
have previously been aware of him sitting in the notary's office, listening to the second- and third-hand account of his
hero's activities, and although he warns us from the very beginning about the difficulties of what he is doing.

And while the notary was talking, telling the story again for
maybe the tenth time (or at least what he knew of the story, or
at least what he imagined, having, in relation to the events which
had occurred during the last seven months, like everyone else, like
the heroes of those events, only that fragmentary, incomplete
knowledge consisting of an accretion of sudden images (and
those only partially apprehended by the sense of sight) or an
accumulation of words (themselves poorly grasped) or a welter
of generally ill-defined sensations, and everything—words, images,
sensations—vague, full of gaps, blanks that the imagination and
an approximative logic tried to remedy by a series of risky de-
ductions—risky though not necessarily false: because either
everything is only chance and then the thousand and one ver-
sions, the thousand and one appearances of a story are also a
story, or rather are and constitute *the* story, since that's the way
it is and was and remains in the consciousness of the people who
lived it, suffered it, endured it, laughed at it; or else reality is
endowed with a life of its own, disdainful and independent of our
perceptions and consequently of our knowledge and especially of
our thirst for logic—and in that case trying to find it, discover it,
drive it out of hiding is perhaps just as futile and disappointing
as those toys, those Central European dolls that look like old
women cupped one within the other, each enclosing, revealing a
smaller one inside, until you get down to something minute,
infinitesmal, insignificant...nothing at all; and now, now that
it's all over, trying to report, to reconstitute what happened is a
little like trying to stick together the scattered, incomplete debris
of a broken mirror, clumsily struggling to readjust the pieces

getting only an incoherent, ridiculous, idiotic result; or perhaps only our mind or rather our pride forces us to risk madness and run counter to all the evidence just to find at any price a logical relation of cause to effect in the very world where everything the reason manages to make out is fugitive and vague, where the uncertain senses are tossed about like floating corks without direction or perspective, trying only to stay afloat, and suffering, and dying just to get it over with, and that's all...) [pp. 9–11]

Conscious from the start that his efforts at restoration are useless, the narrator nevertheless calls on the direct evidence supplied by his own memory: "I remember how suddenly, with no transition, the weather began to turn hot. . . . And I can see that courtyard in the old barracks where Rose lived" (p. 124). He thus breaks into the narrative perspective of the novel, just when the account of Montès' behavior is becoming linear and, despite the warnings scattered here and there, is beginning to form a logical, consecutive whole. But, in fact, the narrator does not contest this account, he merely confirms it with the "I" superimposed upon the third person narrative. Only in his reflections upon events does the narrator take up the question of veracity raised at the beginning of the book. He plays, therefore, a double role: that of the reconstitutor, the organizer of independent facts, and that of the questioner who doubts the results obtained. About this role he says:

these days, these unknown hours when he appeared like an actor suddenly stepping in front of a curtain, then disappearing again—sometimes fifteen days would go by without my seeing him—suddenly reappearing (what was happening to him between times? where was he going? what was he doing? what was he feeling?: what the rumors suggested? what he himself told me? or thought he could tell me? or might prefer to remember? or thought he remembered? or simply did remember?), apparitions, gossip, recollections, stories, through which we glimpsed only (and it was the same for the others: Rose, the little girls, the boxer, the dismissed bailiff, the uncle, the notary, Maurice?) a sort of plesiosauric reality reconstructed out of fragments, starting from two vertebrae, a frontal bone, a submaxilliary, and three metacarpals fished out of time's gray mud and assembled haphazardly according to individual predilections and tastes, and perhaps after all it was only the vulgar and idiotic adventure of a vulgar idiot, as everyone said , , , [p. 112]

The narrator is caught in his own contradiction. He narrates, he orders events according to a temporal and causal design. He accompanies this narration with a commentary that constantly tends to undo his own work, to reveal its lack of continuity and even of substance. He oscillates continually during the recital from one level to another and thus, without actually destroying the structure of the work, creates in the reader a state of uncertainty.

The novelist's consciousness is in this way made obvious, along with all the doubts and urges for revision that accompany the act of creation. Since Gide's *Les Faux-Monnayeurs* there has been no secret about this process, which has often proved a more fascinating subject than the story the writer is supposed to be telling. But neither Gide nor his followers questioned the writer's need to engage in this process. Nor were they really perturbed about the counterfeit nature of the resultant text. Simon's novel, on the other hand, seems to concern itself chiefly with this latter problem, and with the demonstration of its insolubility. The author's struggle to force the written word into the shape of life produces the interminable and complex sentences, continually interrupted or prolonged by subordinates, by parentheses that are sometimes double or triple, by interrogations and unfinished phrases, all so difficult for the reader impatient to get to the point. Equally difficult are the endless qualifications of the already vague and imprecise expressions, such as "it seemed to me," "perhaps," "he could not have said," "it is only a supposition," "maybe," "why not?" and others destined to increase the confusion. In addition we can mention the conditional verbs and phrases, the numerous cases of "if," "or rather," "as though," the verbs hiding in the jungled luxuriance of the paragraphs, disguising action as participles, and the inarticulate conversations that reveal only the distress of the speakers:

"But you..."
"What..."
"What do you mean 'what'..."
"You said 'but you'..."
"Ah I don't remember any more what time did that clock just strike..."
"Him and me that's what you mean..."
"Half past no quarter to no I meant I don't know any more..."
"What did you mean..."
"It must be late I wonder do you have any idea of what time it's g..."
"Why do you pretend to be such a fool..."
"I'm not pretending I was only saying..." [p. 99]

Deprived of the usual punctuation, freed from the bonds of traditional syntax, containing barely the hint, the suggestion of a thought, these sentences are the echo of beings who simplify and confuse at one and the same time actions in the world around them. Montès is notable for "his continual use of the pronouns 'he' and 'she' without any antecedent noun to indicate a specific man or woman, creating a constant confusion of persons, as if he saw the world with some sort of myopic distortion, so that it was populated by vague silhouettes of two-legged creatures differentiated only because they wore a skirt or trousers" (p. 154). All of his experience can be likened to a linguistic hash:

. . . that incoherence, that brutal, apparently absurd juxtaposition of sensations, faces, words, actions. Like a story with the syntax—subject, predicate, object—missing from every sentence. Like what any newspaper article becomes (the bleak, monotonous, grayish alignment of tiny characters which all the world's anguish and action is reduced to) when your eyes happen to notice the torn page wrapped around a bunch of leeks, and then, by the magic of a few truncated, incomplete lines, life recovers its superb and arrogant independence, becomes again that disordered abundance without beginning or end or order, the words fresh again, freed of syntax, that stale arrangement, that all-purpose cement the copy editor pours out like a sauce, a sticky *béchamel* to bind, to glue together somehow so as to make them tasty the ephemeral and disparate fragments of something as indigestible as a stick of dynamite or a handful of ground glass: thanks to which (to the grammarian, to the copy editor, and to rationalist philosophy) a man can swallow, along with his morning coffee, his soothing ration of murders, violence, and madness arranged from cause to effect. . . . [p. 184]

Language reduced to a sort of pap would correspond to the magma of formless facts that constitute reality, and the "editor" or novelist would be the one to glue all these facts together sufficiently well to make a recognizable whole. The suspicion remains, however, that by gluing them together in another order, you might have another whole as valid as the first one. Or another. And another. Where then is the "truth" for the novelist? And is it even worth the trouble to look for it?

And he stood there without moving, thinking perhaps: "If only I could understand...," and again, later: "But is there even something to understand?"— . . . mutations. That's it. Isn't that all it is? You know: cells or something that hang together in another way, and then there's some tiny modification, one microscopic change more or less, but it's always the same thing, since it goes on living. And then?" [pp. 247–248]

"It goes on living." Of the traditional "slice of life" only the most general characteristic remains, the one that assures that the living thing is formed, transformed, de-formed, and re-formed. All the rest is insignificant, serving only to prove its own lack of importance.

Yet the author of *Le Vent* leaves us between two concepts of the novel. The first is the almost-Flaubertian novel, whose protagonists blindly fulfill their separate destinies, surrounded by objects that serve as signs of their character and their fate. The Innocent, who is both poor and potentially rich, who sees nothing as others do, wears an old raincoat and carries, like an extra eye, an incongruously expensive camera. In the bare bedroom of the shabby hotel, the servant Rose, who has nothing, washes cheap colored ribbons to adorn her children's hair. The gypsy is dressed in worn but flashy clothing and flaunts his body in the stale atmosphere of a boxing hall. Cécile, the spoiled cousin, drives automobiles dangerously. Her sister, the self-righteous matron, carries her big belly ostentatiously like a symbol of respectable motherhood. Their father, Montès' uncle, a man of few and fixed ideas, lives in a house whose walls are hung with sabers, where "the furnishings had apparently not been changed since at least the Second Empire" (p. 115). An accumulation of carefully observed details and gestures authenticates the lives of all the characters and animates the heterogeneous, noisy population—policemen, street vendors, gypsies, children—in the windy, dusty streets of the town.

Nevertheless, the true-to-life appearance of everything described in the novel is perhaps only a façade. Perhaps it is all like the stage setting for a Spanish play, "one of those *autos* by Lope de Vega or Calderon" (p. 118), in which everything is deceptive and the actors play according to a well-known rite, a comic illusion that will disappear. In its place is left only the sight of those equally unreal beings, the actors counting their money—but the money is fake, and who are the actors? And in the end, does it have the slightest importance? What is important is that the rite be accomplished, that those engaged in the drama move according to a pre-established rhythm, that they circulate within a form, which remains after all the rest has changed.

Behind the façade there is another kind of novel, based on questions raised by the first, realistic version—disturbing questions about the authenticity of the writing, the role of the writer, and the necessity of the novel. We are forced to realize that not only is the "story" something created by one who never lived it, but that the one who *did* live it, even continuously, is not worthy of our confidence because of "his fundamental inaptitude for being aware of life, things, events, except by the intermediary of his senses, his heart (an inaptitude we ordinarily correct, remedy by an intellectual effort devoted to caulking up the time sequences that have escaped our perception" (p. 153). This "inaptitude" is, of course, not peculiar to Montès, but is by inference part of our human condition.

The strategy of substituting a linear "filiform" time for the "clotted magma in which the moment is a spade cutting into the dark earth, revealing the innumerable swarm of worms" (p. 172), is practiced by the creators of texts; they make deceptive ensembles which allow our rationalism and the nature of language to impose an order and a regularity where none exist, when we should on the contrary be aware of "time alternately telescoping, standing still or expanding" (p. 153). The characters of *Le Vent* are constantly aware of this elasticity, this disconcerting irregularity in our understanding of the moment:

Montes suddenly feeling as if time were moving terribly fast, as if something had just opened a valve henceforth impossible to close, hearing the powerful liquid rush of time, irreversible, impossible to stem or stop now, hurling itself with a disastrous and irremediable racket   [p. 75]

and later:

and it was as if you could see time itself welling up with the sweat, the hum of time mingled with the hum of blood   [p. 92]

Even if the characters are not conscious of the presence of time, they record its absence, or rather, the inexplicable gaps in their experience. The text gives many examples of these sudden leaps in time: "And then, suddenly, with no time between, it was daylight" (p. 152); "He seemed to pass with no transition from the night Maurice had come with his threats . . . to that moment when, shoving aside the policeman . . ." (p. 185). The "no transition" represents a considerable break in the continuum of the "story." The fluid quality of this continuum, on the other hand, is suggested by the use of the present participle, a use that becomes the hallmark of Simon's writing. This technique plunges much of the action into a viscous, indefinite state, without beginning or end, like the "magma" from which its details are drawn.

On the two levels of direct reasoning and experimental writing Claude Simon comes to grips with his novelist's trade. In *Le Vent* he clearly circumscribes the sensitive areas that he feels must be explored by the writer: the possibility of truth in place of mere verisimilitude in narrating, the ambiguousness of consciousness and memory, the questionable reliability of evidence from oneself and others, and the workings of time. From this moment on, he will be absorbed in probing these questions and in determining the relationship between them and the curious activity known as writing. Each step in this research will have its experimental proof in the shape of a novel.

3 L'Herbe

In *L'Herbe*[1] Simon returns with urgency to the problem of Time, the Time that each of us lives and fills and that ends by devouring us all. Are we capable of understanding this temporal condition, does a single being live untouched by the terror that the thought of it inspires?

Simon imagines such a being: an old woman in the process of dying who emits "that intoxicating and probably imaginary fragrance of virginity, of freshness, and of accumulated time. No, not wasted: worsted or rather surmounted, tamed: no longer that hereditary, omnipresent and omnipotent enemy you watch, terrified, as it advances and flows past with such pitiless slowness, but an old familiar traveling companion, perhaps hated and feared once, but so long ago that the recollection of such fears is like the memory of those childhood panics which now merely make us smile..." (p. 12).

This old woman, Marie, has not used her time as most people do, for their own profit. A peasant's daughter who grew into a village schoolmistress, she has devoted herself, with the help of her sister and double—now dead—to the education of a younger brother who finally becomes a university professor. Of her sacrifice, of her refusal of all personal indulgence, nothing is left but some cheap jewelry and her account books, in which line by line, throughout the years,

1. See note 27 of my Introduction.

she has noted the minute details of every expense, of every profit. Not work, or solitude, or even the war has affected her inflexible resolution, or forced her to complain. Without expressing the slightest emotion, the slightest reproach, she has come to die in her brother's house, driven out of her own home by the monstrous mechanism of war. Her brother, growing old and desperately ill himself, lives a grotesque caricature of life with his aging, snobbish wife, who drowns her jealousy and terrors in alcohol.

Scrutinizing this work of time, incredulous and revolted, Louise, the daughter-in-law of the elderly couple, witnesses their pitiful arguments and the prolonged death agony of the old woman. Young, beautiful, on the point of leaving a gambling husband for a lover, she is held back by the spectacle taking place in the old southern house, situated in the midst of the magnificent, melancholy, autumnal countryside. Has the dying woman found out how to vanquish time, Louise asks herself, has her total abnegation a meaning? Is the great "T" formed by the sunlight filtering through the shutters in the sick room the sign of Time's victory?

All around Louise the traces of defeat accumulate, aggressively. The Autumn gives a hint of winter, overripe fruit fills the countryside with the smell of rotting. In the salon the ornate clock that marks time is like an over-decorated tombstone. In the hotel bedroom where the old couple stay in town there is another clock, monumental, absurd, and stilled—"the essential thing being the fact of the face and the hands, that is, the notion of a closed circuit inexhaustibly travelled," for "there is no need to know the time . . . but to have the consciousness of time passing constantly present to the mind" (p. 77). In the combat against time the old mother-in-law—an ornate ruin herself—displays her painted face and flaunts her jewels, which she loses, absurdly, in the train washbowl (the train itself being time, passing and repassing on the same track). The young woman, gazing in her mirror, becomes aware of the old woman on the other side of the wall. In contrast to the frivolous image of the young lady with the poodle, repeated endlessly in diminishing perspective on the cheap box in which the dying woman keeps her meager treasures, the hard, virginal body on the deathbed is stripped little by little of its human attributes until it is a mummy without sex and without age.

What is necessary to vanquish Time? Virtue, courage, inflexibility, or simply indifference and harshness? Louise will not discover the answer. Poring over the old, neatly kept account books that she receives, along with the treasure box, from her dying aunt, she learns only that there is no "Time rediscovered". At the most, a sort of accounting can be made, like the lists of debits and credits which divide time into "edible" sections that reveal no feelings, no disappointed heroics, only the taking in of nourishment and the expending of energy and money. All the rest is unrecorded, and perhaps unimportant.

Seen in the terms of one woman's life, all the events and actions that are part of it make Time appear as a grotesquely overwhelming force, crushing the pitiful obstacle of the individual's existence. Is the daily battle for survival during an entire lifetime to be seen as heroic or futile? How is the real accounting to be made? The principle of causality, which consists of adding facts to facts, events to events, to furnish an "explanation" for any given situation, can reach the heights of absurdity. Was it necessary for all of Europe to lie in ruins and for France to be crushed under a conqueror's heel, for an old woman to come to her brother's house to die after a life of sacrifice? And if such a relationship between cause and effect is disproportionate, when does it begin to acquire any proportion?—were the fields and rivers of France created for the express purpose of forming a décor for the dying youth of the country, "as if their bushy banks, their high poplars, their stone bridges speckled with black moss, had been conceived and created for all eternity only for this, as if to constitute the last vision printed on the retinas of the young men doomed to die" (p. 25)? Yet pathos is made up of such disproportion. How legitimate is it to indulge in sentiment over the fate of one being caught up in History, with a capital H, or in her own history which interests no one except Louise? Louise herself is puzzled by the nature of her interest.

The whole of Marie's life could be merely "a vulgar story." However, Louise's curiosity leads to an ever-widening inquiry. By trying to understand the meaning of time in someone else's existence by reconstituting it with the help of the few clues she possesses—the treasure box, the account books, some pictures showing the sisters and their brother in their youth, then the latter's wedding day—Louise grows into a consciousness of the relentless passage of time and then into a consciousness of that consciousness. But she cannot see the grass growing: only at certain moments is she in a state of awareness.

The inquiry on the subject of time is therefore double. This novel shows us to what extent time in the lives of others is subject to our imagination and its historical constructions, and also how fleeting, elusive, and unreal is our own time. Louise's reconstruction of Marie's life is interwoven with episodes from her own present existence. She has immediate personal problems to resolve, yet people and events from the past emerge and disappear in her mind, very often blurring her perception of what is going on around her. In her concentration on Marie's story, she seems to lose sight of her own. Her most intense experience is not described. Only the aftermath of love-making is depicted; and when Louise is struck by her husband, the blow itself is not recorded, only "the hand back where it was when he had hit her" (p. 135). Eventually, even her love affair is somehow brought to an end because of her absorption in Marie's fate. Louise's effort to see what happened to someone else has fatally interfered with her ability to live and be aware of her own history. "No one makes history, no one sees it happen, no one sees the grass grow," says the epigraph to this novel.[2]

The narrative perspective of the novel is very uncertain. Although most of the reflections seem to come from Louise's consciousness, sometimes she is engaged in what is apparently a straight dialogue with other characters. Occasionally, it is difficult to determine whether Louise alone is responsible for certain observations. For example, the meditations of the father-in-law at the dinner table, comparing his son's hands to those of his dead father, can hardly be part of Louise's experience. At other times, an anonymous narrator seems to speak, for instance, in a long description of a traveler's experience in a train. Louise is described in the third person, yet we are disconcerted as to the source of observation, since at times we feel strongly that the narrator is Louise herself, so intimate are the thoughts and feelings that the narration conveys. Nevertheless, it is in the mind of Louise that the fusion of the different elements in the novel takes place. Conversations, memories, speculations flow into one another in her consciousness. Time accumulates in sequences—present, past-in-present, imaginary past, future—juxtaposed in increasingly complex patterns. At any given moment this cumulative consciousness appears both to reflect the world and to be part of it, implying both change and permanence:

That terrible machine for assimilating every new situation

2. From Boris Pasternak, trans. Richard Howard.

which is not only man and his consciousness, but everything (people, objects, trees, sky) contained in that consciousness, reflected by it, that is, both constituting it and enclosing it; the modification—or the disappearance—of one of the elements being immediately compensated for by a series of tiny modifications (contractions or dilations) in the articulations of the other constituent parts, so that another whole is created at that very moment, differing by its compensation but whose weight, whose total volume are exactly the same. [p. 88]

In *Le Sacre du printemps* Simon speaks of the world as "a kind of mechanism in which no single cog can move without setting all the others in motion." This mechanism is now presented in *L'Herbe* as something unstable, organic, impossible to conceive of as fixed; an ensemble of shifting, variable fragments, making up both an inner and an outer world. If the novel as a genre is considered as a reproduction of such a totality—a question implicit, but not resolved in *L'Herbe*— we can suppose that the closed, unalterable machine in which all the parts fit inexorably and explicably into one another (that is, the traditional novel), is to be replaced by another mechanism, far more subtle, one that allows for an apparently infinite number of possible relationships between the constituent elements. A work conceived in this fashion acquires both pattern and fluidity, whereby the novelist can combat the twin dangers of rigidity and disorder, dangers already present in Simon's mind, as the epigraph to *Le Vent* clearly shows.[3]

The idea of constant modification within an ensemble also precludes arrangement of component parts into fixed sequences of cause and effect and therefore nullifies any attempts to bestow absolute meaning or significance on any one

3. This epigraph from Paul Valéry, "The world is incessantly threatened by two dangers: order and disorder," becomes increasingly important in the development of Simon's work. Translated by Richard Howard.

arrangement. Louise has at her disposition a certain amount of data concerning her aunt. What she does not have is a rule for assembling all the parts. She can isolate certain signs and increase their importance. They can equally well be, from the point of view of other persons involved, totally insignificant. For example, an old photo makes Louise imagine that Marie, for her brother's sake, refused the attentions of a suitor and deprived herself of love and marriage. Little else supports this view, and the account books are silent on the subject. Marie's actions can add up to heroic self-sacrifice—or to insensitivity for practical reasons. The objects connected with Marie—the box, photo, cheap rings, and necklaces—reflect her and each other as in a series of mirrors, but they reflect no meaning. The enigmatic, hunchbacked guardian (the village deathwatcher), who stands guard over Marie, is a sign that she is already closed off in the muteness of death.

The novel is filled with circular and intertwined forms—bracelets, necklaces, rings, baroque ornaments, "arabesques" of birdsong—that emphasize the repetition and endlessness of Louise's inquiry, of the world around her, and of all experience. However, Simon has not entirely translated his work into terms of variable pattern and rearrangement. In *L'Herbe* the structures of the outside world and of unrelated consciousness interfere with the unique whole of Louise's thoughts. Traditional elements are still discernible in the novel. The anecdote, first of all, although veiled by the immediacy of Louise's perceptions, is still recognizable and has considerable pathos, suspense, and drama. The characters are clearly drawn, and their past and present precisely identified. Their bodies and gestures are described, and their acts are given motivation. The reader is not actively invited to take part in their emotions because these emotions are subliminal. Nevertheless we cannot help feeling sympathy for the sad destiny of the old woman, the frustrations of the young wife, or the tragicomical struggle of the old couple. Besides these elements, the lush setting has an irresistible, sensuous appeal, and the descriptions of the outside world, filtered by fine perception, contain passages of detailed realism. These passages, however, deserve rereading for more than their descriptive content. If we consider the following, we find unexpected additional wealth:

then Louise moved, stretched, turned over on her stomach: lying now at full length on the ground, clinging to the earth, thrusting, burying her face in the cool grass as if to print it on the ground, breathing deeply the powerful and harsh smell of grass and earth mixed (but not tears: her eyes closed, dry), merely breathing, filling her lungs with the pure smell of earth, then releasing, relinquishing, still lying on her stomach, but her head turned, able now to feel the meshes of crushed grass stamped on her cheek, and in front of her eyes the field extending, the thick wild grass silhouetted like brushstrokes of Chinese ink against the fading sky, and on one of them (also drawn or rather condensed by one of those subtle oriental brushes) an insect about the size of a pinhead, complex and bristling, perched on its many feet, the carapace striped with tiny green lines, its minuscule and delicate antennae moving while it stopped, hesitated, started again, continued its patient ascension, the blade of grass gradually, imperceptibly bending beneath the imperceptible weight—or perhaps it was an illusion, for it didn't move, didn't even tremble when the insect disappeared: the carapace, the hard wing-cases suddenly opening, releasing the delicate and transparent wings the color of new grass, Louise looking up, trying to follow it, losing it among the monotonous cloud of gnats still suspended, tirelessly whirling in front of the sky that was pink now, and against which, between the branches, she could see silhouetted the dark mass of the house on top of the hill, darkening by degrees, the windows not lit up yet, then the hallway light turned on, Louise able to see (to divine) for a second the massive, misshapen figure heavily climbing the last steps of the terrace, stopping for breath a moment (imagining him sitting till then in the shadowy summerhouse, not working any longer, the white pages covered with fine handwriting scattered in front of him on the table, vaguely phosphorescent in the shadow, the parallel lines of words growing increasingly indistinct, blurring, running into each other until they were nothing more than vague strips . . .) [pp. 209–210]

Such a passage reveals not only the descriptive talent of a writer who has a painter's eye, but also some of the special techniques of Simon's writing. Within a carefully structured text, which appears to render a slice of the outside world, a fine network of connections exists, based on the initial image of the grass. Louise has been lying with her lover in the woods, and earlier the strong erotic link between the grass that lies crushed beneath the pair and the pubic hair that lies exposed after the act of love has been amply emphasized. The grass also covers the world in which Louise is buried both physically and metaphorically. It is all of the world that she can see, and in its exquisite detail she can discover nothing but the indifference of nature. The passage of the insect leaves no more trace than the passage of man, for the grass will spring back into place once she has gone.

The delicate links between these thoughts are in the writing itself, in the words that lead from one image to the next with rich precision. As the grass itself suggests the painter's brush, the brush requires the ink, and the ink suggests both the blot that resembles the insect and the investigation into the mind that makes the image. In the French text the insect itself has "multiple" legs, so fine that they resemble the "multiple" grass, and its wings are grass-colored. The fine lines on its shell, the *stries* eventually lead, by the use of the same word, to a combination of the idea of writing, where its ancient oriental history is evoked by the *encre de Chine,* with the fine

script on the sheets of paper in the *kiosque* or Chinese pavill-
lion that serves as a summerhouse. The image of the insect
climbing patiently up the stem connects also, by a weight inversion (the *poids imperceptible* leading to the necessity to
gravir lourdement), with the old man, the writer, climbing
heavily up the steps. Framed in the grass the house, with the
unlighted windows at the top of the staircase, takes on its true
perspective. The exquisite oriental silk screen that we see, with
its fine, naturalistic strokes, is heavy with implications for one
who loves, lives, and writes in the remorseless natural world.
We have here a remarkably clear example of the way in which
a passage of descriptive realism can shift from the "idea" or
signified content to the signifier or sign, with its multiple and
intertwined ramifications.

The rich sensuousness of the book, however, often obscures
the inner network that holds the narrative together. The
horizontal line of the "T," the chronology which Louise tries
to establish across the years, is continually meeting the down-
stroke, the vertical plunge of the moment into its own depth.
The influx of sounds, sights, and odors at each moment carries the signs that will bring us back again to the research on
the horizontal. With Louise, we discover that this interchange
is unending, until, eventually, the last train leaves in the night,
taking with it light, sound, and movement. In the last words
of the novel, "there is nothing more."

We are to conclude, then, and it is no surprise, that Time is
victorious. But we are also to conclude that Time is not made
up, as we tend to think, of aligned and self-explanatory events.
It is, on the contrary, a dense tangle of moments of consciousness, or perceptions that we cannot register as perceptions
until they are gone. Our efforts to combine these into History
are doomed to failure since we can never capture a totality of

time within a single consciousness, much less render it into language. "If to endure History . . . ," says the professor, "is to make it, then the dim existence of an old lady is History itself, the very substance of History" (p. 31). However, we do not and cannot know what constitutes the existence of an old lady.

In his effort to sharpen our awareness of these problems, Simon has made a tremendous assault upon the fortress of traditional language. The analysis of Guicharnaud is pertinent:

In the long sentences, similar to a series of deep pulsations, of organic waves, the most striking features are: (1) A superabundance of logical tools such as "donc", "de sorte que," etc., but stripped of their normal functions, emphasizing the desperate effort of reason to affirm order, actually the débris of reason's defeat—for what really binds the sentences is internal, somehow independent of such words (2) A superabundance of comparisons, made up of terms which do not exactly coincide, introduced by "un peu comme," "à peu près comme," continued by other comparisons beginning with "ou plutôt comme," completed by what might be called attempts at comparisons, rejected in the formula "non pas comme . . ." (3) A superabundance of present participles, replacing clauses which in any normal style would be in the past definite. Hence acts and gestures are grasped while happening and not as completed. The imperfect tense can produce a similar effect, but the advantage of the present participle is that on the one hand it does not create the expectation of a decisive act (in the past definite) and is not relative but brutally absolute; on the other, it makes the action expressed by the verb into an act separate from the subject and at the same time a quality (momentary) of the subject, a protoplasmic excrescence of it.[4]

What is the lesson that *L'Herbe* has to offer the novelist? The rejection, already explicit in *Le Vent*, of the carefully

4. Guicharnaud (see my Introduction, n. 28), pp. 105–106.

constructed "story" dependent on psychological "truth" and traditional links between cause and effect is strongly reaffirmed here. Simon prefers to bind the elements of experience together in another system whereby sensation, image, thought, and word form associations that may be infinitely variable and unexpected in their effects. The devices he uses to render the apparent discontinuity of time and the fluctuations of perception appear in *L'Herbe* with greater intensity than in the previous novel, but the need to explain their use has disappeared. A very important effort has been made to discover and reveal the topography of the consciousness, that strange crossroads where perception, idea, and language meet and fecundate one another. This kind of exploration will henceforth absorb all of Simon's powers.

4 La Route des Flandres

In *L'Herbe* Claude Simon confirms some of the discoveries he has made as an experimental novelist. Following up the logic of *Le Vent,* he examines all the stages of construction of a story, postulating this time that the author of the story has at his disposal—as is indeed the case for all authors—only evidence provided by a single consciousness. His work then consists in organizing this evidence. While this point of view presents nothing new for the history of criticism, in his next novel, *La Route des Flandres,*[1] Simon imposes it under extremely stiff conditions, excluding testimony from any source other than the central character's awareness of events. In seeking to discover what happened and what is happening, this character and the reader are denied access to any independent store of knowledge. They are enclosed within an area of experience circumscribed in time and space.

Obviously, the information collected by the consciousness has a tendency to organize itself very conveniently in the shape of anecdote. Louise in *L'Herbe* reconstructs all the sparse evidence about the dying woman into a potentially pathetic story. Things fall into a pattern that can be interpreted: the old woman comes to die before Louise's eyes; the

1. Paris, Editions de Minuit, 1960, translated by Richard Howard as *The Flanders Road* (New York, George Braziller; London, Jonathan Cape, 1961). All passages quoted are from this translation. This work was originally titled *Description fragmentaire d'un désastre.*

treasure box, the account books, the photos come into Louise's possession, conversations are heard through the walls. Everything becomes available, with almost no intervention on Louise's part. At best, she displays a growing curiosity and indignation, an excitement of the senses over the pertinent phenomena that lead a not very altruistic mind to reflect upon their meaning. Moreover, all the action is exerted on Louise from a distance. She is influenced by the life of Marie without having exchanged many words with her or discovered how correct her suppositions may be about whether the old woman's life was one of heroism or indifference. Nearly all of this life took place before Louise became a member of the family, and she is trying to perceive events that happened long ago. Suppose, however, that she had been interested in someone much closer to her own life? Someone whose actions and their effects had been subject to a long period of observation, someone who could finally be caught and questioned? Would she have been any more certain of "how things were"?

We know already from *Le Vent* that the answer will be "No." *La Route des Flandres* represents a remarkable step forward in the analysis of this denial and also in the search for techniques for illustrating it in the novel. In one brilliant arrangement are gathered most of the devices that can be used to tackle the problem of truth in writing, and for this reason alone the novel is invaluable for the purposes of critical research.

Recording (this is only the first of the problems) the inner voice of memory, one man recalls a series of events in which he was involved and which are known as "historical"; that is to say, some of the fighting during World War II. As a counterpoint to these events, he also records the images of his desire for a woman he has never met but who has been part of the lives of two of his companions. What will this inner voice have to tell, how will the story it relates be organized, and what phenomena will be selected from the mass of available data? What possible connection can be established between the conscious arrangement of language and the interminable murmur that repeats, deforms, and unceasingly redistributes the images furnished by all the senses and reverberating endlessly in the mind? In what time does this inner unfolding take place, the "now" which fades into the *"déjà vu"?*

Following deliberately in the steps of Proust, Joyce, and Faulkner, Simon takes up the task of pursuing this indefinable something that speaks, recalls, represents, and observes itself along with everything else, and yet appears separate from the being who thinks he owns it. This separateness is clearly shown in the subject Simon has chosen: Georges (possibly the husband of Louise, but before their marriage) remembers the events of the 1940 defeat of France and particularly those involving a distant relation of his who is also his company commander, a certain Captain de Reixach. The captain's wife, Corinne, becomes for Georges an object of fascination, although he has never met her. Georges' viewpoint, however, is not always exactly the same. He begins as the first-person narrator, but then, apparently seeing his own actions at a distance, appears in the third person. When a sudden emotion takes over, or when his imagination runs wild, the first person re-emerges. In addition, he is doubled by another character, Blum, the argumentative Jew who is his companion in the regiment and in the prison camp after they have been captured. Blum is possibly a convenient partner in conversation invented by Georges, who needs to speculate on the people who interest him.

These people—Captain de Reixach, Corinne, and their jockey Iglésia who is also a companion of Georges and Blum —once had a banal place in Georges' life. He knew the de

Reixach family through his mother who was related to them, and he received his first confused impressions of them through her interminable chatter:

> Presenting themselves this way then, through a woman's exasperating prattle, and without Georges' even having to meet them, the de Reixachs, the de Reixach family, then de Reixach himself, alone, with that cohort of ancestors crowding behind him, the ghosts surrounded by legends, whispered rumors, after-dinner stories, pistol shots, notarized documents and clanking spurs that (the ghosts) melted into each other, superimposed in the smoky and shadowy depths of the old cracked paintings, then the couple, de Reixach and his wife, the girl twenty years younger than himself whom he had married four years before in a murmur of scandal and whispering over teacups, provoking that explosion of outrage, of uterine indignation, of jealousy and lubricity that comprises the inevitable accompaniment to this kind of event. [pp. 58–59]

Seen through the smokescreen of gossip and of imagination stimulated by stories and family portraits, the de Reixachs are surrounded in Georges' mind by a haze of speculation long before he ever meets any of them. Yet the actual story is ordinary enough. Corinne de Reixach, much younger than her aristocratic husband, deceives him—perhaps—with the jockey who rides his master's horses much more skillfully than their owner does. De Reixach is killed at the beginning of the defeat of France, brandishing his sword while a machine gun blast cuts him down from his horse. Georges ends up in a German prison camp along with Blum and the jockey Iglésia, from whom he draws meager information about the supposed affair, nourishing his starved fantasy with visions of a voluptuous and provocative woman. Around the main characters circulate the soldiers and peasants, the latter providing a tale of cuckoldry that doubles the story of de Reixach and Corinne.

In different strata in Georges' memory, then, are various

scenes: scenes from the disastrous campaign of 1940, when his cavalry regiment is annihilated, from the cattle train that takes him into captivity, and the imaginary scenes involving Corinne, mixed with the real ones that derive from his final encounter with her after the war when he finally becomes her lover. To these must be added a number of subsidiary imaginary scenes, such as the ones connected with the portrait of de Reixach's ancestor, who is supposed to have killed himself and whose painted face bears a stain that suggests the wound caused by the fatal bullet.[2]

All of these scenes are carefully ordered, appearing a number of times at several key points, so that the narration is conceived in the shape of a cloverleaf.[3] The motionless world of captivity in the center balances the active world of the imagination and memory. Outside the camp certain objects are described that serve to generate movement in the narration each time they reappear. For example, the dead horse, which the defeated soldiers pass, combines the themes of nature, destruction, and transmutation; it connects with the cavalry and with the horses on the racing field. They in turn evoke the colors—coral—of Corinne, the pink cloth left on the hedge by peasants fleeing the battle zone, the jockey, the race, the curtain with the peacock on it at the window of the seduced peasant's wife, and finally desire itself. The theme twists in and out through numerous layers of events, gradually weaving them together in a solid piece. Throughout the whole

2. This portrait is hanging in Simon's country home. A reproduction of it can be seen in *Les Lettres françaises* (Oct. 1960), p. 12, and in *Entretiens,* No. 31, p. 120.

3. See "Les Secrets d'un romancier," *Les Lettres françaises* (Oct. 1960), p. 5. "I wanted to construct my book like a cloverleaf, with a center and three unequal loops. The dead horse is in the center of the cloverleaf" (my translation).

narrative the dripping rain and the sound of horse's hooves mark the progress of time. Once more the grass grows thick in the battlefields and in the camp grounds, bringing memories of more erotic foliage.

Around these key scenes and objects, reflections, metaphors, and semantic variations cluster more and more thickly, so that toward the end of the novel the attraction between one group and the other creates great density in the text. The linear quality of narration is definitively abolished. Whatever may be the points of departure—perception, memory, or invention— the text never moves in the direction of a "story," but, on the contrary, toward an even denser proliferation of images about these generative points.

Georges cannot think, therefore, of the death of de Reixach without evoking an ancestor who is supposed to have died in the aftermath of an unsuccessful war—but by accident (or was it suicide, just as de Reixach's bravado may have been a form of suicide?). De Reixach is associated with his unfaithful wife (Corinne), with her lover (the jockey Iglésia), and with the internment camp. The theme of the unfaithful wife mingles with that of the seduced peasant woman, the theme of Iglésia with that of the everpresent horse and with the idea of seduction. Between these groups of images there is continual interaction. The infidelity of Corinne is transferred to the wife of the ancestor, the sensations of Georges' body being crushed in the cattle train on the way to the camp are repeated in bed when he makes love to Corinne. In the camp, the Jew, seen first as Blum (whose argumentative character reminds us of Proust's Bloch), then as an anonymous storekeeper, later takes the shape of the usurer and chief of the camp underworld; he finally reappears by gratuitous inference in the story of the ancestor, as a hypothetical moneylender. Corinne is actually likened to the horses, since she is a *"femme-alezane"* (woman

—bay mare), ridden by Iglésia. Little by little, new links are forged between every theme and thought in the novel, until, as in Valéry's *Agathe,* one cannot touch one element of the book without causing the whole structure to vibrate.[4]

Much more than a simple game of associations is at stake. As Merleau-Ponty perceived, speaking of the effect of a color:

"There is a significant virtue in the texture of this red, a qualitative texture in the first place. After that, the experiences of which it revives the feeling have been lived *through* it (like things through their names) and that is what ensures—it is this archaic structure which ensures—that it will always be the mediator of these experiences. Because our experience is not a flat plane of qualities, but always to be invoked by some fetish or other acceded to by the intercession of some fetish or other."[5]

The object, the fetish, the generator, that stimulates the mind at the beginning of each scene, contains an inexhaustible variety of latent, superimposable combinations, that is, they can be seen like transparencies one behind the other. The peacock embroidered on the peasant woman's curtain could be the swan of Leda, the dove or faithful pigeon abandoned in the fable, the "headless duck" of de Reixach's ancestor—a sign each time accompanied by a story of stolen or faithless love. The horse, living, trotting, racing, sick, or dead, precipitates images of time, whose passing can be heard in the hammering of hoofs like the destructive dripping of the rain. It is also

4. Claude Simon relates that, during the final stages of composition of this novel, he used colored threads to represent each theme, weaving them together to make the design visible to his own eyes (from an interview with the author).

5. Maurice Merleau-Ponty, "Cinq Notes sur Claude Simon," *Médiations,* No. 4 (Winter 1961), 5–9, reproduced in *Entretiens,* No. 31, pp. 41–46. Merleau-Ponty recognized the similarity between his own theories and Simon's work and used *La Route des Flandres* as an illustration in his courses at the Collège de France. These notes were to have been included in a book that was never completed. My translation.

connected with sex, death, nature, and metamorphosis. None of these combinations take precedence over the others; they form groups that tend to combine with other groups. They offer no explanations and no parables. These combinations in all their density impose a pattern on the narration, but that pattern signifies the failure of the mind to impose on them all collectively a satisfying order, or a definitive meaning.

Long before he chose as an epigraph for *Le Vent* the aphorism by Valéry, "The world is incessantly threatened by two dangers: order and disorder," Simon revealed in his writing his preoccupation with this division. The room of the old Jew in *Gulliver* is a chaos of heterogeneous objects; the student's room in *Le Sacre* is, in contrast, bare and empty, as is that of Max in *Gulliver* during his years of renunciation. In *Le Vent* Montès, who could have been a rich landowner, lives in destitution, and the disorder of his tale is reduced by the narrator to a synthetic arrangement. In *L'Herbe*, the spartan order of old Marie's life and room is contrasted with the confusion and wastefulness of her relatives. The disorder brought by war in *La Route des Flandres* makes itself felt everywhere, but most of all in the prisoners' camp where creatures deprived of almost everything have nevertheless assembled a quantity of disparate articles. The physical disorder, which in all of Simon's novels reflects a profound disorganization in the lives of his characters, and, more deeply, a disorganization of the author himself faced with the demands of life and the "story," now finds itself in equilibrium with a new order. This order of ensembles or groups allows the mind, otherwise the victim of chaotic impressions, to perceive images and themes in clusters, which combine in this novel to reveal a careful overall design.

The new order that takes shape from these clusters is not, however, an order of simplification. The density and variety of the combinations preclude simplicity. This density results from a constant, persistent, recurring attempt at precision. The text of *La Route des Flandres* is remarkable for the extraordinary number of comparisons and rectifications introduced on almost every page; they serve not so much the purpose of adornment as the aim of narrowing the ever-elusive definition of *what* exists at any given time. The narration thus contains numerous expressions such as "in other words," "perhaps," "or rather," "as though," "like," "it seemed to him as if," "it made him think of." The desire to capture not reality itself, but the formations created by reality in the mind, leads to a restless correction of statements, for example—"(in other words the woman in other words the child he had married or rather who had married him)"; "(and probably not so much because he loved her but because he had to or better still because he had to because he loved her)" (p. 10)—in both cases these adjustments are placed in parentheses like the additions of an anxious speaker wishing to clarify every detail.

The comparisons that crowd into the text outweigh the metaphors, as though the author were only too well aware that each attempt to grasp the real is a step away from it; new elements of explanation are introduced and form new layers that screen off the original phenomenon, each time an effort is made to assimilate the unknown to the known. The metaphor is based on the assumption that one illuminates the other. The comparison, however, particularly when persistently repeated and corrected, suggests an uneasy circling around a point impossible to determine or the existence of a zone where precision fails entirely—like the mental state of the soldier crushed with fatigue and defeat:

I saw it for the first time . . . staring at it through that kind of half-sleep, that kind of brownish mud in which I was somehow caught . . . something unexpected, unreal, hybrid, so that what had been a horse (that is, what you knew, what you could recognize as having been a horse) was no longer anything now but a vague heap of limbs, of dead meat, of skin and sticky hair, three quarters covered with mud—Georges wondering without exactly finding an answer, in other words realizing with that kind of calm or rather deadened astonishment, exhausted and even almost completely atrophied by these last ten days during which he had gradually stopped being surprised, had abandoned once and for all that posture of the mind which consists of seeking a cause or a logical explanation for what you see or for what happens to you: so not wondering how, merely realizing that although it hadn't rained for a long time—at least so far as he knew—the horse or rather what had been a horse was almost completely covered—as if it had been dipped in café-au-lait and then taken out—with a liquid gray-brown mud already half-absorbed apparently by the earth, as though the latter had stealthily begun to take back what had come from it, had lived only by its permission and its intermediaries (in other words the hay and the oats the horse had fed on) and was destined to return to it, to dissolve again in it, covering it then, enveloping it (like those reptiles that begin by coating their prey with saliva or gastric juices before swallowing them) with that liquid mud secreted by it and which already seemed like a seal, a distinctive mark certifying its provenance, before slowly and definitively engulfing it. [pp. 25–26]

The attempt to seize the precise outline of the image only causes more images to spawn into a sort of nebula from which shapes emerge, sink back into the mass, and dissolve before re-forming into new figures. We are reminded of Georges' reflections about the horse (the central image of the novel), which, he says, will dissolve and be transmuted into other elements, which in turn will be combined into new and different structures. The process is without beginning or end, and all we can do is note its succeeding stages.

The metaphor, on the other hand, is absorbed into the text

in the form of relationships that govern the movement of the narrative. The idea of woman, for example, is associated with the idea of a mold, from which toy soldiers could be stamped, as though she were the earth itself, the "original crucible" from which mankind comes forth. At the beginning of the book, the word *semblable* (like) is retained in this comparison, whereas at the end the link is suppressed, and only the transition from the original element to all the components of the book is registered. Lying in bed with Corinne, Georges reflects:

Wet mold from which I had learned to stamp pressing the clay with my thumb the soldiers infantrymen cavalrymen and cuirassiers climbing out of Pandora's box (a race armed booted and spurred helmeted) spreading across the world the armed spawn they had a crescent-shaped metal plate hanging around their neck by a chain sparkling like silver, braid, silver fringe there was something funereal something deadly; I remember that field where they had put or rather penned or rather piled us: we were lying in successive rows heads touching feet like those lead soldiers stacked in a box, but when we first came it was still virgin undefiled so I threw myself on the ground dying of hunger thinking The horses eat it why not me I tried to imagine to convince myself I was a horse, I was lying dead at the bottom of the ditch devoured by the ants my whole body slowly turning by a thousand tiny mutations into a lifeless substance and then it would be the grass that would feed on me my flesh nourishing the earth and after all it wouldn't be so much of a change, except that I would merely be on the other side of its surface the way you pass from one side of a mirror to the other where (on that other side) things may go on happening symmetrically, in other words up above it would go on growing still indifferent and green just as they say hair goes on growing on dead men's heads the only difference being that I would be eating the dandelions by the root our dripping bodies exhaling that sharp pungent odor of roots, of mandragora, I had read that shipwrecked men that hermits eat roots acorns . . . [pp. 262–263]

Inextricably mixed with the idea of the woman's body are

various intermingled thoughts of fertility and a fatality as old as time, of the destructive race of soldiers issued from the womb, of the prison camp, of the hunger of the prisoners, of the grass in the field where they lay, of the horse that eats the grass, of the dead horse that molders and is eaten by the grass, of the equilibrium of life and death, of the indifference of nature and (through untranslatable verbal connection with *pissenlit* and *gland*) of the sexual parts that resemble grass and acorns.[6] The opening metaphor of the passage progressively rejoins the thematic content of the book, engendering along the way new metaphors that form an accretion—for example, the idea of hunger leads to shipwrecked men, acorns, and sex. There is even a negative recall, through the grassy "virgin field," of Corinne, who was by no means a virgin but who is the "mold" that prompts Georges' thoughts. Corinne's husband, de Reixach, dies brandishing his "virgin steel" (perhaps another sexual image).

Such a text illustrates abundantly the new order in the writer's work. The heterogeneousness of the images of the outside world melts into the homogeneousness of the writing, translated into an almost uninterrupted flow of words that continues, generally unpunctuated, except by insertions (parentheses) and half-stops (colons, incomplete sentences, and paragraphs), and unchecked by the usual rules. Sometimes the stream spreads out through subsidiary channels; sometimes it makes a bend following the fantasy prompted by one word (dandelion—root—mandragora—shipwrecked—acorn), a bend that turns back, however, to the original direction, while encompassing a major theme in the work. The feelings of expansion and containment are emphasized also by the flow of tenses,

6. This passage has been analyzed in greater detail by Stephen Heath in *The Nouveau Roman,* pp. 175–177.

the past emerging from the repetitive past imperfect—in layers as it were—or given by the omnipresent participle a sense of sustained incompleteness.

Here, then, ends the traditional composing of the novel. Story, plot, adventure are still present, but they are no more than the storehouse from which vital images are selected. All attempts to arrive at a solution are a waste of time. "How can we know and what can we know?" asks Georges. The writer can merely record the flowering and fusion of the image within a fluid, changing, already decomposing milieu.

How can the reader deal with a book that fails to furnish the usual aids for understanding? He may try to reconstitute a story that will correspond, more or less, to the data given in the novel, make suppositions as to how, why or when Iglésia was or was not the lover of Corinne, and imagine how Georges spent his period of captivity dreaming about this unimportant mystery. Will these speculations illuminate the "psychology" or the "character" of Georges? Hardly. We understand that he is obsessed by a number of thoughts that, retrospectively, cast light upon a given period of his life. If we examine the order and frequency of these thoughts, we may think that we can identify a certain kind of man: sensual, curious, and imaginative, very susceptible to the passing impression, closed within his memories, a builder of fantasies, a questioner constantly separating himself from the self who questions. Such efforts to see Georges as a person are, however, likely to be vain, because we do not know who Georges is. As we note at the beginning of this chapter, he oscillates between the "he," the "I," and someone who is neither. In Merleau Ponty's words:

The language of Claude Simon . . . indicates a certain relationship with one's self.

You no longer read I or he
Intermediate persons come into being, a first-second person
intermediate moods (present participle with a value of "simul-
taneousness")
this is absolutely incomprehensible either in the classic conception
of I think or in the concept of selfhood as annihilation: for then
I can hold and design the circle of selfhood—These uses of
language can only be understood if language is a being, a world,
if the Word is the circle.[7]

Georges is not only this "intermediate person." He is the
author of his own text, and like all authors he lends his voice
to the characters that he creates. Since we have no independent indicators in this text of what is true and what is false,
we have no standards by which to measure his statements. In
the no man's land of the indefinite pronoun, the reader follows not a person called Georges who speaks and interprets
the events of his life and the life of others, but something that
speaks sometimes as Georges, sometimes as another, and sometimes only for speaking's sake. Events and "character" are the
accidents of this speech and change as it changes. The narrative, distributed in the grammatical sense between "I," "he,"
and "you," spotlights the difficulty of deciding who is the
speaker, and emphasizes the modifications in the attitude of
the speaker to the self. Neither the tale nor the teller has en-
during characteristics but changes along with the telling. For
Georges, even the "research" with Corinne will not help him
to reach any conclusion. "That wasn't the way, that is, with
her, or rather through her, that I will reach (but how can
you tell?) perhaps it was as futile, as senseless as unreal as to
make hentracks on sheets of paper and to look for reality in
words perhaps they were both right, he who said that I was
inventing embroidering on nothing and yet you saw the same
things in the papers too" (p. 301). Writing does not neces-

7. Merleau-Ponty, "Cinq Notes," *Médiations*, p. 6; *Entretiens*, p. 43.
My translation.

sarily lead to the discovery of the truth about the writer or his subject matter. This is why Georges speaks so bitterly about his professor father's pursuit of knowledge by composing books.

We may prefer to resolve the issue by considering people and events as though they were part of a general design, just as chiefs of staff see the horrors of war like part of a pattern on a map. In this fashion we have at least an organized whole to give us the feeling of being in charge. In the very midst of defeat and disaster Georges envisions a military chart:

the hills represented on the map by tiny fan-shaped lines bordering the wavy line of the crest, so that the battlefield seems covered with sinuous centipedes, each corps represented by a little rectangle from which is drawn the corresponding vector, each bending back in this case to assume virtually the shape of a fishhook, in other words, the barb facing the rear of the part of the line forming, so to speak, the stem, the tip of the curve thus described coinciding with the point where contact had been made with the enemy troops, the whole of the battle which had just taken place therefore could be represented on the general staff map by a series of fishhooks arranged in parallel and with their points turned west, this schematic representation of the movements of the different units not of course taking into account the accidents of the terrain nor the unforseen obstacles occurring during the course of the fighting, the actual trajectories having the form of broken lines zigzagging and sometimes overlapping intersecting each other and which would have had to be drawn at the start with a thick vigorous line then diminishing thinning out afterwards and (like the maps of those wadis which are initially in spate and which gradually—unlike other rivers whose width constantly increases from source to delta—disappear vanish evaporated drunk up by the sands of the desert) ending in a dotted line the points spreading out farther and farther apart then vanishing altogether. [pp. 304–305]

The attempt at schematisation (we shall see the schema

become increasingly important in the novels to come) trails off here into nothingness. The reason is that the schema cannot provide the sort of information that Georges is looking for, as he rides with the group of exhausted, uncomprehending soldiers past the farms with their string of picturesque, evocative names. The individual accident does not appear in any plan showing the general scheme of events. The greatest tragedies (lost battles, wars) can be organized tidily into patterns of existence, which will tell us nothing about "human" truths. The farms with their unique names are not shown on any map, just as no particular soldier can be discerned on the schematized battlefield. Georges' special problem leaves no trace in the overall disaster.

Critics usually recognize, both in *L'Herbe* and *La Route des Flandres,* the profound effect of Faulkner on Simon's art, and rightly so. This effect can be felt in the long, convoluted sentences, in the dislocation of time sequences, in the uncertainty of viewpoint, in the ignorance, bewilderment, or resentment of the actors, in the conjectural tone, and above all in the atmosphere of almost cosmic doom. However, in Faulkner's narrative a central, significant, individual drama (albeit of universal scope) gathers around itself finally the fragmentary evidence which, piece by piece, is presented to us. In Simon's work, on the other hand, the drama never takes place. At most, the author suggests it when Louise realizes that she will not leave her husband, or Georges admits that he will discover nothing from Corinne. And, unlike Faulkner's work, Simon's novel offers no violent, terrifying resolution of the agony, no individual breaking-out or breaking-down of the damned circle. His anguish is of a different kind, one that consists in the absence of resolution and in doubt that such a thing as resolution exists. Georges will never know whether he has "embroidered" his story on nothing, whether his invention has been "drunk up by the sands of the desert." Far from bringing elucidation, the text he elaborates refuses to resolve itself in information. It demonstrates instead that it is the enemy of information, either because of its power to breed new texts (as, for example, Georges' preoccupation with the idea that de Reixach's death in battle might have been a suicide prompted by Corinne's infidelity leads him to spin more and more fantasies around the death of the ancestral de Reixach) or because of its tendency to peter out and vanish in the deserts of the imagination.

We are left, then, with the narrative itself. Clearly, the "meaning" of the narration lies only in its own constitution. A number of very decisive steps in the evolution of Simon's novel have been taken in *La Route des Flandres*. We have discussed the creation of the "intermediate person" that allows Simon to introduce subtly graduated changes into the perspective of the novel. Such changes are also the function of the time sequences, which are managed in this text with such skillful effects of "fading" and overlapping that we might say Simon creates also an "intermediate time zone" between scenes that occur and recur on different occasions. In addition, the generative image, already present in *L'Herbe* but less well-organized there, is brought to the foreground in *La Route des Flandres* and made the principle of construction of the whole novel. The result is a narrative of such coherence and power that any attempt to separate the interwoven images from one another is an act of mutilation. This close texture is reinforced by a procedure that will eventually become a characteristic feature of Simon's work: the use of the word image on the level of the work's total structure. Here, for example, the term *chevaucher* (to be astride, to straddle) recurs with its cluster of meanings (Georges is astride his horse, or Corinne, or time). The organization of the text is also a *chevauchement*—a straddling of one part over another, of one time over another, as the themes converge and separate. The hollow—*creux, moule*—, diversely represented as a ditch where the soldier hides, the molds for making toy soldiers, the woman's sex, is a sign for the final discovery of the book—at the heart of things is a void, and nothing is sure or certain, except the "incoherent, casual, impersonal and destructive work of time" (p. 320). Other such transfers in function of the word image can be recognized in the monotonous circling of the themes in the conversation of Georges' mother, like insects around an epicenter, or in the race where riders and goal are intermittently obscured from view, or in the curtain that rises and falls, concealing in a frustrating way an event that cannot be ascertained—all these are images of the actual structure of the narration. The fantasizing of Georges in the prison camp is perhaps no different from our conjecturing in the prison of forced ignorance, and the war that rages cruelly and absurdly in the rich and beautiful countryside may resemble the destruction wrought by time and our efforts to capture life through knowledge. These are not allegories of any desired truth, but structures that relate endlessly to one another on all levels of writing.

Claude Simon is already far from his early preoccupations. The search for a point of view, which hampered his first works, has led him to examine precisely the necessity or the possibility of finding one. What is there in the mind, which allows, invents, or presupposes any particular point of view? Is there not simply a tangle of memories, a forest of perceptions, a world of fantasies stimulated by the senses and the word, forming a whole forever complete and forever changing? How can this chaotic, undefined mass be reconciled with itself, or with similar "magma" (as Simon calls it) in the minds of others? Georges ends by confessing that he cannot *know,* that he has perhaps invented the whole story of Iglésia and Corinne. But in that case, what of the story and history, what of certainty and the belief that in the life of each and every one of us something has happened?

We may perhaps have recourse to the advantages of collective thought, to the adjustment of individual memories with those of the group, in order to construct a truth by intercorrection, and we can perhaps build in this way, by dint of constant verification, not a story but History. Up to this point, Simon has faithfully followed the path of the novelist who constantly tries himself and tries his métier. He will not avoid the test of historical confrontation, for it will be vital for the formation of his art. In the preceding novels Louise and Georges have been trying to find out what happened at some time in the past to someone whom they did not know. The protagonist of *Le Palace* will try to discover what happened to himself at a specific moment in history.

5 ❦ Le Palace

Even to seasoned readers of Claude Simon's novels, *Le Palace*[1] sometimes appears rigid in form and difficult to understand. It does not lend itself to romantic extrapolation as freely as *L'Herbe* or *La Route des Flandres*. Few of its passages have the sensuous appeal of either of these novels, or even of later ones. No countryside lushness colors the narration, no fresco of horsemen in full flight brings movement to the page. There is nothing but the shadow and the denial of feminine presence. Long lists of objects, apt to discourage the reader wary of excessive *chosisme*, enclose an action that turns impotently upon itself like a vortex. The entire narration is bathed in the Spanish Civil War atmosphere of *orina-esputos-sangre*—urine, spit, blood—without Hemingway heroes to relieve it. Yet this novel represents an exercise of the utmost importance both for the art of Simon and as an example of a practical, structurally exacting exploration of an urgent and disturbing necessity for the novelists: the need for *altérité* (otherness).

This necessity, we know, is present in any novel. On the level of "characterization," every novelist must decide to what extent he is "other," disguised as a first person observer, or

1. Paris, Editions de Minuit, 1962, translated by Richard Howard as *The Palace* (New York, George Braziller; London, Jonathan Cape, 1963). All passages quoted are from this translation.

divided in a number of varied *personae,* or both. On the level of "time" he must discover the variations of otherness in the remembered and reconstituted past. And, if he wishes, in the areas outside calendar time—imagination, dreams, memory— he may reveal how the combinations of otherness on various planes of space, time, and thought blend and shift and blur incessantly into all the selves issuing from the self. When he has to deal with the world of objects, he encounters a number of delicate problems, the most obvious of which is the question of objectivity and sympathetic identification.

Every teller of even the simplest tale must face, however unwittingly, at least some of these difficulties. The assumption of omniscience on the part of the author is full of risks; it can lead to skepticism on the part of the reader. The pretense of ignorance is no less troublesome, for it can raise the tormenting questions of the narrator's presence and the authenticity of his account. Simon's novels provide us with an excellent example of how an author progresses with regard to this dilemma.

In his early works Simon supposes that the partial ignorance of events on the part of his characters is balanced by the total knowledge of the author. *Le Tricheur* and *Gulliver* postulate omniscience in the novelist, as, to a large extent, does *Le Sacre du printemps.* The questions of *who* tells *what* and what is the final version, if any, comes to the fore in *Le Vent,* where the narration is continually interrupted by expressions of doubt and by speculations about the probable inexactitude of what other people relate. In *L'Herbe* and *La Route des Flandres* this question of the dubiousness of external evidence is not resolved, because the author uses a point of view conditioned by a single character who interprets what he perceives according to the terms of his own experience. Attempts are made by characters like Louise and Georges to penetrate what is foreign to them by combining the evidence and building theories or by merely speculating. In *Le Palace* a systematic effort is made to examine the difficulties inherent in the question of otherness, both for the novelist and for his *personae*.

The novel is constructed, like *L'Herbe* and *La Route des Flandres*, around the perceptions and memories of a single actor, called, as in *Le Sacre*, *l'étudiant*, that is, one who is learning. This personage goes much farther in his interrogation of external reality than do the central characters of the two previous books: they remain fascinated by the mystery of the lives that surround them and speculate endlessly on probable meanings. The student, on the other hand, is driven by the need, not only to discover the link between himself and the others and their respective pasts, but to incorporate this total experience into a coherent whole that would finally make sense. Each person and fact would have a contribution to make to this whole, if only he (the student) could grasp exactly what did happen. He therefore expends his efforts, with increasing intensity, in the pursuit of the phenomena that emerge within his consciousness—men, things, and events, which properly combined would give him the right to a place in an understandable world and time. He thus interrogates (1) a world of objects whose presence seems to him to contain the secret of internal change, (2) a personage whose past experience forms a double memory within his own, (3) a "historical" event, (4) a stranger who, also in the past, makes sybilline pronouncements on the meaning of action, but remains strangely elusive, (5) a being whom he identifies as himself at another time and who is separable from what he is, or was. All these characters live and move in a milieu that can be called not only a story, but also History. For one or another to exist convincingly, the disparate elements in the searcher's consciousness must fuse and lose their otherness in a new identity, in order to create something *comestible*, that is, properly blended out of the right ingredients. History, in short, should be the art of serving up other people's leftovers.

It is, indeed, a question of History, with a capital H, real and experienced. The author approaches this question, however, from a position of doubt and uncertainty, in a far more radical fashion than in the previous three novels. We may be able to record memories and thoughts and perceptions as they pass through consciousness and endeavor to turn them into coherent accounts. To attempt to square these accounts with those of other, equally non-objective beings is far more difficult. Yet only in this way can History be composed, on the supposition that to know what actually happened to one participant in the Spanish Civil War must in some way make possible a reconstitution of the total event or, at least, contribute toward such a reconstitution.

The person who ruminates this question remembers having been in Spain, having known some of the combatants, having seen at least a minor episode of the war.[2] Fifteen years later he returns and tries to distinguish in his memory what belongs to the past and what to the present and discover what happened, if anything happened at all. He realizes that when someone has been closely involved in historical action, in any action, he is, like Fabrizio at the Battle of Waterloo in *The Charterhouse of Parma,* very far from knowing what occurred. He is even farther from being sure, when he returns

2. Claude Simon points out that the name of the city is never mentioned and that the action could take place anywhere. The names on the tram stops, for example, do not correspond to Barcelona and this is important. However, the American dustjacket refers to Barcelona, and the photographs and other references in the special number of *Entretiens* make it difficult not to think of this specific city.

to the scene, what time, repetition, and reconstruction add to or subtract from the original sum of experience.

The term "revolution" appears in the epigraph and is defined by Larousse as the "locus of a moving body which, describing a closed curve, successively passes through the same points." The consciousness that registers phenomena in *Le Palace* is a verifying consciousness, seeking to determine the relationships between original perception and recollection stimulated by a return to the same point in space. But this consciousness is caught in the trap of presentification. If the student's memories correspond with what is perceived now, possibly the "now" corrupts them. If there is a difference between "now" and "then" is not that difference also the product and the trick of time? What had the student "been unable to see" that would explain why he cannot reconstruct the past as it had been? Is the "same" point of a closed circle in reality the same? What invisible accounting explains the difference between an event and the memory of that event?

The protagonist of this novel would like to resituate himself at exactly those points in his history that correspond to the spatial coordinates that he recognizes. But memory is not faithful to the cycle of events as they occurred; the mechanism of recollection, set in motion by the flight of one of the ever-present pigeons in the city, brings back first a collection of furniture in a hotel room where once the protagonist stood with four other members of the Spanish Republican Army to watch the funeral of a murdered general. Looking out over the wartime city, standing alongside his former comrades, he sees himself suddenly become completely foreign and absurd:

Then he saw himself, that is years later, and he, that residue of himself, or rather that trace, that stain (that excrement, so to speak) left behind himself: the ridiculous person one sees stirring, absurd and presumptuous, over there, far away, as though through the wrong end of the opera glasses, gesticulating, eternally rehearsing at memory's behest (and even without its behest: bursting in without even having been asked to do so . . .) [pp. 24–25]

At the same instant, however, while confronting the past, the student sees himself also in the eyes of those who have no wish to remember, those inhabitants of Barcelona who ignore their past and reject the man who reminds them of it. He is forced to leave the bar where he has encountered the unsympathetic stare of a barman and a prostitute, and, as he goes, he feels the beer he has just drunk in his stomach "like a kind of foreign body, unassimilable and putrescent" (p. 33)—as though his nausea resulted from the incompatibility of the different elements he contains: the uncertain past and the indigestible present.

Although he senses, at the very beginning of his search, that History, and his history, must be something destined solely to be consumed by the unwary, "carp or History" (p. 148), sacred and odoriferous, a dish to appease the dissatisfaction of having no part in the feast, he persists in his attempt to reenter the "tangential derivative" (p. 148) of the outside world, in the hope of finding his place in it. He turns for help to the apparently immobile, changeless objects that seem to bear the indelible imprint of the past, when the actors in the bygone story have already been replaced in our minds by the absurd puppets that our memory recalls.

Le Palace, then, is built around the jumbled objects that serve as witnesses to the past and the present. The first chapter, "Inventory," begins the catalogue of these objects: the fifth and last, "Lost Property Office," returns to them and shows clearly that the meaning of "object" eventually extends to people and their actions; the student, his companions, the city, the war, are all "lost." These two cataloguing chapters are like a material framework for the three others that deal with action during the revolutionary period.

The first instinct of the student is to consult the material evidence, as it seems more solid and trustworthy than the people, who are "unexpected and even slightly unbelievable, slightly unreal, slightly out of date . . . immobilized or preserved as in a photograph, in that kind of petrified and grayish matter which is the past, that gelatin which keeps things and people indefinitely, as though in alcohol" (pp. 39–40). A minute scrutiny of the objects in the bedroom of what was once a luxury hotel, where the student met with his Republican Army companions, is not reassuring, however, for the inventory is far from being a simple list of things seen at a given historical moment. The shoddy pieces of furniture in this room have been assembled from various sources and are themselves suggestive of a mobility that contradicts the idea of permanence. Their appearance is disturbing because they do not seem to belong where they are, and because they evoke the vanished splendors and the luxurious outfittings of the millionaires who used to frequent the hotel. The splendor and luxury have gone, but a few details—wallpaper, moldings, decorations—keep the ghosts of the departed guests hovering around the shadows of the former, elegant furnishings. The nondescript, heterogeneous chairs and tables that have replaced these furnishings are, however, equally non-existent except in the mind of the student, for the hotel has since burned and been replaced by a utilitarian bank building. Everything has been moved around in accordance with what seems to the student a constant rule of change, "another law . . . rather like that of U tubes, according to which the level of the contents in the various vessels must everywhere be equal, by virtue of which History was constituted not by simple migrations but by a series of internal mutations, of molecular displacements" (pp. 16–17).

Since History appears to demand this constant redistribution of objects, these displacements must be more than accidental removals. Mobile objects are the component molecules of significant ensembles. The pieces of furniture in the hotel room no longer have the relationship with their surroundings that they had previously, hence their function has changed. The table may have been a refectory table from a convent or a school; the chairs were once a bishop's diningroom chairs; the pink silk sofa looks as though it came from a brothel. Now they are all assembled and used by an equally heterogeneous group of republican army soldiers. Thus, change has occurred on visible and invisible levels. The continually shifting tables, sofas, and chairs are like the particles in the Lucretian poem that combine and separate continually to make up everything in the universe, yet compose an unalterable sum.

Now the furniture and the room have vanished with the hotel and can provide the student with no evidence about the past. The apparent durability of objects has failed to protect them, and him, from the effects of time. Preserved in the gelatine of memory, however, are also people, witnesses whose account may help to reveal things as they were at a specific point in the recurring cycle. As they appear to the student in his recollections, these people are outwardly objects among other objects. But they use words and actions to indicate the presence of an inner reality concealed in the outer shell. Do these words and deeds make it possible for the student to break through into the universe of History?

Two of the characters in the hotel room remembered by the seeker for truth have a special relationship to him, and a complementary relationship to each other. One is the stranger, the foreigner par excellence, the mysterious wise man who disappears before he can be questioned, the combatant who generates doubt about the value of action and ideas, who reflects disillusionment and cynicism like the barman and prostitute in later years. The American—nothing more is known of him than his nationality—projects this doubt from the past into the present of memory, even with regard to himself:

perhaps he didn't say anything, perhaps the American had said nothing either, perhaps nothing had ever happened, perhaps there had always been a bank there, perhaps they had never really existed, they (the American, the schoolmaster, the Rifle and the one wearing an officer's uniform, unless it was a policeman's—he (the homunculus, the student) didn't know how to tell them apart very well yet—thinking "Student! Good God: student!" with a kind of rage . . .)   [pp. 36–37]

Almost immediately, the angry uncertainty in the student's mind is countered by the recollection of another being who is very different. This being is so like all those belonging to his race that he is almost indistinguishable from them, he has a memory that sheds no doubt on the authenticity of what is recalled, he believes enough in his cause to kill for it. He is the *homme-fusil,* the man-gun or Rifle, who relates in detail the assassination he has carried out for the anarchists.

The student recalls sitting in a railroad carriage listening to the Rifle's story, at first with great attention. As he listens, however, the mass of information that accompanies the tale becomes so great that even the story teller has to reduce his story to a schema roughly drawn in pencil. He does this to make his meaning clear and to show the relative positions of all the actors in the drama. The effect of this simplification and of the exactness of detail is, however, continually lessened by the listener's wandering attention. The recital of the *homme-*

fusil is at first only interrupted by the thoughts of the listener concerning the life of anarchists in exile. These thoughts soon give way to reflections on the sights perceived from the train in which the two men are symbolically seated, then to further meditations which these thoughts awaken, and finally to the distractions caused by a dizzy car trip through the war-torn city

The rhythm and number of these interruptions continually slow up the pace of the Rifle's story, restoring to it the density of multiple experience that had been taken away by the schematization. In this way the simple act that, in reality (if there had been such a thing) took only as much time as is necessary to get out of a taxi and to pay the driver, occupies numerous layers of consciousness. The Rifle himself is first of all conscious, both during the act and during the recital of the act, of the extraordinary elasticity of time that allows such a quantity of physical and mental events to happen in so short a duration. This primary observation is reinforced by the maneuvering of the student's consciousness. At first interested in the obscure lives of the anarchists, which he reconstructs while listening ("and the student could see it all, just as if he had stood in the shop" [p. 55]), he is distracted by the train whistle which reminds him of the Far West, and then by immediate reality, the rainswept railroad depots that open on to the horizon of the battered city, which the travelers later traverse by car. Then later still, the sight of a statue commemorating the deeds of an explorer evokes a vision of new continents full of broad forests and multicolored birds. This outward sweep allows another world to penetrate into the interval between the beginning and the end of the assassination, an interval perpetually growing longer during the story, stretching out to infinity in the mind of the student. This dizzying enlargement is reflected in the pages where the author describes the speeding car, the spinning roads around the wildly mobile statue, the annihilation of the sense of direction:

he saw through the windshield something made out of stone, marble, and metal mingled in a complicated fashion and that came toward them with the speed of a locomotive, naked women, tritons, prows of ships, cornices, all mixed together: this slid abruptly to one side, horizontally crossing the windshield from right to left, reappearing through the left window, the student expecting to see it pass and disappear to one side whereas on the contrary he could now distinctly make out the impassive metallic face of a siren and a stone entablature that continued to rush towards him, larger and larger, still at the speed of a locomotive. [p. 90]

The speed of the car seems to animate the monument, just as the student's fancies bring life to the printed pages of an encyclopedia that describe the explorer's achievements and the resources of the rich lands he discovered. Both monument and print are really motionless signs that have to be transformed into action by the speed of perception and thought. As memory recalls them, the occupants of the car are also signs, permanently animated or suspended in the imagination of the man who remembers them:

as if immobility, a scornful impassivity where somehow the complement, a paradoxical, obligatory element of speed, so that he seemed to see, after the car had crashed as it could not help doing from one minute to the next, their three bodies or rather the ghosts of their three bodies calmly continuing, unconcerned, indifferent and sitting on nothing, advancing endlessly at terrible speed into the deserted and illuminated city. [pp. 99–100]

The student listening to the Rifle's story reflects, then, that its turbulent action can be recorded only by a series of fixed, schematic compositions. He imagines the Rifle fleeing from the scene of his crime like a character in a comic strip cartoon, in which certain conventional lines suggest rapidity, "the scene articulated by one of those illustrators specializing in such things, the immobilization, the perpetuation of the tumult, the twisted expressions of horror, stupefaction or rage" (p. 102).

In his effort to break away from the absurd immobility of a memory invented by him for someone else, to penetrate, by restoring movement, "that invisible sliver of time that separated two universes" (p. 105), the student tries to put himself in the place of the Rifle and to recreate the flight with all its sensations. Both he and the Rifle are obsessed with the weight, the immanence, the incoherence of "that enormous series, or rather mass, or rather magma, or rather maelstrom of sensations, sights, noises, feelings and contrary impulses rushing together, mingling, superimposing, impossible to control and to define and which had surrounded a man's death with all the pomp and ceremony and abundance necessary" (pp. 107–108). Whereas the Rifle appears to be communicating in all sincerity an experience that is his own, the student is trying to absorb this experience into an already filled consciousness, and, at the same time, to pierce the hermetic wall barring him from a foreign universe. This contradictory movement is accompanied by a physical and mental malaise rendered by the images of severance, vertigo, and redistribution of weight. At the high speed of the car, the fragile body of the Rifle suddenly weighs "a ton."

The chapter on the *homme-fusil* is like a ballet on the theme of memory, danced to the rhythm of variations on time and space: memory immediate and direct, memory of memory, memory of another's memory, reconstruction of imaginary memories, and the total of all these variations. This play of continuously renewed relationships between he-who-remembers and the world composes the warp and woof of mental time, that elastic material as close to zero as to infinity. This contractile and extensible matter, endlessly forced into new patterns, appears with more or less fluidity according to motion, speed, the quantity of details available, and the displacement of perspective. How fast does History happen? Does it "happen" at all if one can be back at the "same" point in time? Has memory any value other than being an immediate phenomenon? To what degree do images born from association obscure those of a past that may be more mythical than true? The problems of Heraclitus and Zeno merge into phenomenological data. What interest have they beyond that of providing convenient structures for thought?

The memory of the Rifle obviously cannot be more simple and less schematized than his listener's. The Rifle has been relating one event, and the student in turn recalls another event, which has a positive-negative, active-passive relationship with the assassination: the burial of Santiago, a general who has been killed under mysterious circumstances. In one case we have a man, alive and present, who has put someone to death; in the other, a man, present but no longer alive, who has been put to death. Both events demonstrate the difficulty facing any writer of stories ("historical" or "fiction") and also the *mise en abyme* of the whole novel. A violent act, supposedly significant, is perceived by one participant and recorded by him for himself and/or another. This perception is henceforth doubly modified in both minds: it becomes schematized, for easier recollection, but it also loses its real contours, fading into other perceptions that spread and dissolve like the ripples in water where a stone has fallen. The meaning of the event grows weaker, and the evidence of the perpetrator of the act becomes the evidence of hearsay, and then hearsay of hearsay, congealed in language but contaminated by forgetfulness and lack of attention. In this way, the dead who took part in historical acts of violence, sooner or later turn into schematized and heraldic memories. They are "those characters of History or legend who died long ago in a battle or a holocaust, not holding back the onrush of invaders, guarding a pass, saving some nation or city whose name or location no one knows any more . . . but who doubtless died for the sole purpose of being represented centuries later, and not even a likeness (for who knows the faces of dead heroes?)" (p. 138).

Implacably doubt of its authenticity creeps in between the original act and the effigy we raise to it in our mind. In the face of this common treachery, how can we judge? "And among them, of course, are the good and bad uncles, but which one's the good one here?" asks the American. The person caught up in the action naturally answers, like Alonso the schoolmaster: "*Nosotros:* we others" (p. 121). But the person already at some distance from this central point begins to see the action as one of the phases of eternal flux and reflux. More prosaically, the action is like one of the streetcars that make the trip from one end of the city to the other, following a route that endlessly repeats the same turnings. This explains why the chapter that follows the story of the Rifle and includes the recollection of the Santiago funeral inevitably leads to the moment when the student stares at the streetcars and asks the anguished question:

But what was it? What was it? No doubt there was something he hadn't been able to see, something that escaped him, so perhaps he too could gain a footing, get inside, gate-crash this tangential comestible and optimistic derivative of metaphysics baptized carp or History, by means of which, if you knew how, you could apparently derive yourself in a manner that was if not agreeable and coherent at least satisfying, as was proved by that excremental derivative of reason baptized rhetoric, and after all it couldn't be so difficult since so many people managed it. [pp. 147–148]

Truth, Reason, History, thanks to the terrifying and regular shift of the totality of phenomena, become only artificial stops along the route; we cannot prolong them. Horror, indignation, individual rights, all are lost in this flux because "no doubt out of routine, custom, formality, because apparently to keep this old lump of mud and water turning required a periodic ration of children crushed under beams, disheveled women baring their breasts and with bony hands pulling away stones and rubble, in return for which the seasons returned more or less regularly and sun, rain, wind and frost divided up the time in an endurable fashion" (pp. 139–140).

Fatality is at fault. But something worse exists than the fatality whose elements can be counted and added up to an exact and overwhelming total, and that is the fatality which denies man even that vain satisfaction and afflicts him with a destiny he cannot manage to define and which constitutes a senseless, meaningless sum, never equal to itself.

In the darkness of the fourth chapter the student pursues the uncertainties that make up the sum of his own existence. These uncertainties bear the traits of the enigmatic American as he is seen during the preceding day, lounging in the café, uttering disillusioned words that seem to deny the meaning of his presence among the combatants. Against the background of blank hotel windows and the hot and sticky blackness of the city, this presence is in itself a dubious thing, since the student is not sure whether the stranger is in the hotel at all, whether he is occupying a room alone, or, finally, whether the room the student is watching is really the right one. Trying to recall during the long night hours the events of the day before, the student can only find two pieces of material evidence: the empty cigarillo case, with its exotic designs, which the American has given him, and the newspaper, the source of general information, which behaves like an unstable and moving thing, an object that has to be captured and held under an ashtray.

Neither piece of evidence provides any information about the ill-defined personage of the stranger ("he always managed to look as if he hadn't slept or changed his shirt for two days but never more than that—so that he must have used a razor, slept, and changed shirts at some time or other, but when?" [pp. 151–152]), who does not believe in the progress for which he fights ("It's the same everywhere you know. You should travel" [p. 168]), and who appears to have some key to the student's inquiry but remains constantly inaccessible. Instead, the inquirer only catches sight of the ambiguous, shadowy form of a naked woman; instead of metaphysics the simulacra of pleasure. And instead of the knowledge the American might have given, the schematized and flowery tableaux on the cigarillo box offer, in the way that the dictionary gives information about the explorer in the second chapter, manageable fragments of distant reality—like the crumbs of tobacco that the student tries to make into a cigarette. These far-off, static pieces of truth cannot be integrated into a whole that can be consumed. In the end, the troubled watcher is triply deceived: first, by his mind that has not been able to recall correctly which room is the American's nor discover whether the latter was ever there or ever with a woman; second, by his body, which after suffering and sweating all night, drops into sleep, just when he should have been awake and alert; third and above all, by time—he has heard the striking away of the hours at night, but time is suddenly lost in sleep, so that when he wakes, it is too late for him to seize his prey.

The second and fourth chapters are accounts of the effort made by one consciousness to absorb the foreign substance of other minds, to adapt and serve it up in an "edible" fashion.

It can be ingested only with difficulty. The foreign material must first be reduced to capsule form and then served with a homemade sauce, as it happens in the case of the Rifle. The American, on the other hand, offers pure poison, leading to nausea and rejection. Yet consciousness, by definition, assimilates this material or perishes. All the persons or objects in the novel have, in the end, to be made of the intimate substance of the student himself:

the student (that is, the one who had been the student) able to hear them—that is, if, as they say, a man is constituted by the sum of his experience, able to hear that part of himself which had the form of a lanky American . . . having a dialogue with that other part of himself which had the form of a bald man wearing something that looked like a uniform . . . both of them occupying that part of himself which had the form of a little square of the old part of the city with, closing one of its sides, the obscure façade of the church . . . and on another of its sides the still open bar of the requisitioned hotel where they (the American, the Italian and the student—or rather those three parts, those three fragments of himself which were an American, a Rifle and a young fledgling) were lying. [pp. 171–172]

This homogenization of others in the student is balanced, however, by an internal fragmentation, which becomes progressively marked. The "homunculus" is not simply someone who took part in these events, not simply someone who, fifteen years later, evokes this participation, but at that time, or in what he remembers of that time, he is also himself cleft in two, especially at moments of crisis. At one such moment when he discovered that the American was gone, "he quickly stepped back . . . so that the part of himself which was struggling with the door there in the hallway suddenly stopped, now content merely to stand there opposite the door as a moment before . . . while the other part of himself, consisting of muscles, flesh and blood, on all fours on the floor, was busy feverishly picking up the butts and pieces of scattered matches" (p. 201).

The Rifle fleeing from his crime has the impression (or the student listening to him has the impression) that his body runs mechanically without consulting his mind—"his body (his legs, his heart, his lungs) still running so to speak outside of himself . . ." (p. 107). In the same way, a profound separation exists in the being of the student who, after the experience and doubt of the dark night, tries to rejoin his comrades:

> Then he managed to move, which a moment before he had thought impossible, doing so now not only without effort but even, so to speak, unconsciously—as if something other than his will: reflexes, mere muscles, had come of their own accord to the aid of his failing spirit, his failing mind, so that while the latter was still wondering what he would do next, he was already watching himself cross the threshold . . . at the same time that he could hear his own voice, casual too, talking so to speak outside himself, autonomous, irrepressible (just as that thing which a few moments before was laughing irrepressibly, everything in himself seeming to function separately and so to speak on its own account, as in that fable about a man whose intestines, lungs, heart, arms and legs suddenly began, with a kind of anarchic insurrection, functioning independently). [pp. 220–221]

This separation of mind and body is so contrary to life that it has to be countered by a constant effort to integrate internal and external faculties. The being of the student is scattered all over the universe of the novel, acting anarchistically beyond his control. He is the Rifle who carries constantly turned towards his own head the instrument of death. He is the American who, equipped with only a revolver and unquenchable cynicism, joins in a battle in which he does not believe. He is all the others—the faithful followers of the cause, the militants, the survivors, the old men in the square, the nurses and their fiancés, the children—he is all the men driving their old trucks or stacked in the streetcars, suffering because they have been amputated of their weapons, all resembling each other interminably, sons of the same race, inextricably mingled, a million copies of the same recalcitrant self.

This residue of so much consciousness only reminds the student of an absence or rather of an inability in himself to grasp "what he had not been able to perceive." If he turns again to the wandering objects of the Lost Property Office, he learns only that man's absence leaves no void. The building into which he tries to enter with difficulty is as full as ever. The American disappears, leaving no perceptible gap, but not before he has shown the student that even the supposed secret of objects is composed of absence. As he sees articles thrown from the windows of a store that sells religious paraphernalia, the searcher (feeling once more that strange detachment from himself "as if someone else, a kind of idiot, a stammering fool, an imbecile parrot interrupted each time he opened his mouth" [p. 144]) exclaims:

"But nothing else? Nothing else? Only cardboard wings? Nothing else?"
and the American laughing again, saying:
"Isn't that enough?"
and the student:
"But nothing else?"
and the American:
"You don't think that's enough?"
and the student:
"But nothing else!"
and the American:
"Listen! It's what it is, isn't it? What more do you want? Something else? What: 'something else'?"   [p. 145]

In this way the student discovers the final trap. Our concept of otherness acts prismatically on what is, so that even if we could break through "that invisible sliver of time that separated two universes," we could not discover the secret law of the "internal mutations," but only that whatever we had imagined to be there is not there and has been diffracted to some other point out of our reach. The triple interchange of perception, imagination, and reality is never to be resolved into a neat formula, and the "something else" so desperately sought by the student is meaningless.

The impact of *Le Palace* comes from the manner in which Simon explores the territory of the individual consciousness, establishing its limits and their points of suture with possible structures in the novel. Simon is the explorer and colonizer of the memory, returning to regions already revealed by his predecessors, but offering a comparative method of exploitation. The construction of any novel demands that the worlds of others be taken into account. The novelist can try to capture and absorb these worlds; he can force his way into them, he can imagine shared experience. Simon shows his protagonist attempting these methods and failing. In an effort to assimilate the history of the Rifle, the student is able to grasp only a series of roughly drawn schemata and is thrown back on himself. When he tries to break down the barrier between himself and the stranger, the door will not yield, and the stranger is not there; when he wants to return to the daily life of his comrades, to work and eat with them, he sees that a part of himself refuses to follow his own instructions. Objects are not what they appear to be nor what they are imagined to be. The present world, when he comes back to it, is already separate from him. So every attempt at absorption or expansion is frustrated. It is not surprising that the book is filled with images of indigestion and nausea—failure to assimilate—or of expulsion and hemorrhage—dispersion of the vital forces.

The student, in fact, is almost continually in the position

of the person in Sartre who peeps through the keyhole and reacts according to what he sees, but who has not yet discovered the meaning of his own function in the eyes of others. Those who speak to him do not seem to perceive him as they are perceived. When the eyes of the barman and the prostitute fall on him, they are accusing, hostile as towards an outsider. The shouting of the barman and the scorn of the woman push him back a great distance and force him to return to a nonexistent history where the only glance that can reach him is his own. Thus, he sees himself as the double of all those he observes; however, far from reaching a happy integration of it all, which might be called Philosophy or History, this return to self indicates a pathological estrangement leading to death.

He is not allowed to integrate himself into the entirety through the eyes of a third person, whether it be a narrator or another character. The narrator is never distinguished from the student himself, and the use of the third person pronoun, which places a distance between the being and itself, adds to the confusion when it is freely used for all other male characters and objects. For example, whether the unspecified reflections in parentheses during the story of the Rifle are those of the student or the Rifle, or attributed by the student to the Rifle, is difficult to determine. This confusion is a device used by the novelist to convey the uncertainty of the student, but it also represents the ambiguity of the novelist himself.

The interrogative pronoun *quien,* which returns like a refrain throughout the text and is associated with the idea of death, is charged with a solemn significance. Always printed on perishable material (newspaper, billboards), it appears in a foreign language (Spanish) and asks a question concerning life and its extinction (who killed?). This *who* also implies *what,* which in turn points to a terrible, impersonal truth: "so that the real translation (that is, what everyone really read) wasn't 'Who has killed?' but 'What has killed?' as if they were wondering in astonishment about the name, the nature of an infection, a disease" (p. 125).

The *who* who is called the student offers variations of himself, none of which is complete. We do not know what the man who lived the adventure and the man who later tries to fit his memories exactly over the traces of the event have in common. No narrator will tell us, for that would require joining the two parts in a false whole, and would suppose omniscience, or the partial "I" of the historian, based on the subjective "I" of the participant. The one who acts and the one who reflects on the action become quite separate as soon as the re-flection takes place: "something in him which had no need of a body, of limbs in order to move across the room again, going out, running back down the hallway, counting the doors once again and checking the number on the little oval enamel plaque while at the same time he seemed to hear the wooden panel echoing under the furious assault of his feet while, clinging again with both hands to the doorknob, he turned and shook, turned, shook, knocked, turned..." (p. 201).

The printed word therefore is presented as the final mockery. Before the eyes of the student the newspaper unfolds "as if it were opening in response to a facetious and sarcastic will," thrusting before him the demand, in capitals, "QUIEN HA MUERTO?" (p. 202), a question which, in its ambiguity, queries the sense of any action. (The Spanish phrase, as it appears in this truncated way, can mean either "Who killed?" or "Who has died?") Language itself and even the paper it is printed on have no respect for persons.

History falls under the same accusation as the simple story, being merely an attempt to avoid the problem of otherness by providing a schema of what occurred or by substituting an interpretative *who* for all the incomplete states of consciousness which it implies. Heroes are only pictures on billboards, varying according to the light of day. Reports are words that twist and die absurdly as soon as they are articulated. It will always be impossible to know what others did and thought, even that other who was one's self before becoming the being reflecting on that self. What then can be concluded about Causes and Battles? What is their legacy, if not a heap of jumbled ruins in the midst of a life that continues willy-nilly, after having received "its periodical ration" of horrors, to repeat itself stupidly and incomprehensibly?

The writing of *Le Palace* translates the anguish caused by this question into a vertiginous, non-progressing movement, full of vortices turning about a void. The book is centered on the funeral procession, which appears not to advance ("seemed to oscillate in place, motionless and twinkling" [p. 113]), surrounded by spectators who cannot be heard ("like particles of silence" [p. 123]), gathered into a crowd that cannot see ("like blind men . . . this one had no alien, external objective" [pp. 124–125]). Around this "historical" event, deaf, blind, motionless, is furious motion: the Rifle runs for eternity after his crime, the occupants of the car are hurtled forever through the empty city, the student runs in pursuit of the American, the crowd rushes into the hotel to escape the rain. The sum of all these movements is nil. The swirling curtain of pigeons, a sign of temporality within the eternal, rises and falls at the beginning and the end of the novel, leaving men and things indistinguishable from what was there before. The saying "Plus ça change" has lost its banality here, however. In *Le Palace,* the more things change, the more obvious it is that we shall never know what "ça" was, because it will always be something different from what we are thinking now, and therefore cannot be "the same."

The novel is carefully structured on all levels as a demonstration of this thesis. The inventory of the beginning becomes the Lost Property Office of the end; things and men end up dispossessed of their original functions and relationships to each other. Between these two catalogue chapters, which serve as a frame for the silence and immobility of the funeral, the different actions of the protagonists swing back and forth in human space and time. These actions take place in the dark—the train trip at night, the meditations in the obscure hotel bedroom—and are projections of endless attempts to join two extremes, the man of faith in action with the man of doubt who acts. The daylight world of chapters I, III, and V is the world of schism in which the student feels first the separation due to time and last the separation from existence itself. At the heart of the work lies silent death, and the question without an answer: "What was it? but, what was it?"

The rigid structure is like a straightjacket to hold in place the flaccid, formless, crumbling substance of beings without consistency. The stylistic details that characterize Simon's writing—long series of participles, highly convoluted phrases, parentheses, complex paragraphs, repetitions, abstractions, cinematographic changes of distance—are all present in force in this book. So are certain fetich-images: pigeons, newspapers, the anonymous woman's body seen by the voyeur, horses, the car ride. Typographical effects depending upon the emphasis in capital letters of certain key words or groups are frequent, as are the truncation and the stupefying repetition of certain expressions. The one word that signifies grammatically union, strength, and the future—VENCEREMOS—appears mutilated on bits of paper, repeated on torn posters, making us aware by its physical presence—like the QUIEN HA

MUERTO of the newspaper and the ORINA-ESPUTOS-SANGRE of the pharmacy—of the futility of fixed signification.

The predominating verb tense is the imperfect, which contains the indeterminancy of the overlapping tenses in narration. A few preterites break up this narration when there is a shift of scene, as in the change from present perfect to simple past after the conversation in the bar or a symbolic intervention occurs, as when the pigeon interrupts the phantasmal meeting in the last chapter. At the end, however, when the student puts into words his objective—to join his former companions in death—this simple past is transformed into a conditional ("then he would enter . . . they would all be there . . ." [p. 248]), and then—for the first time—into a present, as the unrealized past and the dream future meet and cancel out.

In the end, the student has no real companions, except the shoeblacks in the washroom, who are like so many underworld rulers, reigning over human remains, decay, and excrement, and horribly disguised, like many ancient gods, as wretched creatures devoted to the most humble occupations. "The ceremonial row of shoeshine boys with their crow-black hair" (p. 252), throws a mythical light on the entire narration. Through some awful decree, despite desperate efforts made by man to join his fellows as he rushes toward his absurd and imperceptible destiny, he can have as witnesses only these dark deities, in the shadow of the bird of doom.

Claude Simon denies energetically that he offers any message or expresses any metaphysical point of view in his books. If one wishes to look for them, traces of personal disillusionment on the historical and the political level can be discovered in the choice of material and in the organization of *Le Palace*.

The Civil War or the parliamentary regime may well have been the "little macrocephalic corpse dead before its time because the doctors hadn't agreed on their diagnosis and thrown into the sewers in a shroud of words" (p. 21). Indeed the book ends on the same tragic image of the city bleeding to death from its abortive birth. But a book, by its existence, is a positive fact. The student of literature is justified in passing beyond ideologies and seeking the relationship between the problems raised and the solutions accepted in the context of the novel.

Simon has attacked vigorously all the problems he has raised since *Le Vent,* and he has turned each one into a practical demonstration. The novelist's problems—the story, evidence, memory, and the misdeeds of time—are woven into the narration as part of an experience, the experience of someone who is trying to make them part of his own reality. Simon has also faced an existential problem that derives from and dominates all the rest: it concerns our entire mode of being in the world around us, in the midst of other beings and objects that seem relentlessly alien. How can a single consciousness reconcile its subjectivity with that of others? How can it be one with itself? How, in short, can it be so situated as to recognize itself as being in and of the world?

These questions have been vital to the philosophers of the twentieth century, and to none more than to the late Maurice Merleau-Ponty, who recognized in Simon's art an apt illustration of his own observations concerning language, perception, and the relationship of the ego with the world. *Le Palace,* in fact, might well be considered a discussion of some of the theses that Merleau-Ponty advanced twenty years before about the interchange between the Self and the Other.

The discussion in this novel, however, is entirely in negative terms. The student, who continually attempts to discover his place with regard to others and in the world, fails in his quest because his consciousness, while perpetually turning inward upon itself, never reaches the still point of total solipsism. It is neither engaged in the true dialectics of Self and Other, nor blessed with the "absolute density which would free it from time."[3] Time, far from being the external source of this ambiguity, manifests itself always at the point of contact with the Other. In the eyes of the Other the student becomes aware of the *now* that denies the *then,* or the past impinging on the present, or time itself immobilized by distance and myth.

If he could see only what takes place in his own consciousness and blend into his own organization everything that presents itself—makes itself present—to it, he could say with Valéry's Monsieur Teste that he can see himself seeing himself existing.[4] But he cannot imprison himself within the hermetic Self, any more than he can accomplish the transcendental act that would return him to the world. *Le Palace* is, significantly, the only novel by Simon in which the physical act of joining—love-making which momentarily and desperately allows both a union and the defeat of time—is present only as an incompleted shadow-play. For the student, Time is a suppurating wound, and the Other is the main source of his suffering. To find acceptance, he must first pass into the timeless region of death; then he would finally relate to others:

they would all be there, the schoolmaster, the Italian, the bald man, the American, with their indecipherable, exhausted, calm and passionate faces . . . exuding something invincible, something indestructible (not a belief, a faith, nor even a conviction, still less the certainty of being right: merely knowing that, good or bad, things could be otherwise), and they would accept him, without smiles, without effusions, without even a visible sign of

3. Merleau-Ponty, *Phénoménologie de la perception,* "Avant-propos," p. vii. My translation.
4. *Oeuvres complètes,* II, 25.

sympathy: nothing but a brief glance, inexpressive, neutral, as if it were natural for him to be there, to rejoin them, although a little late, as if they had been expecting all along, even after so many years, that he would finally meet them here, beginning to talk again about what they had been discussing before he came in . . . [p. 248]

This text reveals everything and shows clearly the nature of the student's search and of his frustrated desire: he seeks not good or evil, or even understanding, but union—to join the others—at whatever the cost—but join.

The import of the novel is not in the discussion of a philosophical theme and certainly not in the enunciation of any creed. The situational dilemma is surely, profoundly, continually, that of the novelist himself, for no novelist can pursue his art without engaging in the dialectics of the Other. Can he play the roles of Ego and Alter without annihilating Self? *Le Palace* is an investigation of possible answers to the dilemma. Here the relationship between fiction and History is of the utmost importance, as it is (although in a different manner) in a later book *La Bataille de Pharsale*. To present History as a perfect, or at least an "edible" product of dialectics is a risky and dubious enterprise. It presupposes a possible resolution of the tensions that must keep every historian continually vigilant. History is essentially incomplete, because for it to be complete, it would have to be constructed from the outside. But why is the exterior construction, which is denied to the historian, not permitted in the case of the novelist, who is responsible to none but himself?

In comparison with the historian, the novelist has a liberty and a privilege of great import: he can refer directly to his source and use it without shame. Where the historian is at the mercy of elements that are no part of himself, the novelist discovers that the irrefutable truths from which he builds his work are immediately at hand in his own consciousness. Why does he not exploit this liberty?

The whole mystery of the realist novel lies in this question. For the innocent realist is often attempting to write micro-history, that is, to do on the scale of the individual what History does on the large scale and thus put himself under the sign of the Other. Should he feign exteriority, he will be reduced to schematization and deceit; should he cling to interiority, then he must resolve the dialectics of intersubjectivity.

In *Le Palace* Claude Simon demonstrates what will happen if the author faces up to the implications of his choice. Already in *La Route des Flandres,* when Georges cries "How can we know? How can we know?" and even "What can we know?", he indicates the difficulties encountered by man in search of truth. Georges is generally concerned with speculations concerning what happened to others, the student, with personal experience involving himself together with others. In both books the essential question of the Story is discussed. But *Le Palace* extends the discussion from the individual case to the general, from the story to History.

The negative results of the inquiry do not, however, put an end to the novelist's activity. He is not, after all, obligated to find out "what happened." He does not have to settle for the optics of Descartes, nor is he condemned to follow the nightmare traces of Kafka. He can return to zero and examine the data as they are presented in their original milieu, without any further effort towards integration into a spurious whole. Claude Simon will turn in the direction of this solution in his next novel, entitled, significantly, *Histoire.* Having demonstrated with rigor and skill in *Le Palace* the impossibility for the twentieth-century realist to retain the traditional structures of the novel—which are dependent upon at least a simulated understanding of "others in the world"—he will henceforth concentrate on the "what" that perceives and writes, stripped more and more of its identifying idiosyncrasies.

Le Palace is therefore not only an important moment in the increasingly subtle relationship between an author and his art; it is also a significant piece of evidence in the litigation concerning the very existence of the novel as an intellectual activity.

6 ❧ Histoire

At the end of *Le Palace,* Simon comes face to face with the extreme consequences of his own logic. If History escapes us through all the fissures in Time, how can we ever undertake the recital of "what happens when . . ."? Must we abandon all attempts at reconstruction and simply satisfy ourselves with registering the ambiguous shifting of the separable pieces that make up the memory? To what extent is it legitimate to impose an arbitrary order on the inexhaustible whole of which we are composed? And what is the effect on that whole of an order that is not part of its nature?

Simon appears to give a pessimistic answer in the epigraph to the new novel that he calls, with apparent irony, *Histoire.*[1] Two lines from the eighth Duino Elegy by Rilke make up this epigraph:

> It submerges us. We organize it. It falls to pieces.
> We organize it again and fall to pieces ourselves.[2]

It—the vast, amorphous, fluctuating accumulation of material that is constantly changing into something else—what can be the relationship of the novelist with *it?*

1. Paris, Editions de Minuit, 1967, translated by Richard Howard as *Histoire* (New York, George Braziller; London, Jonathan Cape, 1968). All passages quoted are from this translation.
2. Epigraph translated by Richard Howard.

One immediate consequence of recognizing all matter as "unorganizable" is the disappearance, in any type of narrative, of a "beginning" and an "end." To learn what goes on in any consciousness, one may break into the movement at a given moment, but what we might find there has no law of logical or chronological development. The only imaginable "beginning" is the marking of an interruption in the regular flux of images, an interruption we most often recognize when we come out of sleep. The waking mind grasps the first perception which, after the night of absence from the remembered Self, allows the consciousness to rediscover the "I" enriched with a world of memories that each day overwhelm it. *Histoire* opens with such a recapturing of the self by means of a moving shadow, that is, the branches of a tree perceived at the moment of waking: "One of them was almost touching the house and in summer when I worked late into the night sitting in front of the open window I could see it or at least its farthest twigs in the lamplight" (p. 1).

The tree is perceived not visually but through the sounds of birds in the branches that provide a thread of consciousness sufficient to draw up from oblivion the multiplicity of images lying ready in the memory. These pre-conscious images are like the reverse side of immediate perception. Before re-entering the day and the present, the mind rediscovers the night, and the distant past it has carried through the night hours. From the tree-framed window, the owner of this memory returns to other scenes, those of his childhood evoked by the calls of the sleepy birds in the foliage, cries which recall the voices of old ladies who used to come to visit his grandmother. He remembers his sick mother with the priest at her bedside, and then the portrait of his dead father over her bed evokes the long correspondence of the mother before her marriage with the ever traveling fiancé, who sends her postcards from every port in the world. Through the postcards, the scene that begins as a square of light illuminating the branches of the tree enlarges itself until it contains "the enormous earth the fabulous sumptuous, variegated, inexhaustible world" (p. 13), and time enlarges itself to contain the time of the dead, those dead "who had passed there that day at that hour precisely" (p. 23).

Dawn is the moment of departure, but this apparently simple moment is charged with the great complexity of memory. Dawn awakens again what is lying heaped up in the darkness, a potential which it stirs and stimulates before adding the contribution of another day of living. For the novelist, this is the point of articulation, the necessary break that allows him to make a false but useful distinction before the mental phenomena fuse once more into a heterogeneous mass. The segment of the book that comes before the real awakening establishes the existence of an obscure and abundant treasure, spilling over into the opening day.

Before entering into this day and a full consciousness of the present, the mind passes through an intermediate stage. Between sleep and waking, perceptions are confused with memories, and the judgment does not yet seek to separate them. Hearing is the first link with the outer world, calling on the other senses. The movement of the leaves, the calls of the birds, the old ladies, the dream of departure long ago, all mingle in a second sleep. Then the body comes painfully back to life and time proclaims its supremacy, for between the gray dawn and the bright colors of a sunlit world nothing explains the dazzling transition. Suddenly the world is there.

When at last the reborn being manages to reunite mind and body—"the inglorious ghost of the human race in frayed pyjamas" (p. 31)—the ritual acts of each day bring back the rites of other days; each gesture is multiplied in the individual and universal memory. Water from an ordinary faucet is the

lustral water of mythical fountains, of rivers of antiquity, the
source and matrix of every living thing.

The being whose birth results from these memories and the
baptismal waters will live a day deprived of heroic incident,
one of those days when "nothing happens." We shall follow
this being step by step through the hours, during which he
takes care of the sale of furniture in an old house that is part
of an inheritance, goes to the bank for necessary papers, meets
an old family friend, has lunch, bargains with an antique
dealer, visits a cousin to get some documents signed, returns
in time to hear an old friend deliver a political speech, goes to
bed and back to sleep. There are no events. But the smooth,
dull surface of this day hides a network of connections of extraordinary complexity. From the contact with the objects in
the house emerges, more and more obsessively, the picture of
expanses of memory. The paths crossing these territories, however, are tortuous.

The renewed being raises his face, streaming with water
from the wash bowl, and sees his double doubly hazy in the
mirror through the drops. His thought turns first ironically to
the Lord's cup in church at mass,[3] then to the impious and
mocking school friend, Lambert, who was always the first to
try everything, including shaving. The thought of shaving
brings to mind all those who shave, the man who was martyred
for refusing to do so, the Latin text that tells the story of this
man, and the uncle who made the protagonist as a schoolboy
study and translate this text. This uncle is Uncle Charles, who
will later be the double or "translation" of the narrator and
who is the pretext for an old and boring family friend to stop
and importune the protagonist on his way to the bank. The

3. The impious mockery of the Mass, connected with the shaving
scene, reminds one of the opening pages of *Ulysses*, as do the school-
room scene and later, in *Pharsalus*, the pigeon-divine dove connection.

narration proceeds from one ordinary incident to another but enfolds in its coils other times and other places, or places escaped from time, such as the strange study-laboratory of the uncle-mentor, where the clock and the calendar no longer serve any purpose and daylight is excluded, yet which remains, in the minutest details evoked by sight, sound, and smell, an ineradicable memory.

Part of this upsurging past overflows and covers the present, some of which is lost in the process of remembering. We shall not know what happens between the morning shave and the meeting with the old man in the street because, in what Ludovic Janvier has so well defined as "the movement of recoil and overlapping," one of the coils of time has obscured another.[4] This movement is continuous in *Histoire*. Immediate happenings are overlaid by recollections from widely separated moments of the past. These recollections are themselves of varying quality and origin, so that their effects in the present are also of great diversity.

We have seen in our discussion of the previous novels that the recollections of Simon's protagonists are most precarious when they deal with the activities of others. Simon illustrates this difficulty in *Histoire* through the device of the postcards that show scenes from the travels of various members of the narrator's family. All that the postcards offer us are "knifelike slices made in duration" (p. 226) in which the fixed shapes of the world through which the travelers move are congealed. The cards which mark the progress of the narrator's father round the world are in reality the memory of an absence, of someone who appears neither in the pictures nor in the narration itself; and their fixity denies the movement they commemorate. They indicate a space to be filled, a space equal to

4. *Entretiens,* p. 75. My translation.

the outside world and to the inner life of others, one which we fill with snapshots of our own, made up from experience completed by knowledge out of encyclopedias, which is nobody's knowledge—just as the student in *Le Palace* fills his imagination with static pictures of the Rifle, or dictionary definitions of an exotic country. By using the postcards to show the fragmentary, paper reality of these memories, Simon underlines their lack of sequence (they spill out of the furniture drawers) and their fragility. The foreign scenes and languages on the cards emphasize not only the distance between the sender and the receiver of the messages they bear, but also the disparity between the few laconic words written on the back of the cards and the exotic experience they supposedly represent. Located forever, with great precision, in a time and space that are not the narrator's, the postcard messages are recollections cut out of their supporting matrix, no longer preserved by a living memory. The life-giver in this case could only be the mother who collected the cards, and into whose womb the narrator, reading the postcards at the end of the book, dreams of returning.

The type of recollection sustained by a living memory is somewhat different. Although static, this recollection recalls the evidence of the senses and mingles perception, feeling, reflection, and memories of memories in a confusion that contrasts directly with the shiny, false, dimensionless surface of the postcards. In Uncle Charles' study—"a fixed universe where time did not move at the same speed if it moved at all" —there is a smell, "a cerement smell, as if it were not only that of the distilled must mingling with the whiffs from the little alcohol lamp . . . but the very odor of the eternal penumbra which prevailed in the office"; there is lighting, "the dazzling October sunlight seething so to speak like some acid between the crack of the shutters . . . the bulb always on"; there is sound, "that crackling of grains of dust accumulated by the wind" (pp. 34–36). This sensitivity to the reactions of nose, eye, and ear makes the inventory of disorderly objects lying about the room and the echoes of distant conversation more than just a detailed recollection of the past and gives the scene a permanent solidity and coherence.

A third type of recollection combines known elements with speculation and the "doubling" of events. Charles, according to the old family friend, deceived his wife with a painter's model in Paris. However the story of infidelity is perhaps the narrator's, and the woman who is several times mentioned in the narration as having thrown herself out of a window is perhaps the unhappy wife, or another woman who killed herself in a similar situation. This memory has as its point of departure an old, blurred photograph showing him (one of the two) with a painter known as "the Dutchman," the model, and the painter's wife. The narrator invents or records reasons for his (their) behavior ("What to imagine?" he asks [p. 229]). He describes in detail the shapes and colors in the studio, the significant patterns of paint on the floor, fanning out in all directions like the motifs in the novel, the attempts to take the photograph which result in a fuzzy shot because the photographer is trying to include himself in the picture—a patent comment on the book itself. But this movement preserves "the lightning-like trace left by the face during its various changes of position, restoring to the event its density" (p. 226). The imagination does its work so well that the narrator ends up in the skin of Charles (like Marcel in that of Swann), and we can no longer tell who asks the unanswerable question: "But what else? What else? Else? Else?" Whose memory is likened to the hazy picture "where contours are not delimited by a line but the volumes appear to emerge from the shadow or sink into it just as they do in memory, certain parts in full light others..." (p. 238)? The sad couple of the unhappy wife and the unfaithful husband, whose memory are they, of one, or the other, or both? ("After all, it does not matter much" the narrator says [p. 229], when discussing the question of exactness.)

Passing from one level to another in these temporal excavations, from reconstituted past to imaginary past, to the past of absence, the novel constitutes a complex recital of an ordinary day. Time rediscovered obliterates the present, which reappears every so often above the debris, only to be submerged once more by new discoveries. The strata at different time levels form a fluctuating line around the basic cycle of the day. The narrator's youth and that of his cousins fades into the time of the dying mother, and then farther back into her youth and that of the fiancé-father. The dates and scenes on the famous postcards are amalgamated in the mind of the narrator who finds them stacked in a drawer in the old house, where the furniture offers yet another layer of unsummoned memories. The "story" that results from this "archeology of thought," as Merleau-Ponty called it,[5] is as far away as possible from plot and anecdote. Of course, a tale could be constructed from the elements given, if we were to fill in the gaps and put things in order. But then it would be the reader's work, not the writer's. The latter has assumed the task of showing where the stratifications lie and demonstrating how every new experience is an act of sedimentation—"to be described in the imaginary world as much as in Perception."[6]

It is less a question, then, of capturing time past and imprisoning it in art—even less of registering the fantasies of an exuberant imagination—than of illustrating with great care

5. Merleau-Ponty, "Cinq Notes," *Médiations,* p. 7; *Entretiens,* p. 44. My translation.
    6. Ibid.

to what extent everything in consciousness is indissolubly held together and how impossible it is to remove the smallest detail without destroying the whole. A single example will show the proliferation of the fibers that grow like living things between one set of images and the next.

The recollection of Uncle Charles' study, decorated with a view of Barcelona, brings to the mind of the narrator a conversation about his own role in the Spanish Civil War and consequently a clear picture of an episode in the war when a carload of soldiers is subject to guerilla attack at an intersection in Barcelona. Once activated, this recollection attracts to it almost everything that happens to the narrator during the day. A sandwich eaten by one of the Spanish soldiers, a hunchback who took part in the fray, the café where a waiter alternately shows and hides himself, all reappear in various ways, first in a restaurant where the narrator sees a hunchback, then a family studying a map of Spain, and later in a café where soldiers are drinking, and a waiter moves in and out of the mirror's reflection. At another moment, the scene at the intersection comes back once more when an old car stalls, reminding the narrator of the battered vehicle used by the soldiers.

Other finer threads in the discourse reinforce even more securely the connection between the different motifs in the narration. The narrator's mother had Spanish friends in her youth, whose postcards in Spanish she kept with the others. She liked to dress up in Spanish clothes and watch the bloody games in the arena. The theme of Spain, with its blood and combat is kept up in all the narrator's relationships—not only with his mother, Uncle Charles, and Lambert, with whom he discusses politics and involvement with the Civil War—but also in his erotic connections. It reminds him of Corinne, his cousin, who criticizes his role in the Spanish War, whose husband is killed in World War II, and who has bloody scratches on her legs after climbing a tree; of the girl he deflowers; of his wife whose ebbing life is paralleled with the slow dying of the city of Barcelona (drained of blood in childbirth, as we know from the image in *Le Palace*). The traditionally Spanish motifs of eroticism, blood, and death are inseparable from the female facts of domesticity and birth. At the end of the novel the narrator, in the blood-red darkness of the womb, is still waiting to be born from the mother long since dead.

There is more in the novel than the recollection of a personal past: for *Histoire* is made up of the memories and experiences not only of the supposed narrator, but of others from the novels of Claude Simon the writer. We recognize people and scenes from *Le Palace,* from *La Route des Flandres,* perhaps even from *L'Herbe*. We recognize the themes of disintegration and mutation, of indifferent and prolific nature, of the ineffectiveness of writing, of the supposed mystery at the heart of things. We rediscover the motifs of the cigar box, the photograph, the comic strip, the bank and its currency, the newspaper titles read upside down and mutilated. Some of the motifs are, we might say, premonitory. Simon will use the image of the old ladies like birds in *Les Corps conducteurs*. The cloud formations and the banknotes that fascinate the narrator of *Histoire* will be important in *La Bataille de Pharsale*. The pinball machine in the café where he telephones reappears in *Triptyque*. Each of these motifs is a generator of further images, not only in *Histoire* itself, but all the writing that follows.[7]

7. A schema of Simon's images is yet to be constituted. He establishes the same connections in his early novels as in his later ones, but in the later novels the generative power of these connections is much greater. For example, in *L'Herbe* the sexual act is associated with the sound of the departing car. In the later novels the sound and the ve-

At a greater depth, another layer of memory and perception stretches between the opposing poles of the narration. Between the strata of personal recollection the narrator interposes long quotations from books by other authors, as if they had remained like solid blocks in his memory. Mixed with reminiscences from school textbooks, passages from two authors, one ancient, one modern, predominate: around *The Golden Ass* of Apuleius cluster the erotic themes in the novel, while around *Ten Days That Shook The World* by John Reed center the revolutionary themes. Eroticism and revolution meet inextricably in the person of Lambert who, as the narrator's school friend, translates the Roman Catholic Mass into obscenities and borrows licentious books in Latin, and later, as a left-wing politician, harangues the whole town over loudspeakers. The works of Apuleius and Reed have formed deposits in the narrator's consciousness, and by choosing to quote long passages from them, each time with the exact wording, he seems to be emphasizing the role these texts have played in his life. He has, in fact, divided his life between the two impulses of eroticism and political action, both unsuccessfully, if not disastrously. His belief in political action took him to Spain. His erotic tendencies have involved him in unhappy relationships with women. We can perhaps conclude that the quoted texts, which are "literature" and foreign, both in origin and in Simon's narrative, serve to bring out the difference between the finished, successful work, written up according to the formulas of History, and the unfinished, imperfect elements of experience recorded in a text in a constant state of evolution.

In a similar contrast between the finished product and the work in the making, the distance between myth and its forms

---

hicle suffice to generate erotic scenes. After *Histoire,* we shall see the development of the generating power of images.

in experience is repeatedly emphasized. On the one hand the legendary past is isolated as a petrified souvenir, like the Greek ruins and museums at Mycenae, where it appears in a completely static form as a printed plan or as objects with undecipherable labels enclosed in glass cases, impossibly remote from the developing tragedy of the narrator and his wife. On the other hand, the legend is grotesquely adapted to modern life. In *La Route des Flandres* the swan of Leda is metamorphosed into the peacock on the peasant woman's curtain. In *Le Palace*, ancient heroes are perceived as villagers fighting for property rights. In *Histoire*, Theseus is imagined as a slick-haired youth with a machine gun, and the Minotaur as the mysterious paper-eating organism of the Bank. The Sphinx interviews a client in need of money, and gods, goddesses, heroes, and kings pose on banknotes or cavort on pillars at the opera or in counting houses. Recorded and consecrated historical and mythical figures are blurred by immediacy, just as Uncle Charles' photo is blurred by movement.

The text of *Histoire* is a mine of references, a mine from which galleries lead down and out into all kinds of time and space—mythical, historical, conventional, and personal—and into which are drawn, through the mediation of the most banal incidents of daily life, the most imposing themes of human existence. The movement then is double: if we are led to see how the majestic mythology of the past terminates in our own feeble activities, we can also perceive how long our shadows may be and how these activities by their very repetition and monotony acquire a fatal grandeur.

Histoire resumes the experience of a novelist who is engaged in checking, one after the other, the discoveries that he has made about his art during the writing of his previous novels. In *Le Vent* he learns not to base the narration on an anecdote that is necessarily baseless and formless. *L'Herbe* shows that novelistic time cannot be reduced to a mathematically correct unilinear computation and that effects and causes cannot be tidily deduced from selected evidence. *La Route des Flandres* and *Le Palace* give the lie to omniscience and explanation based on the assimilation of alien consciousness—that is, "psychology" as it is commonly practiced. *Histoire* is a novel without an anecdote, without chronology, without psychological investigation, without explanation, the logical outcome of its predecessors.

Why then is it called *Histoire?*

To begin with, this narration is a study of consciousness and its internal relationships constantly in a state of flux during waking hours. This study is made up of words that accompany, follow, or precede these relationships, so that occasionally the words themselves create the very structure that they reveal—for example, the obscenities imagined by Lambert during the Mass provide the link between the morning ablutions and the study of Uncle Charles. Sometimes the words separate themselves from the recorded event so drastically that they wring from the writer this cry of despair: "You can no more tell such things than you can experience them again after the event, and yet you have only words, so all you can try to do..." (p. 126). All you can try to do, he implies, is to set up a system of exchange between the consciousness and the Word that will allow maximum development to both. One will no longer be the slave of the other but each will play its essential role in the ongoing story of writing. This is the "story" that tells itself as the narration progresses.

In this novel and the preceding ones, the primary images that appear in the narrator's mind, either directly through sense perceptions or filtered by memory and reflection, are organized around a central "generating point" or theme that

determines their relationship to other images. Each reference
to a theme causes an upsurge of fresh images. These new
elements bring with them clusters of additional components
that form new relationships in their turn and accumulate
until they become constellations of themes and images. In *La
Route des Flandres, Le Palace,* and *Histoire* these constellations are easily recognized. In *Histoire,* however, a loosening
and liberation of the word as generator of new groups take
place. Detaching itself physically from the text, like the newspaper titles and posters in *Le Palace,* the word in *Histoire*
almost playfully decorates its message—like the amusing poster
for the (*c*)*ours de danse* in which "the letters themselves appear to compose a kind of joyous dance figure" (p. 24). Elsewhere, the word appears in the mirror, or in the myriad stars
of the night sky, like inverted signs for the spectator to decipher. Sometimes the narrator plays games with his own
vocabulary: the sea is *plissé* (wrinkled), a word that brings to
mind the idea of age, the "old skin of this old world this old
monster *plissé,* pliocenian, or what, pliocene perhaps nothing
to do with it words which simply resemble one another
plesiosaurus . . ."[8]

The soldier Champenois tirelessly explains the misunder-
standings engendered by his name which others take for a
sign of origin in the province of Champagne; at the same time,
seated near him, the narrator lets his fancy wander along the
roads proposed by the word "Frascati":

> that place what was it called Frascati just outside the town on
> the road to Nancy for a long time nothing but a name a vaguely
> fabulous legendary word in the stories of the veterans of the
> regiment bragging about their binges their conquests to the new
> recruits a moss-green word . . .

8. Page 319 in the French; not translated in the English text.

rustling branches cascades fountains as in those pictures those
prints of ruined gardens in the environs of Rome and at the
same time indissociable from the guard room the men on leave
back at midnight drunk vomiting the stink of wine fiasco not so
different from Frascati and Chianti a sound . . .

Fiaschanti
named for the hill at whose foot it was located, where the road
started up to the monument built on top a kind of obelisk in
memory of the battles fought there during the war
fracas too in Frascati And then probably because of the Italian
sound of the word the stereotyped image not of soldiers in the
uniforms of the last war but of officers sabers drawn and
Algerian riflemen charging with fixed bayonets among the red
and yellow explosion of cannon-balls of smoke whose smell was
identified for me with the smell of incense the scarlet trousers of
the Papal zouaves I could see in one of the four-lobed rosettes of
that window in the chapel Lambert singing the filthy words at
the top of his lungs.   [pp. 283–284]

This free meditation alternates with the explanations of the
soldier Champenois like a litany, that is, the physical illustration of what was going on long ago in the chapel where Lambert ingeniously turned the Mass into a chanted obscenity.
Meanwhile, sitting among the soldiers in the café, the narrator
now recalls Lambert's "severe interrogation" about war and
his lectures on politics. A pair of lovers nearby stir up memories of sexual adventures in the army. Little by little the narrator's thought weaves military, political, and erotic subjects
into one bitter memory of love and conflict, the two poles of
the work.

In *Histoire* the word is not entirely broken up into signifier
and signified, but the signifier has a greater measure of freedom. The pre-established form of the word may easily become
the leader of a play, both ludic and instrumental, between
metaphor and logic. "Frascati" gathers into a bouquet almost

all the themes of the novel. In *Histoire,* however, the game is not yet entirely the whole show. The chronological thread can still be pulled, bringing with it all the dependent structures, including the nontemporal and imaginary ones. In the works to come, these nontemporal structures will play their role fully, freed from any necessary adherence to an external order. For *La Route des Flandres* and *Histoire* an independent semantic pattern can still be reinvented. For *La Bataille de Pharsale* and *Les Corps conducteurs* this is no longer the case.

7 ❦ La Bataille de Pharsale

La Bataille de Pharsale[1] takes up in a radically new fashion the question asked by *Le Palace*. How can we write "history" when all we have are memories and evidence obtained by dubious means? *Histoire* provided one possible answer to the question: perhaps one can catch at that instant and register, with the help of signs, some of the mental phenomena present at any given moment for a single consciousness (a performance, however, requiring great caution and the imposition of artificial limits and organization on unlimited and unorganized material). In *La Bataille de Pharsale* the idea of organization is revised and in some degree made mathematical: no longer is there any question of making up a false total, but simply one of pointing out the generative points of series that emerge, inexhaustibly, each time that the mind begins to function.

Pharsale will not be "an attempt at reconstitution" of a battle. It will be an examination of the series and groups of series that arise from internal and external generators in the work. The battle is by now a well-known element in Claude Simon's writing, an element present in almost all of his novels, as background rather than event, for the battle is never

1. Paris, Editions de Minuit, 1971, translated by Richard Howard as *The Battle of Pharsalus* (New York, George Braziller; London, Jonathan Cape, 1971). All passages quoted are from this translation.

grasped, even in *La Route des Flandres,* in its totality. It is perceptible solely through the scattered manifestations that no warrior has ever succeeded in collecting in one single, coherent thought. "The real Waterloo is neither in what Fabrice, nor in what the Emperor, nor in what the historian sees, it is not an object to be determined, it is what *happens* at the limit of all these perspectives and on which they all depend," declares Merleau-Ponty, adding, "What should be done is to write history in the present."[2]

In Simon's present the battle of Pharsalus is composed—like all the other battles of the Spanish Civil War, World War II, and those which are not called battles but games, matches, lovers' jousts—of memories mixed with foreign substances, the products of the imagination, of reflection mixed with likely details. Yet here the composition is different: the memory is no longer that of someone who has taken part in the action, but that of historians long dead, who have frozen, once and for all, in a language that is dead also, the memory of men defunct for centuries. Who then is the living possessor of these recollections? Only the rare and uncertain reader of these ancient texts. And this reader, often an unwilling student, as he tries to assimilate these left-overs, like the student in *Le Palace,* allows to intervene between this ancient thought and his own, the innumerable events that are the signs of his own life.

Through the procedure of inserting printed records into living memories, the text of classic authors is set in Simon's prose like mineral in growing wood, in the midst of phenomena which radiate, that is to say, which fan out progressively from the point of origin in the consciousness of the writer, forming in a series of continuous ramifications a "bushing"

2. *Phénoménologie,* p. 416. My translation.

effect, a plant-like structure capable of endless reproduction. The battle forever immanent in Simon's thought is at the juncture of several luxuriant series: it evokes not only the conflict of armies, but also sexual encounters, sports, paintings of combats of all kinds. The precise observations in Latin about battles, read with difficulty by the student, are thus diffused throughout his experience as a man, a soldier, a lover, a traveler, an artist.

Both *Le Palace* and *La Bataille de Pharsale* open with the same image: that of the pigeon. For the persistent reader of Simon's work the pigeon has already many implications. It is not the herald of peace; in opposition to the divine dove of which, necessarily, it is a reminder, it is the omen and ever-present spectator of war, its feathered wing suggesting the arrow that slays, whether by that we mean the weapon of war, the more surely fatal flight of Time, or the flying quill that describes the vain attempt in writing to immobilize changing reality. In *Le Palace,* the pigeon swoops down and settles, giving the author time to note details: "one of them landed on the stone balustrade, enormous . . . strangely ponderous . . . with its speckled dark-grey plumage, the back of the neck iridescent, the throat coppery, with its coral feet, its comma-shaped beak, its bulging breast" (pp. 13–14). All of this picturesque realism is transformed in *Pharsale* to conform with a new pattern:

Yellow and then black in the wink of an eye then yellow again: wings outspread crossbow shape and shot between the sun and the eye shadows for an instant across the face like velvet like a hand for an instant shadows then light or rather a recollection (warning?) a recall of the shadows leaping up with the speed of light palpable or at least consecutive chin mouth nose forehead feeling them even smelling them that smell of dry-rot cellar tomb like a handful of black earth hearing at the same time the sound of silk tearing the air rustling or perhaps not heard perceived merely imagined bird arrow beating flapping already vanished the vanes quivering the mortal darts crisscrossing creating a hissing vault like the one in that painting (where was it?) some naval battle between Venetians and Genoese on a blue-black white-capped jagged sea and from one galley to the other the feathered arch humming in the dim sky one of them piercing his open mouth just as he rushed forward sword raised leading his men transfixing him stabbing the shout in his throat

Dark dove aureoled with saffron

But white against the glass the wings outspread suspended in the center of a triangle surrounded by a sunburst of gold rays. Soul of the Elect set free. Sometimes an eye in the center. In an equilateral triangle, the sides, bisectors and medians intersect at a single point. The Trinity, the Virgin impregnated by the Holy Ghost, Vessel of Ivory, Tower of Silence, Rose of Canaan, Something of Solomon. Or painted in the background like the one in the window of that pottery shop, walleyed. Who can buy such things? Chamber pot to receive. Squatting. Riddle: What is oval, moist, split in two and surrounded by hair? An eye for an eye as the saying goes a tooth for a tooth or face to face. One staring at the other. Exploding in a liquid hiss, like a horse. Or rather mare. [pp. 3–4]

The pigeon is no longer described. It is only shadow, light, movement, and immediately it stimulates mental activity that produces the image of the arrow carrying with it the whole series—the battle, the erotic curve, the sea, death, then the divine dove, religion, the stained glass window, the triangle and geometric intersection, the vessel, the eye-vulvula and the horse-woman connections—all born on currents of agressivity and sexuality. Every one of these elements, starting from this condensation in the first two paragraphs, will develop into an essential series in the novel.

In *Le Palace* the pigeon bears with it the memory of the places where it has been, the people who were in these places, and the events associated with them, postulating the search for a "story." In *Pharsale* the bird generates in a few words an ensemble apparently heterogeneous, but whose homogeneity is to be revealed little by little in the course of the reading, this homogeneity depending less on a place, a character, or a story, than on the mind that selects from the "magma" of its memories and perceptions certain points to which everything else relates. These points are then reduced to two: a crisis of jealous love in the life of a painter in Paris and the search for the exact spot where, according to classical authors, the battle of Pharsalus took place. The two points have for an obvious connection the theme of bodily combat, and for inner links the memory of translations done with the uncle who may be the Charles of *Histoire,* who may have had an unhappy love affair with a model who betrayed him with the "Dutchman" in Paris (but the love affair is that of the narrator). In addition, the work that takes shape from the shadow of the pigeon, emerges, as the critic Jean Ricardou has explained, almost naturally from the lines that serve as epigraph to the whole book, the famous verses from Paul Valéry's *Cimetière marin.*

> Zeno, cruel Zeno, Eleatic Zeno,
> Your winged arrow finds its mark
> And flying sings and does not fly!
> The sound is birth, the arrow death,
> And the sun...A tortoise shadow for
> The soul, Achilles running motionless.[3]

The winged arrow, which is the bird, whose fleeting image accompanied by an auditory sensation—the "torn silk" rustling of wings—marks on the motionless page the alternating steps of light and shade, re-presents the winged arrow of Valéry and the sun of Achilles running motionless. All that is

3. Epigraph translated by Richard Howard.

needed to complete Simon's text is the Greek flavor, and this will be added by Pharsalus and the journey in Greece. But it is already more subtly present, we suggest, in the quasi "zenoist" attitude of Simon in his previous works: time without change, movement without progress, an indifferent nature and ever-imminent death forming the bases of permanent preoccupation for the novelist.

The title of the novel, its epigraph, and its first page contain then a program of generators already present and linked in the consciousness and the writing of the author and reinforced by other pieces of "literature." The anonymous personage whose mental activity combines these phenomena is the historian not, of course, of an event that took place two thousand years ago, but of a Pharsalus that is continually producing itself in his mind and embracing the details of his present life—the Paris subway, the cafés, the students at the "Bal des Quat' z Arts," the painters, his jealousy, the journey in Greece, the recollection of Latin lessons—all scrupulously regulated according to the laws of transition that come to light only after a methodical study in depth of the text. These laws allow the reader to move around in a continuum whose perspectives, instead of being explicitly laid out, are to be discovered only after considerable research and effort on his part.

There is no "action" or "movement" in this book, in the traditional meaning of the terms, but instead a continuous broadening around the points of departure. We have thus the sense that a field of vision is being progressively enriched, with new details being continually added, in the same way that a painting takes shape under the artist's brush. The theme of painter and painting is of great importance—it forms a part of the series concerning the jealous lover whose mistress is deceiving him with another painter, and it gives rise to many more series of images referring to colors, pictures, art students, the Parisian studio, erotic scenes, and also to all those dealing with the arrangement of the body in space, the attitudes of models in war and love ("slaughter as well as love is a pretext to glorify the body" [p. 81]), and the geometric analysis of position. Thus, the other field, the field of battle, dissolves into the field of painting, thanks to the detailed analysis in the text of several canvasses showing battle scenes. In the paintings chosen by Simon, the conflicts described so exactly by historians seem to become visible, accentuated by the dramatic highlighting of their painted representation.

The work has its own movement, very different from the traditional linear one, organized around a set of recognizable points. These points are themselves shifting, so that in the three parts of the book, the reader, observing the changing relationships between special signs or landmarks, views them from an indefinite number of possible angles, before he finds himself (just like the reader of *Finnegans Wake*) once again at his starting place. In the first part, under the sign of Valéry, "Achilles running motionless," the search for the exact location of the battlefield controls all the memories, those of sexual misfortune as well as of the Latin texts studied in childhood— and those of other battles, and other texts. Among these memories the seeker wanders vainly, "running" without leaving the territory of his obsessive thoughts where, the subtitle already tells us, he is condemned to remain forever.

"Lexicon," the second part of the work, is introduced by a sentence from Proust's *Le Temps retrouvé* about the appearance of ordinary objects as signs or hieroglyphs that imply much more than their immediate meaning. Here individual words are used as projectiles that seem to explode in all directions with their charge of memory, meaning, and evocation. Michel Butor has observed that a dictionary contains the focal points of innumerable possible narrations. The signs within it

are, in fact, open to an incalculable variety of developments—
hence the dictionaries and encyclopedias, which abound in
Simon's pages. We shall find the *Petit Larousse* here, toward
the end of the book.

The first key word, "Battle," releases a dense cloud of associations, gathered together around the descriptions, first, of
of the supposed battlefield with references to the Latin authors
and, second, in great detail, of a series of battle paintings in
which warriors and horses inextricably mingle and gradually
become confused with a scene from World War II, then with
a scene from a soccer match, and finally, with the "battle
scene" of the lovers. The emphasis here is pictorial; each arrangement is presented through the eye of a painter particularly sensitive to the organization of mass and lighting and to
the sweep of gesture.

"Caesar," another key word, reminds the narrator of the
helmeted Roman soldier seen, for example, on banknotes, those
same banknotes where every fold creates a new series of meeting and diverging lines. The banknotes and the soldier bring
up a family scene at Lourdes, where the narrator's grandmother fishes out banknotes from her bodice to pay the bell-
hop and where Roman soldiers are omnipresent at the stations
of the cross. "Conversation" brings to mind the painter's studio, where the jealous lover questions the wife of the painter
whom he suspects of sleeping with his mistress. "Gladiator"
evokes a crazy soldier who, stripped to the skin, threatens his
companions with his saber, a sudden bizarre phantom from
ancient battlefields. "Machine" offers the image of an abandoned harvester-combine, whose decomposing form and possible functioning are described as carefully as those of a human
or animal model; its disjoined members serve indeed as a
link between the distant economic and industrial world and
the organic reproductive sphere in which it comes to resemble

more and more the creatures whose mechanical acts (ploughing, sowing, attacking, fecundating) it reflects.

"Voyage" introduces the false movement of the train, from which all the themes can be rediscovered in a kind of retreating perspective. Variations of themes already known are provided by travelers or by landscapes and people they perceive through the windows. Travelers look like paintings by Piero della Francesca; the books they read are about war and love; people seen in different places make erotic gestures; names read backward take on a curiously important sonority, especially those with Simon's favorite resonance—"*or*" (which evokes the dominating color, yellow, and the theme of money or exchange)—as in the sign "Verona" seen in reverse from the train. Little by little the whole thematic content of the book passes before the eyes of the traveler sitting motionless, carried away by the rushing train, like Blind Orion being led he knows not where, on a journey with no possible point of arrival except the one he has just left.

With "O" is finally resumed the sense of the reading, which shows how the continuously recommencing series in the text should be considered. On the one hand, each observer's eye is the focal point, O, of an infinity of invisible lines leading to perceived objects O', O'', O''', and so forth. On the other hand O., the observer, moves about, so that the same objects are never to be seen in the same manner:

the movements of space and time mingling, which is to say that for O., moving rapidly from one place to another the world appears at no moment identical with what it was in the immediately preceding moment, so that . . . we must represent the totality of the system as a moving body ceaselessly altering around a few fixed points, for example the intersection of the line OO' with the trajectory of the pigeons in flight, or again that of the itineraries of two journeys, or again the name PHARSALUS figuring in a Latin textbook and disfigured on a signpost beside a road in Thessaly.   [pp. 126–127]

In the third part, "Chronology of Events," the journey in the train provides for the return of all the themes, drawn together by the landscapes that pass in fragments before the eyes of the stationary traveler. At the same time the text opens out on to supplementary memories, further references to passages by Proust concerning World War I, to the art commentary of Elie Faure, to quotations from Simon himself, such as the *Venceremos* and the *Dolor* of *Le Palace* and the war scenes and Corinne from *La Route des Flandres*. "Chronology," evidently, is in no way related to calendar time, any more than the careful information concerning distances between cities visited has anything to do with ordinary perceptions of space.[4] Large areas of recollection, long periods of recorded perception divide one spot from another, one minute from the next. Not only relationships between events in time and space, but also points of view are modified: a wartime scene, told in the first person in "Battle," the translation scene and the erotic passage from Part I, now reappear as in the third person and as perceived by O. the observer—an observer so withdrawn, so emptied of personality, so close to zero that for him the lovers' act becomes a painting with the figures totally immobilized. This scene in turn suggests an allegorical painting by Lucas Cranach entitled *Jealousy* and another by Pieter Brueghel the Elder called *Battle of the Israelites,* both on postcards, one of which O. is planning to send to the faithless woman. In the repeated scene where the young Corinne is carried on her father's shoulders, O. is first the

4. Ricardou points out, however, in "L'Essence et les sens," that Verona is situated at the intersection of the railroad lines from Milan to Venice and Florence to Trento. The idea of intersection in space is important (*Entretiens,* p. 106).

father or carrier, but the second time, the observer watches the "man" carry her; also in the love scene, O. is the woman partner to the "man." The watcher being carried along by the train is like one who sees himself from an increasing distance in memory, looking backwards as he retreats into the present. The scenes he stares at become petrified, hardened into sculpture, which finally crumbles slowly away. As the past scenes congeal, like friezes, the watcher becomes emptier and emptier of personality, until he is only absence.

The book ends with the view of the writer at his table, on which we see the "generators" of his writing: the dictionary, the postcard on which can be seen a renaissance trumpet player wearing a curious, cylindrical hat, and behind him an arm brandishing an axe, a helmet, and parts of interlocking pieces of armor, then a pile of coins, a box of paper clips ("trombones" in French), half red, half yellow, like a renaissance costume. A little earlier we also learned that the table holds a package of Gauloises cigarettes, on which is the design of a winged helmet, a yellow pack of matches ornamented with a smiling man and woman advertising CORN'S AUTO SCHOOL (both the machine-erotic connection and the idea of *cornes*—cuckoldry—are here), a thousand lire banknote engraved with a bust of Verdi and a Gorgon's head, and a *coquille Saint-Jacques,* a large shell used as an ashtray (advertisements for Shell Oil are frequent throughout the trip to Greece). In front of the writer lies a sheet of paper, blue in the shadow, yellowish-white in the sunlight, over which passes the shadow of a pigeon. The writer begins the first sentence of *La Bataille de Pharsale.*

The reader who would really discover the richness of the novel has to dismiss expectation of enlightenment from extraneous events and learn to recognize the laws of transition that govern the text. They have been minutely analyzed by

Jean Ricardou,[5] who sees them as dependent on the interplay between the different systems—lexical, syntactical, and semantic—which function together to make the whole. The impulse that carries the writing along with it may spring from an extended metaphor, such as the *moissonneuse-lieuse,* the harvester-combine which represents both physically and semantically both liaison and the results of generation; from a pun (*"phare"-"sale"*)', from generative proper names (Charles, Charlot, Charleroi, Charlus)', from the oxymoron (Orion, the blind giant seeking the light, the constellation which, when deprived of the O signifying the observer, is inverted to *noir*—black), from repetition, from lapsus, and above all, from the *vocable générateur,* that is, the word or syllable that brings forth whole cycles of sound and meaning. This word usage can appear in a number of ways: as a single word with a single meaning (*isosignifiant isosignifié*), which can appear in varying contexts, as a word with several meanings (*isosignifiant hétérosignifié*), as derivatives of one term having the original meaning (*homosignifiant homosignifié*)', as derivatives of all sorts, rhymes, anagrams, quasi-anagrams (*homosignifiant hétérosignifié*), as terms having a similar or analogous sense (*hétérosignifiant isosignifié*), as terms suggesting associated ideas (*hétérosignifiant homosignifié*), and so forth.

Thus the word *jaune* (yellow) dominates the text in all its meanings and forms, including partial anagrams—*nuage, âne, âge.* Its coloration tinges the whole book, physically and psychologically (death and jealousy). One of its synonyms, *or,* gives both the preferred sonority of the text and the meaning of the third power which, with love and war, exercises its attraction on all other phenomena—gold, money, exchange,

5. *Pour une théorie du Nouveau Roman,* pp. 124–158.

banks, banknotes—the economic factors that play a subdued but persistent role in all of Simon's novels.

If we add to these verbal arrangements the combinations of two or more in blocks or *montages,* which in turn suggest other formations linked in groups of ever-increasing complexity, we can see a geometric progression of possibilities. The groups made up by the description of the harvester or of people coming out of the subway, for example, placed always in conjunction with erotic scenes, take on themselves an erotic coloring that they then communicate to other groups. In extreme examples of these procedures syllables disconnect and reconnect in phonetic groups, a process that accentuates both the mental disorder of the thinker and the persistence of series through the disintegration of customary structures. The following is part of the meditation of the unhappy traveler in the moving train:

profound *statues of Hope and Faith* idiotic would make a nice title too *lasciate ogni speranza la forza del destino* the *tragicacà* of *coscienza* lacerating the hero burning with love for his little dove the great white hunter the poor black bastard too bad so sad send him home to recover O perfect love my little dove is that a sin Lord make me let me my cock in her sweet little cunt whatever we risk compro my sweet little damn building before the monsoon or later hunger the black bastard famine skeletons final solution page 347 about a centimeter of pages left between her thumb and her right forefinger which at the rate of thirty pages or a millimeter per half hour must make about fifteen half hours say seven and a half hours of cacas of con science the whole thing for thirty-five lire or about a centime a page of meta physical but in the end God will know His own calculating she would have at least enough for two evenings nicely worked out in company of beefy males in shorts and tsetse flies and the Lord make me but not yet O Lord then why not take advantage me too ask Him ask him while he sat there in the cotton clouds opposite the Métro entrance the pigeonshit of the Holy Ghost sucking hard on over his head Sodom and Gonorrhea what page *all ugly voluptuous memories he brought away from her alowdhim tomagine the ardent or faintpose she might assume with others result that he missed each plesur tasted wither each cacaress imagined and whose sweetness he had rashly mentioned and each grace he endowed her with since he knew a moment afterward these woodbe tools used to tor turehim,* the sun very low now its horizontal rays entering the compartment slashed coppery then turned green by sifting between the young acacias bordering the embankment then gone impossible to see if he was sleeping his head tilted back on the seat still holding the typed pages the lenses of his glasses reflecting the glittering horizontal speckled rush of the leaves against the setting sun. [pp.121–122]

This extraordinary passage, which begins with a description of the banal reading matter—a love story—of a woman traveler, contains as though in separate spare parts all the essential elements of the book: the obsessive jealousy, brought out by the mangled quotation from Proust concerning Swann's suffering over Odette, the rage and disgust of the lover, the combat between males, the child woman, the motifs of the pigeon and the divine dove, the subway, the omnipresent cloud, the blacks which appear as counterparts of Orion in various parts of the book, the satirical reference to literature which offers "solutions," and finally the puns and jokes, the sentence, the word, the book itself reduced to atoms.

We begin to see now that something quite new is taking place in Simon's work during the writing of this book. In the previous works, living characters, more or less anonymous, bring into the text by their presence whole clusters of experience, references to other times, places, and people in endless progression. Many novelists, Balzac among the first of them, have used this device to imply connections between the characters, connections stretching beyond the scope of the particular novel in which the characters appear. Thus the illusion of a certain density of existence is intensified, giving the characters added dimensions. The searcher for Pharsalus, who appears in the first pages of *La Bataille de Pharsale,* brings with him in this way a series of factual references that recall *Histoire* and emotional references that evoke any and all of the preceding novels, thus enriching the present work with a set of ready-made perspectives.

La Bataille de Pharsale is no longer dependent for such enrichment, however, on the human personage and the objects that surround him. This role has now been conferred upon the text itself. We have seen how Valéry's poem at the beginning opens up the whole book for us. Part II is also provided with an opening program, a quotation from Proust that dwells on the inner significance of outward signs ("I considered closely some image which had compelled my attention, a cloud, a triangle, a steeple, a flower, a pebble, feeling that perhaps beneath these signs was something else I must try to discover, a system of thought they translated in the manner of those hieroglyphs which supposedly represent only material objects" [p. 67]). Part III has an epigraph from Heidegger on the appearance of a world from the understanding of one function ("The tool turns out to be damaged or the material unsuitable...When its unusability is thus discovered, equipment becomes conspicuous...the context of equipment is illuminated, not as something never seen before, but as a totality constantly sighted beforehand in circumspection. With this totality, however, the world announces itself" [p. 129]).

These direct quotations are set above Simon's text so that we can note their importance. Within the text itself others are inserted, some still easily recognizable—like those from the Latin authors who can be identified as Caesar, Livy, Lucan, Apuleius—others less so—like the remarks concerning Poussin and Dürer borrowed from Elie Faure's *Histoire de l'Art*. We have already seen how the alien texts incorporated into *Histoire* serve both to illustrate and offset the main themes and how important it is that they should be recognized for what they are. This is true also of the visible inserts in *La Bataille de Pharsale*, but a subtler function is now introduced.

The illuminating work of Françoise van Rossum-Guyon in "De Claude Simon à Proust"[6] reveals how fragmentary passages from *Le Temps retrouvé*, which appear in the early pages of *La Bataille de Pharsale* at the prompting of the word "jealousy," arise from and dissolve into all the connecting themes in the work of the two writers: jealousy itself, war, eroticism, change, and death. The Proust text deals with the return to Paris of Marcel, the protagonist of *A la recherche du temps perdu*, during the war years around 1916; he comments on the changes in the outward appearance of women, especially in clothes and coiffures, the inward changes in values and social hierarchies, and the thoughts aroused by the deserted, dark streets of the wartime city. In these pages Marcel refers several times to the disappearance of his love for Albertine, but nevertheless he dreams of walking with her through the darkness of the unlighted arcades. A little further on, Gilberte, daughter of Odette and Swann, speaks of the changes the war has wrought in Tansonville, the flowering hawthorn country of Marcel's youth. Taken from their context, these references propagate in *La Bataille de Pharsale* a lengthy series of developments and combinations of motifs.

The cylindrical coiffures of the Parisian women in *Le Temps retrouvé* provide a seemingly frivolous symbol of mutation and lead Proust into a meditation on the effects of change upon various types of character. In *La Bataille de Pharsale* the coif-

6. *Les Lettres nouvelles* (Sept. 1972), pp. 107–137.

fures blend into a number of new groups of images, evoking
the attire of warriors as described by historians or depicted by
painters—as in the figures of Piero della Francesca or in the
costumes of parading students. These in turn arouse more
images of war—destruction, painting, reproductions of warriors on coins, the winged helmet on the packet of Gauloises,
weapons, swords, lances, and genitals. The images refer finally
to general truths of head, heart, sex, life, and death, but, as
Rossum-Guyon points out, not through direct meditation, but
through juxtaposition of objects that provoke such meditation.
The Proustian image spreads throughout Simon's work, but
the spreading is of a peculiar nature.

The sufferings of jealousy, so minutely described elsewhere
by Proust and condensed by Simon in one recurrent scene
where the jealous lover hammers at the closed door behind
which he is being betrayed, are summed up by the narrator
in Proust's words: "I was suffering like..." (p. 12). These
words are part of a sequence in which Marcel expresses the
pity he feels for men on leave from the front lines gazing at
the feasting in the capital, a pity that reminds him of the
sympathy he felt in his youth for hungry fishermen staring
through restaurant windows at rich diners. A phrase referring
to one form of feeling is thus diverted toward another emotion typical of both writers involved. The distance between
the hunger and desire of those deprived of the feast and the
sexually hungry man hammering at the door of the room in
which his ear "sees" the lovers at their enjoyment, is not so
great. The image is merely diffracted from one group to another, just as the function of one sense is usurped by another.

The principle of diffraction is closely followed by Simon
with all the images that he borrows. The cylindrical shapes
transferred to his own discourse from the external source come
already enriched with their own special Proustian significance.

Simon incorporates this significance into his own writing and operates new transfers at unexpected angles to groups not implied by the original image; coiffures become helmets—arms —armour—metal objects—machines in one sequence, and masks—faces—expressions in another. Even the famous *édicule Rambuteau* (outdoor urinal) is included because of its cylindrical shape and leads to one of the more complicated literary puns in the text. The cruder term for the *édicule* is *pissotière*. Françoise, the servant whose speech gives so much joy to Marcel, is corrupted by Parisian pronunciation into saying *pisstière*, omitting the "o"; this vowel is already a significant sign in Simon and happens to be the first phonetic component of the word for hawthorn—*au[o]bépine*. Along the *raidillon aux aubépines*—the hawthorn path—young Gilberte made suggestive gestures to Marcel. From these connections Simon derives the extended erotic play on words: *"raidi"* meaning stiff, and *"pine"* meaning prick (penis). Considering the preoccupations of the narrator, who is obsessed with the thought of the woman he loves copulating with his rival, this transformation is far from being merely a rude joke or a titillating passage. This obsession reactivates a series of signs which then animate what follows.

We can see from this complex usage how Proust's text is absorbed and yet deflected through Simon's narration. It is no longer a question of merely developing a borrowed epigraph in a new discourse. Although each element in Proust is treated like a hieroglyph, no simple explanation accompanies it. Real hieroglyphs are present in the text: the numerous printed arrows, the Greek omega indicating male and female anatomies, the O that variously encircles zero, totality, absence, or finality, and, humorously, the pants legs and the vest front substituted for the A in *pantalon* and the V in *veston*. These are merely surface signals however, pointing to the other signs that lead, not to elaborate expositions on art, or life, or time, but to one another, in such a way that their juxtaposition is self-explanatory. What was Proust is now Proust embedded in Simon, and the images are not so much assimilated, as decomposed and reassembled, as in the following passage where recollections from *Histoire* are gathered with the fragments from *Le Temps retrouvé* into an intense expression of desire:

> pomegranate tree growing against the wall under the window of his office the highest branches overhanging the sill their shadow playing over those shutters always stubbornly closed and he behind them in that sour smell of unfermented wine of alcohol of decomposition like a corpse jealously near the top of the right-hand page wearing those tall cylinders Rambuteau urinals called them pisstières Probably in his childhood he hadn't heard the o we called it the hawthorn path and where you claim you fell in love with me as a child but I can assure you Hands under the kimono . . . [p. 23]

Rossum-Guyon rightly sees the process mirrored in one of the dominating images of the book—the abandoned harvester machine, festooned with its disconnected wires that look like new vegetation growing up within it. Like the tool mentioned by Heidegger, the broken machine announces a whole world and refers both to fecundity and the sexual act, as well as to a mechanical and industrial economy. The machine is also the image of any text in which each part has a precise function with regard to the whole. So in *La Bataille de Pharsale* the Proust text has become a *physical* illustration of its own theme—the dislocation and decomposition of matter by time and conflict. Toward the end of the last section we see workmen dismantling and carrying off parts of the machine for use elsewhere; this passage is immediately followed by a long piece of translation from the Latin and then by another passage concerning bank notes, that is, exchange values. Still later, we are shown a brand new machine waiting in the station at Pharsalus, and new machine parts piled up on the railroad, waiting to be despatched.

The observations we have made concerning the intertextual exchange with Proust can also be made about other borrowings, not only of verbal matter, but of material such as the paintings frequently described in *La Bataille de Pharsale*. These descriptions illustrate themes recurrent in the book, and sometimes appear in blocks, in a stylized and static fashion, as though we were in an art gallery, being given the opportunity to stand back and admire the canvasses. At other times, the figures in the paintings seem to emerge and merge with others belonging to the historical text, as, for example, when all the painted warriors become suddenly alive and incarnate in the person of the crazed and naked soldier of the narrator's war memories, or, inversely, when the imaginary group formed by the lovers behind the closed door comes to resemble a sculpture. Tricks of lighting and perspective bring scenes out into three dimensions, or flatten them pictorially, just like the little cubes in the woman's skirt pattern, which, to the observer in the railroad carriage, seem "alternately to project or recede into a three-dimensional space" (p. 110). In fact, the discussion of the three painters, Poussin, Piero della Francesca, and Uccello in the section "Voyage" turns on the use of space —its depth in Poussin, its restriction in the other two.[7] In Simon's narration, therefore, extraneous matter is deliberately brought out, muted, or modified in its relationships with sur-

7. The narrator dwells on the fact that the English expression "movement *into* space" cannot be translated into French. This preoccupation with depth and enclosure is perhaps one reason why the triptych form interests Simon. A triptych can open out and literally surround the viewer, but the viewer can also withdraw from it.

rounding material, according to the value of exchange or contrast that the author wishes it to have.

By this time we should have become aware of a special characteristic of this writing. When we observe a motif that is drawn into the text from the outside, giving it extra depth, we are made conscious of the text *as text*. In this narration we discover that what we had imagined to be an account of the "real" world—memories, perceptions, ordered observations—constantly refers to already existing constructs or representations of that world. The true source of the text is not "nature" or "life" but other texts, that is, groups of signs that give the illusion of nature and life. Proust sees a cloud or a pebble, not as a cloud or a pebble, but as signs to be read. Simon shows that these signs will not lead us back to "reality," but only to other signs: feelings (jealousy), facts (the battle of Pharsalus), concepts (war) are already codified as texts or representations. The use of the hieroglyphs in the narration makes this clearer and reminds us that the true physical reality is the text we are looking at, a reality confirmed by the use of different forms of typography, italic script, lower-case Roman type, Greek characters, and capitals. To underscore it all, we are not allowed to forget that the passages borrowed from Proust also have a physical being, for we are told how and when they appear to the reader on the printed page: ("Remembering the place: somewhere at the top of a right-hand page" [p. 10]). We are instructed to look at what we are reading as a visible system of signs and are required to recognize these signs as translations or adaptations of other, previously formed systems.

The use of the text within the text is not in itself original—we have only to think of the physically dislocated text used by Balzac in *La Muse du Département*. As far back as *La Route des Flandres,* Simon introduces into his narration part of a "translated" text. But such interpolations mirror the main construction, without disturbing it. In *La Bataille de Pharsale* the process of intertextuality, that is, of using pieces of an alien text as an integral part of a new text, is carried much farther. The translation becomes much more than an attempt to transfer ideas from one language, or from one medium, to another. It is an act of physical transformation, the creation of a new set of relationships. Instead of serving merely as a comment on an established movement of the new text, the borrowed passages enter into it almost as protagonists, and act *in* it, of their own right, as part of the movement. Into the writing texts come and go, speaking not of Michelangelo, or of Poussin, or of Piero della Francesca, but of each other and of their mutual rapport.

The effect on the human actor is decisive, and we need only think of the protagonists of Simon's previous novels to perceive this. The searcher does not create the discourse of *La Bataille de Pharsale.* He is created by it and exists only by virtue of it. He ceases when it ceases and begins again as it recommences. His personal history is subordinate to the signs that compose it. We come to understand that, like him, we exist only in what we can relate about ourselves, and that such a telling is dependent on the elements of translation that we employ, for our lives are written in the terms of pre-existing systems. The narrator becomes increasingly an absence filled with signs that refer to the human condition—he is Everyman in search of the Word which will create him and without which he cannot be.

This novel—like those of Joyce—makes demands on the reader to modify his reading habits and become accustomed to turning them into an act of research, leading to the identification and continual consciousness of the generators in the book and their development. He must be an explorer in a territory loaded with hidden riches, full of surprises and returns to the unexpected, composed of the already known. He will be free to follow the numerous paths proposed to him, in the order that he prefers; yet he must recognize that the detours that appear to offer the greatest choice will always bring him back to his starting point. However free he may feel within the labyrinth, he will not be free to emerge from it without the help of one of the many threads crossing it in all directions. He will be exhausted long before he has exhausted the text, which, on the last page, begins once more the very same game of writing begun on page one.

What is the reward of the reader? What is the battle of Pharsalus?

He who patiently accepts the difficult conditions of such a book shall receive the title of historian, that is, of seeker, having followed step by step, with every detour, the true progress of the mind that reconstitutes the historical present only by re-creating, according to the rules of a very serious game. He will be the true historian, not of Pharsalus, which is jelled into its text, but of the phrase, and of much more than the phrase—the mental mechanisms at the origin of the phrase, which work on the living substance to turn it into literature. Not only man himself, his knowledge, his love, his journeys make Pharsalus. "What happened" is replaced by "This happens"; what is happening is writing.

As for the "real" Pharsalus, it can be either the old, dead, misunderstood text or some unknown field lost in the Greek hills. We shall never know. The point is that it has served as a mainspring for a movement that needs only the presence of the working reader to reveal a continuously new truth.

8 ⁝ Les Corps conducteurs[1]

The principles of novel writing that emerged, little by little, from an effort both conscientious and lucid, were for Simon convincing enough to summarize in a short theoretical work, the preface to *Orion aveugle*.[2] As we read this manifesto, we understand that, with the anecdote and the plot discredited and all idle questions about events banished, the novelist is no longer bound by a predetermined plan of writing. As he remarks: "Before I begin to make signs on paper, there is nothing, except a shapeless magma of sensations that are more or less confused, memories more or less accurate, all accumulated, and a vague—very vague—project."

Simon does not mean here simply putting down on paper, without order or design, in the surrealist manner, everything that passes through the mind. Besides the blank paper and the "magma," a third element is necessary: the act of writing. "It is only when one writes that something happens. . . . It seems . . . that the blank paper and the writing play as important a part as my intentions, as if the slowness of the ma-

1. Paris, Editions de Minuit, 1971, translated as *Conducting Bodies* by Helen R. Lane for Richard Seaver (New York, Viking; London, Calder & Boyars; Canada, The Macmillan Company of Canada, 1974). All passages quoted are from this translation.
2. Geneva, Editions d'Art Albert Skira, 1970. My translations. The text of *Orion aveugle* forms a large part of *Les Corps conducteurs*. They are not, however, the same book, but the generators are the same.

terial action of writing were necessary to allow images the time to accumulate."

In the act that unites the physical and the mental exists the principle of a mysterious fertilization process, of which the product is never "reality"—"description is helpless to reproduce things and always speaks of objects other than those objects which we perceive around us"—but a completely new creation based on the words themselves. If these words at first refer to the memories and perceptions of the writer, soon "each word provokes (or commands) several others, not only by virtue of the images which it attracts like a magnet, but also by its very morphology, simple assonances which, in the same way as the formal necessities of syntax, rhythm, and composition, turn out often to be as fertile as its multiple meanings."

The organization and invention in the novel no longer depend on the original project of the writer but happen, as it were, on their own. Following this trail of words and images "like a traveler lost in a forest, retracing his steps, starting over again, deceived (or guided?) by the resemblance of certain places which are really different and which he thinks he recognizes, by the different appearances of the same place, his trail crossing itself frequently, returning once more through sites already visited . . . it can even occur that at the 'end' he [the writer] is to be found in the same place as at the 'beginning.' "

The primary images, however, are chosen by the writer or at least correspond to his personal myths. We have seen, in *La Bataille de Pharsale,* how the generators of Simon's text are other texts of diverse origin, which communicate both matter and movement to the new composition. From these texts emerge also references to works of art, which in their turn become texts. In *Les Corps conducteurs* the first step is omitted, and Simon's text comes directly from selected and identifiable art works which contain all the elements necessary to generate the text of the novel. These works, twenty in all, are reproduced in the Skira edition of *Orion aveugle,* and we should consider what they are.

The first reproduction is a drawing by Simon himself of the last scene described in *La Bataille de Pharsale,* showing the writer's room and the objects on the table where a hand holding the pen is busy writing. The dictionary, the postcard with the reproduction of a man blowing a trumpet and wearing a high, cylindrical hat, behind him an arm brandishing an ax and someone wearing a helmet, the package of cigarettes (Players, not Gauloises), the package of matches (or paper clips), the shell ashtray, the window opening on to rooftops— all are there. But the money, the sun and shadow, the pigeons are not. Simon gives enough to show us continuity and change and to remind us firmly that we are watching a writer writing.

The frontispiece to the printed text following Simon's declaration of principles—reproduced in manuscript—is a portion (about a third) in black and white of a "combine painting" by Robert Rauschenberg, entitled *Charlene* (which can be seen in the Stedelijk Museum in Amsterdam). A larger portion in smaller detail is reproduced, this time in color, further on in the book, so that we may have no doubts about its importance. This painting is composed of many separate parts and of a variety of materials and is divided by frames into larger and smaller areas. This is how one critic describes it:

"Charlene" . . . has a strong rectilineal and frontal structure. The irregular, boxlike supports, tightly packed, draw attention to their edges. One is conscious of their making, in their sum, the total outside shape of the picture, but the notion of the frame as a boundary between the picture and the outside world—an aesthetic threshold—has to give way to something much more complex. The frames and battens of "Charlene" articulate the *inside* of the picture; they also throw its boundaries far and wide. The wall behind insinuates itself through a hole in the picture and becomes a part of it. And as to the flashing light and mirror, one can imagine them as frames emerging from the picture out into the world, creating a new boundary for it in the space one is occupying oneself.

The concave mirror traps whatever is moving in front of the picture. A red dress or a white shirt, a turning reflection can be caught there swelling and shrinking on its polished curve. It is constantly moving, and by its agency the picture moves constantly too, each value that the mirror traps transforming the values that are painted or pasted in. A blue dress will flash like blue fire, inverting the warmth of the picture; bare arms, a spectacular suntan will spread a brilliant cinnamon that irradiates every red note there.

The real light in "Charlene", inside the picture, puts us in a new relationship in which we might wonder which side of the frame we are standing on. In Amsterdam, where the picture now hangs, the light is high and flat and the flashing bulb is like a sharp, dry point. Elsewhere one has seen the surface of the picture modeled by the light, glistening, dulling, glistening, as it has flashed on and off, and has seen the picture suddenly take on the tawdry inertia of a bedroom wall flicked by neon across the street.[3]

On one of the panels are shown a number of well-known works of art; paintings by Goya, Degas, Van Gogh, for example, are reproduced, and over them drip long streaks of white paint from the panel above. One of Rauschenberg's fetishes, a picture of the Statue of Liberty, can be seen at the bottom. All of the details of this "combine" will take on great importance for the reader of *Les Corps conducteurs*.

A second painting by Rauschenberg called *Canyon* is equally striking. In the center of the lower third looms the great,

3. Andrew Forge, *Rauschenberg* (New York, Harry N. Abrams, n.d.), p. 11.

wing-spread body of a bird of prey perched on what appears to be an iron bracket set on a box held by a wooden stake; from the stake dangles, held by a thick string, a bolster in a striped case. The upper left portion is splashed with white, gray, and black paint and decorated with a picture of a child seated in a bathing pool, the photo of the Statue of Liberty, and scraps of red, white, and blue posters on which can be made out parts of words like "associa," "ocra," "labor." On the right is a metal container, corrugated at top and bottom, with indications of weight and size.

There are enough objects, forms, and colors in these two works alone to provide a considerable amount of text. But many more will be worked into the novel: a montage of a number of dolls' hands in various stages of disrepair by Fernandez Arman, another by George Brecht, of a cabinet with drawers and shelf spaces filled with toilet articles, a toy model of a motorcyclist in front of a house, and nine pigeonholes, one empty, containing colored balls of various sizes and in the center a red ceramic heart. Also included is a photographic montage composed of Andy Warhol's portraits of Marilyn Monroe, the Coca-Cola and Canadian Club signs in Times Square, the sequence showing the assassination of John Kennedy, and pictures of Che Guevara. Another by Brassai, *Ciel postiche,* shows a bare back in half shadow against a mountainlike relief and a dazzling white and dark background. Finally, we have the large montage of Louise Nevelson, *Sky Cathedral,* composed of innumerable rectangles of varying sizes, each containing carefully carpentered fragments that often project out of their frames, increasing the impression of length and height and of enormous complexity and artisanship.

Next in importance to the collages and montages, which already in themselves indicate the approach to the book, are the engravings and lithographs, two of which are beautifully detailed colored copies of eighteenth-century anatomical plates showing a female body and a man's head. Also included are a lithograph, *Christopher Columbus Builds a Fortress* by Maurin, and an engraving showing the signs of the Zodiac—magnificently illustrated with birds, beasts, and mythological figures—taken from the *Atlas universalis* of Andrea Cellari (1708). Then we have an etching by Picasso, showing an old, withered king staring at a huge, intertwined, erotic couple—a page and a woman making love before his sad, round eye—and an engraving from the *Petit Journal* showing the Chambre des Députés in Paris in confusion after the bomb throwing in 1893.

Several photographs are reproduced: an aerial photo of the great serpentine Amazon river in its jungle sheath, one of a wall telephone, one of an anatomical illustration from Larousse, one of the inside cover of a cigar box, advertising Henry Clay Havanas. Finally, there is a composition by Jean Dubuffet, *Caballero* in *"vinyle sur papier entoilé,"* a very gay arrangement of small pieces in red and blue, like a jigsaw puzzle making up a man.

The great painting by Nicolas Poussin, *Paysage avec Orion aveugle,* from the New York Metropolitan Museum of Art, occupies two pages of the book, as well as the cover—and the heart of the novel. For a complete reading of *Les Corps conducteurs,* we must bear in mind each one of these works, for they provoke and sustain all the new combinations that occur during the writing; with them as a background, we can circulate in Simon's pages as in an exhibition where all the objects displayed have become mobile and maneuverable. The images that appear as the writing progresses cannot be foreign to the experience of the writer, for they expose familiar treasures. He does not, in fact, find it necessary to seek material outside the already-constituted sum of his own writings because any given element is potentially capable of leading him as far as he cares to go in "the singular adventure of the narrator." Therefore, we shall recognize features we have come to know very well from the previous novels; however, just as Proust's text directed Simon's to new areas of experience in writing, so every element in these new groups is the "conductor" that will guide the author toward fresh horizons and surround him with an infinite number of images stirred to life by its "charged" presence.

The bodies that serve as conductors lead outward to all the paths of creation through the word. The human body, of which Poussin's Orion provides a splendid example with its muscular nudity, is in itself a universe. In *Les Corps conducteurs,* written under the sign of Orion, the body is present in all its shapes and metamorphoses—the fetus, the child, the old and the young, male and female, black and white, naked and clothed. It is shown in all of its activities—we see it waking, sleeping, running, waiting, traveling, eating, drinking, loving, suffering, and rejecting; in all of its disguises—the naked savage, the soldier, the urban man, the old lady absurdly decked out, the smartly dressed negro, the old king; in all of its perspectives—a giant among stars, a pitiful atom at the foot of skyscrapers; in a variable relationship with all other imaginable bodies, simple or composed, living or inert.

The suffering body of one sick man provides the basic plan, explaining the variety of scenes which pass quickly and in apparent confusion before the eye of the reader. The sickness itself is a reference point, forcing the sick man to realize what he does not normally think of—that his one body is itself a combination of bodies, that its apparent unity can be dissolved into fragments which are themselves separable and capable of redistribution in strange contexts. Coming out of the doctor's office, he sees in the window of a store where stockings are sold a row of disconnected legs, showing off the merchandise. They remind him of the anatomical prints hanging on the walls of the office. Seated, exhausted, on a fire hydrant, but still conscious of what is going on around him, he recalls these prints; but he is also reminded, by a Spanish inscription on the wall, decorated with a cross in runny paint, of an engraving showing some missionaries among American natives. The cross will make him recall the wavering shadow of the airplane on the forest below, seen from the air while he was reading the story of some explorers in the jungle. The landscape seen through the airplane windows, with its winding rivers, will bring to mind once more the veins snaking beneath his own skin and through his own body.

He has taken the airplane to attend a meeting of writers who are attempting to define the role of literature in a world of suffering humanity, and the speech of this assembly is Spanish. From the airplane, the gaze of the traveler moves upward to the heavenly bodies—like negatives of earthly ones —united by the imagination into geometric configurations "forming triangles, trapezoids, polygons"; these in turn are formed into living shapes, "animals, objects, individual human figures, or pairs of figures" (p. 43), the last recalling an erotic theme, swirling in the midst of the Milky Way whose thick scattering of stars is like the seminal act of creation.

We can easily recognize the basic material of Simon's previous work, here regrouped into a universal catalogue, demonstrating that bodies—natural ones like the jungles, the mountains, the sea; artificial bodies, buildings, machines, drawings; and imaginary bodies like the constellations—all enter into a fundamental and complex relationship with the original suffering human body, whose image, as it passes down the street, is projected, continually deformed and obscured, on to all the variegated objects and people exposed in store windows. That this takes place in the New World is not surprising. In Simon's previous novels the Americas always appear as encyclopedic projections of the unknown. Now Simon is attempting an encyclopedic census of the relationships of one universe, reaching out not so much in time, as in space.

Technically it is a New World that Simon explores. Despite continual reference to themes that are constants in his work, he has acquired a new distance in relation to them. The "I," the anxious interrogation, the feeling of helpless involvement in the destructive processes of nature have disappeared. In spite of his suffering—or perhaps because of it—the man who is the center of the movement in the novel remains distinct, separate, indifferent, emotionless about the events of his life, the actions of others. As Ludovic Janvier observes, the text is an absence speaking to another absence.[4] The man barely communicates with the outside world: on the telephone he cannot transmit the message he is trying to send through space. He can only obtain a negative response from his lover. He reads the newspaper upside-down, trying to decipher the inverted words. At the writers' meeting he is slow in following the Spanish of the speakers, which is translated for him by an interpreter.

Why, if we are dealing with relationships between bodies, is there this failure in communication? It is because the instrument—like the defective telephone in the novel—comes between these objects and the "meanings" that we try to give them. For the writer that instrument is the word. Here once again we see the newspaper offering a dead world of print, "continuing to hopelessly display fragments of words or images snatched out of a world of violent, high-flown rhetoric and

4. *Entretiens,* p. 71. My translation.

enclosed in rectangles surrounded by a heavy black border, like death announcements" (pp. 133–134). At the congress, the writers argue interminably about the wording of resolutions concerning the duty of literature to give a meaning to society, but they never succeed in adopting any formula.

Between words and things is a layer of transparent glass, like the glass of the telephone booth, or of the airplane window, or of the storefront windows protecting the merchandise—the same glass that in the museum prevents the viewer from entering the figured world of the artist. This screen, however transparent, prevents any exchange other than visual from either side of the obstacle. Thus, for the spectator, everything appears to be representation or literature. The old themes are transformed: the revolution with its Spanish tinge has become a meeting, inspired by a historical engraving, where Spanish-speaking delegates do nothing but argue; adventure and the quest in the jungle are stories the reader finds in a magazine while sitting comfortably in an airplane that flies high over the wild terrain—or movies to be seen from a comfortable seat in a cinema—; erotic acts are immobilized in films and magazines. The constellations, wild animals, and exotic birds become descriptions from an encyclopedia, and the body itself an anatomical illustration offset with cross-sections and captions.

We should look carefully at what happens to the human personage during this process. In *La Bataille de Pharsale* this actor still carries into the narration his load of memory, imagination, and conjecture, which fuse with the contribution of the assimilated texts. In the midst of the continuous present of the narration we are still led, either by the use of the past tense or by the recurrence of certain scenes, to attribute the sign of the past to certain episodes. In *Les Corps conducteurs* this sign has disappeared, along with the "I" that implies a personal history. Consciousness is recorded through an impersonal "he," who brings to the text nothing but his presence and his physical suffering. If any of the scenes that unfold before our eyes are from the memory of this recording consciousness, we have no way of distinguishing them from others that occur during the narration. An immediate past seems to be established by the man sitting on the hydrant, apparently remembering the shadow of the airplane on the ground. But it is difficult to distinguish the "before" or the "after" of the airplane trip, later it seems to take place at another time, with another destination (North or South America?). The man who telephones in vain to an unknown woman whom he later (perhaps) meets, presumably shares a past history with her, but this is never evoked. As far as possible, the registering consciousness is relieved of all secondary functions—reflection, judgment, feeling, and the idiosyncrasies that distinguish "personality."

In *La Bataille de Pharsale* the protagonist has a tendency to perceive actions and characters like sculptured groups or works of art; he observes them objectively even when this implies personal suffering. In *Les Corps conducteurs* the distance between the spectator and what he perceives is even greater. If the character represented by "he" is jealous, unhappy, or obsessed, we learn nothing more about it than what the representation of the scene tells us. He is no longer the "I" who demands "What happened?" or "What do I know?" (never "What does it mean?"). He suffers, but clinically, without expression. The words combine and separate on their own, on this side of the screen. Only when the physical pain is strong enough to force him into the material world does he stumble into a kind of "landslide" that covers everything, hampering his progress. The greyish, viscous substance gradually rising around him, which stands for the dull, faceless advance of time in the bar and waiting room and which others do not appear to notice, is one of the two important metaphors in the book. The other is the "mask of warm mud" that fatigue and time lay on the face, covering it with anonymity and leaving nothing but the betraying lines and wrinkles.

The denuding of the human character is paralleled by a similar stripping of the text. The mannerisms of earlier works have disappeared. If we compare this narrative with *La Route des Flandres,* for example, we find considerable changes in writing techniques. In *Les Corps conducteurs* the sentences are shorter, restricted to the simple present tense and rarely linked by the repetitive "and." They no longer have an indefinite prolongation through the participle, they do not pause in suspension before conclusion and are seldom interrupted by parentheses. In contrast with *La Bataille de Pharsale,* the more exotic hieroglyphs are absent. Citations of extraneous texts are short, being generally reduced to titles, explanatory captions, signs, inscriptions, and fragments of speeches. Descriptions of art works are absorbed into a narration without sections or chapter headings. The comparison and the metaphor have now become, in an extremely reduced form, fused combinations of images in an apparently straightforward description. In the following example, the images of the woman, the anatomical model, the subway map, the geometrical-geographical pattern all run smoothly into one another:

The woman's eyes stare at him above the edge of the large cup whose contents she is sipping in little swallows. Each time she swallows he can see her neck bulge slightly and the cartilage of her larynx move up and down beneath the skin as the liquid slides down her throat. Above her right breast the towel hanging from her hand forms three oblique folds spreading outward like a fan. . . . Crossing her chest in a horizontal line at the height of her armpits, the towel allows one to see only the upper edge of the opening in the form of a cello case protected by a panel of plexiglass, behind which one can make out large red and blue tubes which fork off in different directions and intertwine. Beneath the smooth skin of her neck a very faint bulge is the only indication of the location of the outer cervical blood vessels, which swell imperceptibly with each invisible pulse of blood. Narrow blue, red, and yellow stripes, only a few fractions of an inch wide, indicate on the map the various subway lines, dotted with little white circles at more or less regular intervals. The system as a whole is laid out in approximately parallel lines, which occasionally bend slightly inward or outward, though in the southern portion of the city they branch out and intertwine in complicated loops and curves. [pp. 134–135]

The metaphor no longer consists in raising one term to the level of another, but in leveling all materials in a common substance. In the same way, the anonymous, expressionless actor is released from purely personal detail into the universe of human myth, which transcends any individual event. The ceaseless rituals of life, love, suffering, and death are constants in every existence, and man has inscribed them on all the objects that surround him, celestial or earthly. This myth takes place incessantly in the present, repeating itself in all the motifs, large or small, that are subject to perception.

The fragments of perception pasted together make up static groups where temporality and movement have no place. It is true that the world appears to offer the specifics of time and action. Postcard images, like that of the missionary engraving at the beginning, are transformed "from referential static to historic shift," as Janvier puts it,[5] that is, from description into narration in which something apparently happens. The traveler flies over different countries, arrives somewhere, flies off again. The writers prolong their meeting well into the night, until weariness is evident, and the hall filled with smoke. The

5. *Entretiens,* p. 77. My translation.

explorers in the jungle continue to advance, decimated by sickness and the enemy. The central character walks through the city streets, going somewhere. But, of course, all of this is frozen time and movement. The traveler, the explorers, the walker never definitively arrive anywhere; the meeting never ends, and the same speeches are repeated over and over again. The sun and the moon are always in the same place, the constellations turn around one another. The airplane, apparently immobilized in the immensity of space, is no different from the old lady who advances so painfully that her progress can scarcely be observed. In the streets, the flood of cars and pedestrians monotonously follows the same rhythm. The hands of the clock are motionless. And the sea, mass in motion, is itself plunged into the atemporal: "The white overcast seam connecting the mineral desert and the desert of water is also motionless once again. The eye cannot discern the movement of the tossing waves or that of the foam spreading out over the sand on the shore or breaking against the sunbaked rocks" (p. 166). The "tumult like unto silence" of which Valéry writes in the *Cimetière marin* is parallel to the movement of Achilles that has become immobility, or to the giant Orion who "will never reach his goal, since as the sun rises higher and higher in the sky, the stars outlining the giant's body are gradually growing paler and dimmer, and the fabulous silhouette motionlessly advancing in great strides will thus slowly fade and eventually disappear altogether in the dawn sky" (p. 187).

The registering mechanism, "the pale bulging eyeball, firmly held in place by its red roots, with its iris, its cornea, its vitreous humor, its aqueous chamber, and the thin membrane of the retina on which the images of the world fall, gliding across it and replacing each other one by one" (p. 187), makes none of the distinctions that would be necessary to establish progress. It does not know whether the images registered are grandiose or absurd. The eye is indifferent. What it sees finally, when man at last falls towards the waiting earth is "microscopic debris, motes of dust, stray hairs, little hairs coiled up in spirals, horsehair . . . strewn over the pink, mauve, almond-green, or pale yellow patches, with the parallel gray strands of the warp and woof showing through in those places where it has been worn threadbare" (p. 191).

The eye is indifferent, but the artist is not. In the incessant flux of images, he recognizes the sign that facilitates the transition from one scene to the next. This sign, always visual, transcends all the possible meanings of the elements that compose it, or, as Simon explains himself:

if one element (let us say, for example, a black horse) dominates or attracts to itself other elements both by what can be called the morphology of the sign in itself (black) and its meaning (horse) one must *always* sacrifice the meaning to plastic necessities, or, if you prefer, to the formal ones, that is to say that, *before any other consideration,* the black (and the pattern of the design) must agree (by harmony or dissonance) with the elements that border it, *without anyone asking* what (for example) a horse might be doing in a bedroom or next to a priest in his chasuble, rather than galloping by the seaside or in a field.[6]

The artist therefore makes a collage—or rather, to adopt the play on words made by Claude Lévi-Strauss, a *bris-collage*[7]—fragmenting perceptions to reassemble them in new, unprecedented, harmonic arrangements. Far from suffering from this fragmentation, the "meaning" of each group is enriched, for as Simon observes:

there occurs at this point a phenomenon that appears to be some

6. *Entretiens,* pp. 26–27. My translation.
7. *Bris* in French has the meaning of "breaking" (n) and *collage* that of "gluing, sticking." *Bricolage* applies to do-it-yourself activities, often implies inventiveness.

sort of miracle: that is to say, there will appear as well (like a "bonus" one might say) a significant opening of perspectives, an ambiguous meaning, uncertain and *"tremblé,"* as Barthes would say, not explicit, but often richer and more fertile (or charged) with vibrations than that which would have been set up between two elements chosen only with relation to their meaning (horse-beach or horse-field) and whose manipulation has revealed, despite the connection between the latter, a formal incompatibility.[8]

In art bodies touch and become conductors where, in the world on the other side of the glass, this would be an impossibility. In the plastic arts they can be made to meet directly through their representation. And in the writer's world their representation—the word, that instrument recently judged an obstacle—can also form new and unexpected contacts, illuminating "miraculously" the original phenomenon. The eye with its indifference, the word with its impermeability, combine to turn perception into creation.

The collage is constructed, then, not at the expense of the signifier, but by transforming it and enriching it in a manner unforeseen by logic. It would be better to speak of a series of collages, composed of essentially the same elements, highlighted each time in a new fashion, and making up one constantly variable whole. The Serpent appears in the sky, in the jungle, like a "big worm" in the body, like a caterpillar, a river, a flag, or around the neck of the old woman as a "boa". The cross section is cut in the human body, in a building, in a subway train. Old ladies, legs, travelers are "skewered" in rows. Instead of being limited to one meaning, the signifier opens out in space, illuminated in different ways according to its surroundings. Such a liberation makes it impossible, however, for it to tell any one "story." The close connection with meaning dissolves, making room for the "play" between the

8. *Entretiens,* pp. 26–27. My translation.

parts of speech and for the transition that replaces the metaphor.

The only movement is that of the text itself, and the action does not concern the objects described but the advance, the swerving, and the retreat of images among images. An allusion to a development that seems irrelevant at the time, often prepares the appearance, two pages later, of new groups composed of the elements we have already encountered.

We have here much more than a simple game of associations. For example, the longitudinal crosscut of a skyscraper under construction raises in the mind of the spectator in the street—because of its hygienic, *imputrescible* appearance—a kind of negative picture, that of the condor feeding on rotten flesh. The scraps of meat hanging from the beak of the scavenger recall, however, the colored fragments of posters dangling from the board near the building being torn down and replaced. The word "meeting" perceived on one of these poster scraps brings back the writers' congress where "the speech deals mainly with considerations or declarations having a certain social and political import, in which nouns with a rather timeworn air about them, not unlike the faded colors of the posters, such as Liberty, Revolution, Solidarity, or Unity, reappear frequently. Two animals carved from a single large block of mahogany, a condor with a bare neck and a leopard, frame a shield" (p. 25). The condor, however, is already phonetically present in the text on an earlier page, where the airplane traveler, seeing the mountain surge upward, thinks of "some fierce, gigantic reptile with a legendary name, that of a titan, a mining company, or a constellation (A*con*cagua, Ana*con*da, Andromeda)" (p. 21)—the titan referring back to *Orion*, the mining company to both the serpent and the building to be occupied, the building to the mountain, the syllable *con* to the erotic object and to the notion of relationship. The condor and the building are related to the constant elements of destruction and construction that are the great underlying movements of the narration, of all narration. Hence the meeting, combining, and separation of signs is much more than a mere surface pattern; it implies the making and unmaking of the universe.

In the legend of Orion, the hero, blinded by the son of Dionysus, whose daughter he has violated, carries off the fire god's apprentice to help him find the dawn and restore his sight. He is later attacked by a scorpion and then killed by Artemis, who has been tricked into believing that he has seduced one of her priestesses. Artemis then sets Orion among the stars, to be eternally pursued by the Scorpion.

Simon's use of this story leads to many interpretations. Orion, the seeker of light, will become light itself, not the light of day that shows everything, but only the dim outline of an immense pattern, where darkness is an integral part of the total design. The eye that sees and does not see in the gloom gives him his being, just as the being of the book emerges from the pattern formed around the obscurity of words. The world is communicated to Orion through the little person perched on his shoulder, naming in his ear what he cannot see. According to these indications, he advances toward a light that he cannot reach, since he himself must disappear before arriving. The very name of Orion is rich in implications—it has the ancient meaning of "mountain" and appears in the book as the immense rocky shape looming up before the airplane, and also as the skyscraper, dwarfing the humans below and underlining Orion's double connection with earth and sky. The initial "O" and the syllable "or"—which are so particularly significant for Simon—recall the anonymous spectator called O., and also the wealth and the banknotes that represent the folds and intersections of destiny. When spoken, the name Orion awakens echoes of "orient" (and deserts are often mentioned) and perhaps *horion* or blow on the ear (the ear of Orion has become his guide to progress, so words must strike our ear before we can make progress in understanding).

Orion's essential implication in his surroundings is indicated in the carefully detailed description of Poussin's painting.

Although the rules of perspective have apparently been followed so as to give the viewer the illusion of depth, the painter, seemingly working at cross purposes, has also deliberately incorporated a great many tricks of perspective in his canvas, thus destroying this feeling of depth, so that as a result the giant has become an integral part of the pasty magma of earth, leaves, water and sky surrounding him. Orion is not advancing in an upright position, with his body forming a vertical axis in relation to the plane of the path he is following, as would be the case, for example, if one were looking at a chess piece standing on a square of a chess board, surrounded by nothing but empty space on all sides. He appears, on the contrary, to resemble a figure in a bas-relief, firmly imbedded in the décor that is intended to frame him or serve as a background for him. The gigantic body either stands out from this natural landscape or sinks back into it, depending on the play of light and shadow, but never becomes entirely detached from it. The soil, the branches of the trees, the clouds are also cleverly highlighted or shaded, so that at times the portions of the body in shadow (the right arm, the back) or in the light (the shoulder and the left arm groping in front of him, the left leg stretched straight back) stand out in clear outline, whereas other portions (the right leg striding forward, the midsection of the body, the hand holding the bow) blend into these areas of light and shadow and merge with them. The landscape thus fails to create the impression of a plane perpendicular to the canvas. On the contrary, it forms bumps and hollows and projects certain of its elements forward, not according to their proximity or distance, such as would be the case in conventional perspective, but rather, only in accordance with the requirements of this rhetorical style of composition and expression. These elements cease to be sky, pebbles, leaves, and instead become an environment, or more properly speaking, a matrix. They are not gaseous, mineral, or vegetable masses located at varying distances from the viewer like the receding planes of a stage or film set, but mere accidental lighting (or color) effects, accenting the reliefs (the salient contours) of a dough of uniform consistency kneaded into a single rough mound. Though distant objects, the hill on the horizon, for example, where the path reappears, winding its way up the slope, are drawn in smaller scale, they nonetheless seem to form part of the foreground because of their strong contrasts and accents. The rock ledge jutting out over the hill, with certain patches of it in glaring light and others in deep shadow, the thunder-clouds with roiling black folds, are exactly similar in nature to the muscular, craggy back of the giant stuck fast in this clay out of which the creator has modeled forms of the animate and inanimate world that are indistinguishable from each other. [pp. 62–63]

This text is fundamental for the understanding of Simon's techniques in *Les Corps conducteurs* and for the interpretation of the myth. Like Orion, the sufferer is caught in his surroundings and like him is made of the same substance, by the same creative gesture, as everything around him. All the beings in the text are indissolubly linked to their background and to each other. The skyscrapers link heaven and earth and are reflected in the water. The beasts in the jungle are repeated in the heavens. The mustachioed man on the cigar box has the same physiognomy as the people at the writers' meeting. All are bonded together in one large, baroque composition.

This lesson of Orion is repeated in a plastic sense in a work of Louise Nevelson, one which illustrates by structural means what Poussin has done in paint. Although elements from Rauschenberg and Brecht—the bird of prey and the red heart, for example—can be recognized, as individual motifs in the text, Nevelson goes beyond the motif by showing the actual organization of matter. Her *Sky Cathedral,* a massive piece (344 x 305.5 x 45.5 m), composed like much of her other work of pieces of wood shaped or worked into every imaginable form, but grouped in special relationships by rectangular frames, unevenly but harmoniously built into rising columns. The eye is thus caught by the minute detail that characterizes each group—one, for example, is made up of long, thin, parallel strips, another of rough rectangles and wedges piled on top of one another, a third of hand-turned, rounded, or curved objects—as well as the huge general design that integrates them in the total work.

Louise Nevelson allows us, as we are informed by the introduction to the catalogue for her show at the Galerie Jeanne Bucher in 1969,

to see—starting from raw material devoid of plastic qualities and evocative power, through the proliferation of shapes, hollows, planes, through the tension introduced into their relationships and combinations—a defined magic space, or rather, the realization of a magical act. . . . The geometrics of Louise Nevelson produce a hypnotic effect in space by subordinating it, through harmonics which burst open the rigid framework of the piled-up box constructions, liberating essential rhythms. The combinations of short and long rhythms, the subtle interplay of active angular shapes and passive rounded elements, modulate in counterpoint. The orchestration of light and shade values, of depth and relief, of planes and projections, maintained within a completely unified thought, develops an overwhelming dramatic tension. Nothing seems left to chance; nor does anything seem to follow a previously determined plan, so easily does the work appear to breathe.[9]

Louise Nevelson has also produced works entitled *Homage to the Universe* (1968) and *Rain Forest Wall* (1967), both containing the same elements of arresting detail and inspiring

9. *Louise Nevelson* (May-June 1969), n.p. My translation.

architectural design and both suggesting correspondences with Simon's work. No doubt this type of construction is closest to his wishes. It implies both the physical reality he is describing and the universal structure he intuits. One passage from *Les Corps conducteurs* illustrates the connection between one and the other:

The glass façades of a number of the skyscrapers have lights on around the clock. Their thousands and thousands of windows, arranged in vertical rows one atop the other, separated by thin steel horizontal strips, rise to dizzying heights, forming towering walls that gleam like diamonds. The tops of certain of these skyscrapers are surrounded by dense heat waves, tinged a dirty pink by the reflections of neon signs. Others, however, are plunged in total darkness. Deserted by their daytime occupants, they have been relegated to the realm of shadows. Behind their dark façades, one can almost see their superimposed office cubicles, their corridors, like row upon row of pigeonholes one atop the other in the darkness, filled, like the gutted rooms of abandoned houses about to be torn down, with a clutter of useless objects. Rickety tables, chairs with broken legs, cabinets with sagging carved doors, rolltop desks, rusty typewriters, sofas with prickly horsehair stuffing and backs upholstered in cracked moleskin, exposed beams, plaster acanthus moldings, balustrades, blades of overhead fans, all the debris, identifiable or not, is covered by the dark of night with a uniform layer of black paint. [p. 65]

In *Orion aveugle* this passage is printed opposite the reproduction of *Sky Cathedral*. But besides this visual correspondence, an even deeper one matches the very intent of Simon's work. The use of previously employed material, the organization into groups and cells, the relating of the individual cell to a massive construction plan aimed at transforming our appreciation of space, all this is common to both artists. Simon, of course, is working with the word and the printed page, but he too is using his techniques of assemblage to change our feelings about space, to "burst through the rigid framework" of association. Like Nevelson, he includes in his groupings old, worn objects that are revitalized by redistribution, and like her, he makes it impossible to exhaust the force of that redistribution with one brief glance. In each grouping, something new is always to be found. The prospecting, in this New World, is infinite.

The prospecting is very important. It has brought us to the end of a long road, where we discover that the novel has been stripped, little by little, of its original trappings and the "weave laid bare"—purified, desensitized, and decorative. In these last pages, the sign recovers its value of sign, liberated from fixed epistemology. We learn nothing about the stylized outside world; we merely follow the traces that its representation leaves in us, and we are asked to believe that the reorganization of the signs making up this representation is, in the end, the true object of the novel.

9 ⁝ Triptyque

When *Triptyque* appeared in 1973,[1] the reviewer in the magazine *Express* greeted it as "du déjà vu. Ou presque."[2] The comment is both accurate and unjust. By now, the reader has learned to recognize and relate to previous apparitions the images that once more faithfully return: the erotic scene, the clouds, the posters, the machines, even the names of Reixach and Lambert. But he should also have learned that the image plays a role and that with each new appearance its function is subtly altered to infer new relationships within its sphere, just as actors take on new parts, or characters in a series show up in different circumstances. We must look beyond our own recognition to discover what fresh combinations the new text has to offer.

Just as the movement of the different elements in *Les Corps conducteurs* begins in the pages of *La Bataille de Pharsale,* so the activity in *Triptyque* arises from reflection upon this same movement in *Les Corps conducteurs.* In *Pharsale,* the initial impetus given by the action of one text upon another is diverted towards the production of new groups of images formed by the interaction of the original series. This formation leads directly into *Les Corps conducteurs,* where such

1. Paris, Editions de Minuit, 1973. All passages quoted are in my translation with the permission of Viking Press, Inc.
2. No. 1126 (Feb. 5–11, 1973), p. 51.

groups are related endlessly in mental and textual space, as multiple series of repeating and variable structures build up from primary representation. In *Triptyque,* this structuring is itself called into question.

Of course, a "something" is represented. Here, this something is made up of recognizable and even explicit narrations —three, to be faithful to the title, plus a fourth which is a kind of commentary on the others. It is not hard to distinguish events in a village, where a couple of boys out fishing spy on a pair making love in a barn and cause, indirectly, the death of a child. Mingled with this strain is one about a pair of lovers in an urban setting and a wedding night spoiled by a drunken husband. A third is about an older woman in a plush Riviera hotel who appears to be asking her wealthy lover to save her son from a drug charge. At intervals between them develops a long circus scene, featuring a clown and his companions and a monkey.

The novel, then, offers pictures which tell stories; and apparently there is no attempt to make the stories other than what they are—banal, linear, straightforward, with no suggestion of "character," with no mystery about what is going on. People and events are images, perceived in the text according to certain laws of attraction—that is, the images often prompt and interrupt one another, one story supersedes the one being told, as the visual series develops—but perceived clearly, evenly, and indisputably at the moment of telling.

Only, of course, story telling is not the purpose of this novel. What is actually happening in the text? The title leads us to expect a painting of sorts. We know that a triptych is a three-paneled work of art, used as an altar piece (we recall *Le Vent*); the two side panels, which generally develop and enrich the motifs of the center or main panel, can be fitted over it. The intent of Claude Simon was originally, it seems, to write a novel based on two series of elements that could not be reduced to any realistic schema or pinned down to any definable time or space. However, an encounter with the work of the painter Francis Bacon caused him to substitute a triple series in the book, developing in each of the three parts motifs that grow simultaneously and feed on one another. If we remain on the level of the "stories" however, whatever their number, we shall discover almost nothing about this novel.

The first paragraph offers, as usual, a number of clues:

The postcard represents an esplanade planted with palm trees lined up under a too-blue sky by the edge of a too-blue sea. A long cliff of dazzling white façades, with rococo designs, bends inward gently following the curve of the bay. Exotic bushes, groves of canna, are planted between the palms and make up a cluster in the foreground of the photograph. The canna flowers are colored in loud red and orange tones. People in light-colored clothing come and go on the breakwater which separates the esplanade from the beach. The printing of the different colors does not exactly coincide with the edges of each object, so that the raw green of the palm trees runs into the blue of the sky, the purple of a scarf or a sunshade invades the ochre of the ground or the cobalt of the sea. The card is placed on the corner of a kitchen table covered by an oilcloth with yellow, red, and pink squares. [p. 7]

Here is an immediate warning that we are confronted with a representation—and not a very accurate one—in which all the elements are intensified, in colors that run off into one another and blur the lines of separation. Almost all the basic colors of the spectrum, or the palette, are mentioned. There is a glimpse of rococo design. We are made aware that this representation is part of another decor, which in its turn will be described. That we are being provided with a metaphor for the novel that is to be is not hard to imagine.

The next brief description of the table, on which stands a

dish bearing a dead, skinned rabbit, recalls a still life painting. But this immediately gives way to a camera approach through the kitchen door, out through the courtyard and orchard, along the path through the village towards a waterfall and a barn. The "one" directing the camera is very scrupulous about the scope of his picture:

From the barn one can see the belltower. From the bottom of the waterfall, one can also see the belltower but not the barn. From the top of the waterfall one can see both the belltower and the roof of the barn at the same time. . . . Lying in the field above the waterfall, one can see the grasses and the flower clusters standing out against the sky, their stalks sometimes swaying in the wind, those of the grasses, which are more flexible, bending slightly, the flowers bobbing stiffly back and forth. From this angle, the flowers are bigger than the belltower. In fact, one cannot look at the tower and the flowers at the same time. If one looks at the flowers, the belltower, in the distance, appears like a blurred grey rectangle, drawn out lengthwise, with a purplish triangle, also blurred, on top. . . . If one stares at the belltower, the stalks and flower clusters in their turn change into blurred shapes gently swaying, forming acute-angled triangles whose uncertain sides alternately cross and part.   [pp. 9–10]

Perspective, clarity, and limits of vision, we conclude, depend on distance, position, focus, and the scope of the recording instrument. The concept is not particularly new, if we are speaking of the visual arts, but it deserves more reflection as a commentary on a *text*. There is to be no omnipresent, all-focusing eye, no seeing what goes on behind one's back, no simultaneous registering of widely separated phenomena to suggest cause and effect. The two village boys who spy on the couple in the barn can see just as much as they can make out through the crack in the wall, no more.

The apparent innocence of description—the Stendhalian mirror reflecting the roadside—is a blind. On the shining river surface, "the reflection of the sky and the dazzling clouds make it impossible to distinguish the river-bed" (p. 15). Sometimes, however, other objects—fish, old pots, the river mud—can be perceived and, when two village boys lean over the water, are seen *through* the reflection of their heads (p. 13). Here we have the image of the image. What we see, through the heads, is a representation modified by the quality of the material substance that projects the image toward us, by the lighting that picks out this image, by the mechanism that registers it. As we read this text, the functioning of each of these parts and their role in the construction—and in the de-construction—of the text becomes more and more apparent.

In the first section of the triptych the insistence on types of representation is repeated in obvious ways: by the postcard, the filmstrips, which one of the boys is examining in his room, the posters and the double spectacle of the cinema and the circus, the spicy engraving of a maidservant seduced in a barn, the painting of wrestlers surrounded by onlookers. Almost at once, however, something disturbs us. We are disposed by habit and tradition to assume that these recognized representations are imposed on a background of "reality," that is, something serving as an unchanging field of reference. But then we observe that the boy who is peering at the filmstrip or "still"— in which appears a person who, later, seems to be part of a film in progress at the local movie house (which is the barn) —is perhaps no more "real" than the piece of film. In the movie we see a room where engravings hang on the walls; one of the engravings depicts an erotic scene showing a maidservant being tumbled in a barn, and through the fanlight of the barn, two laughing boys are peeking at the scene. We have already seen the boys peering between the slats of the barn at a similar sexual encounter. A doubt begins to arise in our mind. Who is being represented to whom? In the sequence boy-film-cinema-engraving-barn-boys, where is the logical stopping place?

That the answer is to be denied us becomes evident in the second section. At first, a boy is struggling with a geometrical problem that involves finding the relationships between the angles of a triangle inscribed in a circle with tangents (already an erotic design in *Pharsale*). The beginner in drawing also learns to judge distances and work out perspectives and relationships in geometrical terms. However, the boy never solves his problem, which in its last form is seen scratched out. Simon now shows us why.

The perspectives that we are tempted at each moment to take as true ones turn out to be each an illusion of another and fade into one another almost as quickly as we can adjust our vision. The stills—which the two boys are now looking at in the field and which are perhaps the same as those in a scene from the movie—show a naked woman lying on a bed. She is first described from the point of view of the movie camera director, whose apparatus looks down on her as she lies in a painted décor. But she is abruptly changed into an anatomical painting, with her muscles outlined in Venetian (Venus) red, washed over with lighter shades, and with her head unfinished. Immediately the studio reappears, and then the boys. Are we to assume that the boys occupy the central viewpoint? A few pages later, we discover that the movie camera is also taking shots of them in reverse; it is moving backward and including everything that has just been described, as well as a scene conjured up by the circus poster on the barn into which the boys are peeping:

. . . while as the camera keeps moving, the two bodies get further off, as if sucked back, growing smaller and smaller, sucking in with them the circus ring, the lion tamer with his shiny boots and hair, the leaping tigers before the bars beyond which, in the blue half-shadows, crowd the rows of invisible spectators. Soon, also, appear the head of the clown, the roaring lion, the tarred barn wall, its roof, the edge of the wood, the sloping field, the path to the sawmill, the vertical poplars at the bend in the river, and, beyond the orchard trees, the first village roofs over-looked by the belltower. [pp. 90–91]

So we (the invisible spectator) make behind the camera the inverse trip that was made outwards from the kitchen into the hamlet at the beginning of the book, and we find ourselves again with the boy in his room struggling with his angles, tri-angles, circles, and tangents. A little later the camera follows in a "long traveling shot" the two boys as they rush across the field after spying on a young girl changing into her bathing suit. The camera's movement is emphasized on the last page of this section, when it slowly closes in on an old woman selecting from a rabbit hutch the animal that will be the centerpiece of the still life we observed at the beginning of the book.

Meanwhile, another thread in the narration shows a couple making love against a wall, at night, under the street lamps. The man of the pair appears to be the bridegroom from a wedding party that is getting inebriated in a local bar, and also the sheep-faced young man on the movie poster, portrayed looking sulkily at a tearful bride. The woman of the night couple seems to be the barmaid from the same local bar. All of this turns out to be, however, a story in a book being read by the actress in the hotel where a movie is being made. Her companion, perhaps the man who appears in some of the stills that the two boys are examining in the field, also appears tem-porarily described as an unfinished painting. The hotel and the bay lined with palm trees are seen—like a copy of the original postcard—as a lighted panel, with winking electric bulbs, above the jukebox in the bar where the members of the wedding party are getting drunk.

Regularly throughout this section the clown and his companions pursue their antics—jokes and tricks grotesquely representing elements in the other narrations. The components of the text come one out of the other like objects out of a conjurer's hat, except that the hat itself is a product of the objects that emerge from it. Through one representation another can be perceived, like the world as it appears to the boys looking through the transparent film with another world in it, while they themselves are seen through another film. This cinematic procedure recalls Buñuel's *Discreet Charm of the Bourgeoisie,* in which dreams emerge from and contain one another unceasingly.

All varieties of representation are in evidence—painting, engraving, posters, billboards, postcards, stills, transparencies, moving film, painted sets. One particular element is emphasized in this second section, just as focus and perspective were studied in the first. This time, our attention is drawn with persistance to lighting.

In each scene the source and intensity of light, its focal point, and effect on coloration are carefully indicated. The varieties of illumination are meticulously graduated, from the pinpoint in the darkness to blazing sunlight. The faint glow of a cigarette lighter with which the drunken bridegroom hunts for his lost keys under the car colors his face in shades of pink and black; the same coloration is given by the table lamp to the face of the actor in the hotel bedroom. The headlights of a car or a motorcycle, the downward sweep of streetlamps, and circus or movie spotlights pick out subjects pictorially (the French word *pinceau* is used for a beam of light and the painter's brush, and also for the artist's brush when the make-up of the actors is being repaired). Strings of blinking lights, interspersed with patches of darkness, follow the passage of a car on wet pavement, the descent of an airplane, the curve of a bay, the streets of a town. The surface of a window gives a shiny cameo effect to a man standing behind it. Reflections shimmer from water and mirrors. In contrast with the night scenes, brilliant sunlight picks out the flesh tones of the two boys running half-naked through the countryside and concentrates in the vivid coloring of the little girl caught, like an impressionist painting, in a bright, natural setting:

Swaying in the breeze, the tangled branches are stirred by faint movements, rising and falling, revealing and concealing alternately the hair, the face, the shoulders and the arms of a young girl standing behind a bush. The skin, extremely white and milky, seems to concentrate all the daylight on her, or rather, as in overexposed film, to shimmer faintly as if she herself were a source of light. The face, haloed by orange-gold flame, is freckled. . . . Dark blue, with shining spots of sunlight, a kingfisher rapidly skims along the water. . . . Clusters of pink and purple flowers, with long stalks springing up horizontally at first and then bending over towards the light, grow between the stones. [pp. 118–119]

Shadows are as important as light. They are often linked with movement. The still life of the skinned rabbit that opens this section also takes on the appearance of motion from the shadows cast by a single swaying light bulb. The clown picked out by the spotlight has two grotesque shadows that cavort beside him. The movie posters seem animated by the shadow of leaves projected by the poor street lighting. Sometimes shadow itself is both actor and movement. "Some time ago too the shadow of the hill has crossed the river, invaded the meadow, crossed the path to the sawmill, and now it is climbing the further slope, covering the barn. It has even got beyond the edge of the wood, and begins to climb the high rocky cliff which rises vertically, towering over the scree-covered, scrub-grown slope" (p. 159).

If the swaying motions of nonhuman objects often give the illusion of life, human and animal actions, on the contrary, often appear mechanical. Sexual activity is constantly linked to machines such as the motorcycle, the locomotive, the street-car (on which the words "Men-women" actually appear in an advertisement), the old baby carriage, and assorted agri-cultural implements. The noises made by these machines often accompany copulation. And the machine can and does func-tion badly, or break down altogether, disturbing once again our illusion of "real life." A film taken from a boat is jerky, not only because of the rise and fall of the water, but because the projector is worn. It breaks down completely during the screening of the film about the couple in the hotel and later during a sexual encounter, so that we are abruptly reminded by the freezing of the image, and then by the uneven, spas-modic start of the mechanism, that what we had accepted as flesh and blood reality is merely a set of objects perceived as combinations of light, shade, and color, activated by a defec-tive machine.

The slowing down or speeding up of the succession of images introduces the thought of time—or rather, of our conscious-ness of time—for to calculate duration from the succession in itself is not possible. Only an interruption, only a sud-den disturbance in the smooth flow can awaken this conscious-ness and its discomfort will then make us aware of ourselves as spectators of the show. The sudden jerk, the discontinuity, the hesitation between the emission and the reception of the image also correspond to the uneven nature of our attention to the outside world; our attention does not always coincide with the rhythm of events or is sometimes distracted, suspended in mid-air, like the cat pursuing the mechanically advancing chickens, "pausing . . . sometimes halfway through a step, one paw motionless in the air, then renewing its progress by completing the movement it had begun, like a movie actor when the film gets stuck and then starts up again" (pp. 92–93). Sometimes the connecting movement is lost altogether, so that the links in a "continuous" narrative disappear. The quality and persistence of attention is also a factor of artistic production—indeed of the production of the world for the consciousness—and depends on the relationship between the projector of the image and the receiving apparatus.

The absence of connecting evidence is illustrated almost immediately in the third section, where we see the two boys attempting to decide on the order in which to arrange a number of stills from the movie about the couple in the hotel. One picture is too ambiguous to be placed chronologically and this causes an argument. There is no way of telling where it really belongs in the story, or if it really belongs at all. Besides the problem of order, the question of rhythm also comes to the fore. Suddenly, in all of the narratives, the pace is speeded up. Things begin to "happen" and approach climax or catastrophe. The machine, at rest during the first part, is now a majestic and powerful locomotive in motion, a streetcar, a noisy truck. Longer passages from the "stories" carry us along at a faster pace. "The water runs rapidly with a silky sound, almost imperceptible, stirred by faint ripples along the banks or by whirlpools which swirl on the surface and escape, carried off by the current. . . . The little monkey accelerates, imitated by his human rival . . . the rhythm of the piece being played by the orchestra accelerates also. The level of laughter rises by one degree" (p. 194). When the film gets stuck again, the urgency is conveyed by the frame catching fire: "the eye, until then absorbed by the moving shapes then slowly becomes conscious . . . until, as though to confirm the impression of catastrophe, there appears a dazzling white spot, whose burned edge rapidly spreads, devouring without distinction the embracing bodies, the tools and walls of the barn, the lights coming on then, the screen now empty, dull and uniformly grey" (p. 195).

Too excited by the excess of movement, visual perception temporarily blanks out and then substitutes for moving pictures static engravings—the ones on the wall of the room occupied by the movie actress.

But the film starts up again, as it always does, this time with a darkened décor. Night has taken over, and sounds replace objects, but they are related to one another in the same generative fashion.

The earth, the whole world seem swallowed up by a layer of thick, palpable ink, which can be felt like a liquid in contact with the eyeballs, the face, even the limbs. In the crowding darkness, the even, continuous splashing of the invisible waterfall, re-echoed by the invisible rocky cliffs and the sides of the valley, seems like an audible solidification of the silence, of time without dimension. Powerful, fixed, and omnipresent, it provides a kind of foundation for the strident chanting of the crickets, invisible too, which weaves something like a second sheet of silence, steady, monotonous, on one piercing, barely-modulated note. Sometimes, frightened by someone approaching, or to recover strength, one of them, then another, suddenly stops, giving place then (like a curtain opening on to another curtain) to the same strident call weakened by distance, but continuous, repeating itself from one distant spot to the next in the darkness, like a series of relay stations spaced out on all sides in the immensity of the vast night suddenly grown still more vast.   [pp. 206–207]

As the light slowly returns—the moon rises, flashlights glimmer along the sides of the river, the lights of the hotel gleam, the bride in the room with her drunken, sleeping husband stares at her reflection in the mirror—the various catastrophes are consummated. At the same time, a new series of connections is established, which effectively prevents the reader from ever assuming the full daylight of logic. With the movie camera once more moving in on the face and body of the actress on the bed, we discover that the film advertised on the poster, showing what seems to be an ill-fated marriage, is possibly made from the novel she is reading. This postulates a link between the illustrations and the supposed story, even though Simon tells us "there is no continuity between the various pictorial elements" (p. 217).

We can neither deny nor confirm a continuity that the mind constantly creates among all the disparate elements invading it. The boys in the field are once more looking at the stills from the hotel movie. The fragment they have been unable to place—that of a man in a dark suit with his hand on the doorknob of a bedroom—leads into a scene in which he enters the room, glances at the woman who has fallen asleep over her novel, and sits down to finish a large picture puzzle. The puzzle, when completed, shows a village in a valley, with river and waterfall, barn, belltower, sawmill, orchards, two boys fishing, cows and flowers—in other words a replica, stiffly frozen, of the opening scene. We realize that the third section is, as might be expected, a structural inversion of the first, with variations in detail and perspective. In the first part, the clouds themselves are like parts of a puzzle, changing shape and breaking up in the sky. In the third part, the man sweeps the whole scene, itself become the puzzle, off on to the floor where it breaks up into multiformed pieces. This is the end of the movie. The usherettes open the door of the movie house, and the invisible spectators file out into the windy night, lit by feeble, swaying streetlights. However, they (we) have not quite escaped. One car, decked with wedding ornaments, remains like a question mark in the silent, unpeopled darkness.

The warp and woof of the text is made tight, not only by the interwoven themes, but by a web of inner connections based on the word and the image. Visual and auditory images bind many scenes together, so that we cannot meet one without evoking the other or others. The focal gleam on metal, for example, relates the knife the old woman uses to slaughter the rabbit and the scythe with which she cuts grass to feed it with the shining of the moving, destructive hatchet in the last section, which in turn recalls the raised ax in *La Bataille de Pharsale*. The silky sound of water where the trout swim evokes the soft swishing of the luxurious cars, moving along the bay as silently and as smoothly as fish. The skinned rabbit is not very different from the naked woman on the bed, especially when half-covered with a cloth, like a sheet. Its jerking movements before death are reiterated in the movements of the copulating lovers. The ever-present circle or hole into which disappear various objects—the trout into a vase lying on its side, the river into a cavern—is a perpetual sexual image. The squeaking wheels of the baby carriage in which the old woman collects food for the rabbits, while the boys watch the love-making in the barn, is matched by the clattering of the streetcars, the clanging of the trains, the rumbling of the truck during other such scenes. Olfactory images are linked with visual ones: the smell of the mushrooms surrounds the dead rabbit with the odor of nature in the deep woods, combined with the scent of decay; the phallic shape of the mushrooms corresponds to that of the male member (in conjunction with the naked flesh of the rabbit or the woman) and to the baroque shapes of the luxury hotels.

Lexical connections are almost inexhaustible. The clown's entire first act is based on the play on the word *marteau* ("hammer" and "crazy"), where he clamors for a hammer to nail down his gaping boot—a further play on the expression *gueule d'empeigne* (the mouth of a shoe vamp, that is, a wide-mouthed, ugly face)—which "barks" at him; at the same time he accuses the partner who brings him hammers of various sizes of being crazy. The same witticism is used, unconsciously, by the barmaid trying to reason with her drunken lover, just after she has caught the heel of her shoe in the streetcar rail. A more tenuous but essential connection is suggested between the word *encrage* (the process by which the printer fixes the colors in reproductions) and the scenes of boats at anchor—their *ancrage* presupposing the possibility of being moored to one spot, a possibility denied both by the absence of the actual word in the text and the sense of the whole book. Innumerable other word plays bind the motifs inextricably together on levels of sound and meaning, constantly stimulating research on the part of the reader.

Another kind of net is woven by color. A breakdown of the shades mentioned—and scarcely an object is presented that is not carefully defined in terms of color—shows that groupings can be established according to basic tones and their variations. A range of natural objects is situated in the orange-brown-yellow part of the spectrum (predominant as we already noticed in *Pharsale* and particularly characteristic of things that are natural and mortal; yellow is also a funereal color in France). Objects made of natural materials also belong in this group: straw hats, a clay bowl, sawdust, wooden boxes. The countryside is seen in shades of green, "acid," or "olive" when perceived through film. White objects stand out—façades, clouds, skin, butterflies, shirts, flowers, clowns' faces—often immediately matched with their opposite in shadow—the white clouds on page 13 are followed on page 14 by black clouds of chimney smoke; a man wearing a black suit converses with one in white; in one seduction scene black stockings are worn by the girl, in another, white; the motorcycle, the locomotive and the car, which are associated with the sexual act, are black, while emphasis is laid on the white skin revealed during the act, and on the white wedding favors. Black and white mark the extremities of vision: "Moving lines of an intensity ranging from white to black sweep through the luminous shaft in harmony with the motions of shadow and light on the screen" (p. 33).

Red is also often contrasted with black, as in the circus posters, the butterfly, and the ladybug, in the clown's grotesque make-up, and in the rug on which stands the man in black. The red of the rabbit's blood and that of the boar killed by the huntsmen in the first section stands out on the face of the battered bridegroom at the end. Flesh tints abound wherever the body itself goes beyond nudity into intimacy—in sexual organs, in the stripped muscles of the rabbit, in cows' udders, in lips. A selection of bluish-mauves includes also stripped flesh, flowers, tiles, faces, bricks, scarves, parasols (the *ombelles*—flower heads—merge into the *ombrelles*—sunshades). One could classify the entire text strictly according to the position of each object in the spectrum or on the palette.

To draw the threads still tighter, certain passages hint—but only hint—at the formation of interpretative links. One of the boys who has been looking at photos of a naked girl and peeking through the hole in the barn picks an apple, and after biting into it, throws it away because of its bitter taste. Later, the boys step on a serpent in the grass. The clown in the circus, who forces his partner to get down on all fours and run on a leash, followed by a monkey, is clad in a splendid, glittering costume bearing all the signs of the universe—sun, moon, and stars. At all times, the constant, insistent theme of sexual union is matched by the presence of death. The boy, staring at a picture of a naked girl and masturbating, is looking out at the old dog-faced (Cerberus or Anubis?) woman, who is cutting the throat of the rabbit. The disfigured husband comes into the bedroom on his wedding night and sprawls unconscious and bloody on the bed, like the dead boar described in the first section. And the lust of the couple in the barn has as a direct result, we divine, the drowning of the child the serving maid has entrusted to the two boys, who in their turn hand it over to some smaller girls, so that they may go to spy on the act of the lovers. To leave no doubt, the live wire of the wedding party constantly calls for drink to celebrate the groom's farewell to a carefree bachelor's life, using the expression: *"On enterre ça!"*—"We're burying that."

In the night punctuated by lights searching along the river banks, all of nature seems to be occupied in mindless, noisy coupling, in defiance of death:

The little lights dancing back and forth, here and there, clustering, separating again, like fireflies, absurd in the depths of darkness, like the shouts, voices immediately lost in the monotonous uproar of the waterfall, and the deafening chirp of mating insects: the obstinate signals, indefatigably sent out into the peaceful August night by hundreds of stiff legs scraping frantically on armored bellies, ceaselessly calling to blind, imperious, ephemeral union. In the luminous shafts of lamplight searching the banks, the leaves of the bushes bordering the river's edge occasionally appear, a raw, cold, artificial green, against the inky background which immediately swallows them up again, revealed for a moment, roughly snatched out of the secret conspiracy of the night in which can be imagined (lower, more secret, yet as powerful as the noise of the waterfall or of the crickets) something like a palpitation, something as irrepressible as the mating-calls: the mysterious palpitation of the vegetation (imperceptible motions of leaves, not from the effect of a breath of air, but that slow unfolding, that slow twisting, as if they were opening, folding or closing at the very contact, or rather embrace of the darkness), the imperious and incessant circulation of the sap, the secret movements of matter, the multiple breathing of nocturnal earth.   [pp. 207–208]

We recognize not only the ancient theme of proliferating, uncaring nature—where man is a small, mutable part—but also the long, sweeping, suggestive, multibranched sentence that Simon had put aside in his later work. Situated here, however, such a sentence has a very different effect from those of the earlier novels, such as *L'Herbe* or even *La Route des Flandres*. It no longer forms a part of a homogeneous whole, translating the search for a way of writing down the unanswerable queries of man faced with living. This sentence is placed here, among others that are much more objective, as an example, as a masterly illustration of re-presentation through words that carry the heaviest sensual charge and rouse in us the strongest desire to invest the passage with "life" and "reality." Yet the passages surrounding it invalidate this effect, while they reveal to us the mechanisms that make it almost successful.

Many of Simon's critics prefer to discuss his work in the most abstruse terms. We look in vain for these terms in the work itself or in Simon's brief comments on his art. Yet we realize that underneath the apparently simple, archetypical stories lie—half-buried like the pots that Simon's village boys catch sight of in the stream—reflected elusively in the shifting and shimmering surface of this text, several enormous questions. The first we cannot overlook, since it is stated continuously: what is representation and how is it purposefully organized into a work of art? Along with this issue go the related matters of artificiality, illusion, and technique. Less obvious, but clearly formulated, are the questions of continuity and composition. Finally, Simon poses the difficult problem of the reader-critic-spectator or the judge of the representation.

As in all of his previous investigations, Simon does not offer theory, but proceeds by means of example. A representation can be made of anything and composed of any material; it can change according to the ensemble in which it is inserted without changing itself. For example, the jigsaw puzzle represents a village scene; broken up into its component parts, it forms "an archipelago of little islands hollowed out by bays and gulfs, bristling with headlands" (p. 224). It can fade back into the landscape and become a metaphor for the drifting clouds. The eye, we observed in *Les Corps conducteurs,* is an apparatus that perceives indifferently. Only when reflection, interpretation, and judgment follow perception do we run against the twin perils of reality and illusion and through them discover the enigma of art. By using certain procedures in his text, Simon confronts the perils and offers his answer to the enigma.

The very first sentences of the book draw our attention with insistence to the artificiality of a certain type of colored representation. All the shades on the postcard are exaggerated and run over at the edges. Later, the coloring of an erotic engraving demonstrates poverty of resource and execution: one yellow suffices for the straw, the pubic hair, and the boys' curls; one pink for the cows' udders, the male member, the woman's genitalia, her breast, her lips, her cheeks. Glaring artificiality shows up in the circus posters, in the clowns' disguises, in the actors' make-up. In contrast "natural" colors are represented in a range of yellows, browns, and greens that seems to show the greater variety and subtlety of the "real"— until we discover that this too is representation and that its artificiality is merely of a less evident kind. The obvious contrast between poor and crude representation and cleverly maintained illusion reminds us that artificiality and artifice are derogatory terms only if we imply by them that the man-made is recognizable and inferior to something else defined as true or real. But if the real also turns out to be an artifice, as it does here, then we are forced to judge artificiality only in terms of art, for no other criteria are available. If the sky and the sea are too blue, the flowers too vividly colored, the exaggeration may be due to poor workmanship or inferior material, but we can judge these defects, not the likeness or lack of likeness to some unknown original. The aim of the artist, in short, must be to create what is authentic *as art*.

The *encrage*, the term for the application of printer's ink, has, as we have already remarked, a profound, punning relationship with the anchoring or *ancrage* of the boats by the shore and in the canal. Through the suggested homonym it raises the question of the anchoring of the narration to one chosen version of reality—an anchoring deliberately rejected in this text. The poorly applied, unreal colors are themselves a metaphor for the shifting of reality in the book, as we attempt to confine it within the outlines of some fixed truth. The poor representation makes us question not only the idea of an original of which art would be merely a good or bad copy, but also the necessity for pinning down art itself to any one "basic" form.

The effect of unsatisfactory representation is to shock us into reflection upon reality itself, or what we have always taken for reality. Very little is needed today to remind us that what looks so firmly set within well-established contours might dissolve suddenly and flow into the unbelievable. We tend inevitably to forget this and to let our inertia and our desire for ease and order freeze things once and for all into static shapes, in the belief that we have only to fit them together like a puzzle to discover the whole picture. The artist takes it upon himself to remind us that the picture of reality that we accept so easily is one only among many possibilities, and moreover, that he, the artist, is not obliged to offer us a reproduction of what we consider the "real" world.

He can make this point by means of a visual image—such as the *encrage* we have mentioned—or verbally, by representing the irresistible tendency of the mind to create links and continuity between any number of given elements. The posters advertising the movie currently showing, and the one "coming next week" in *Triptyque* are composed of a number of disconnected scenes, with no visible continuity, as Simon carefully informs us. Yet from such scenes—in one group a forlorn bride, a pair of lovers, a guilty looking young man, and two men fighting, in another an anguished middle-aged woman wearing pearls, two men in dark suits, and a frizzy-haired young man who resembles the youth in the first group —are woven two possible complete stories. The first concerns the disastrous wedding night which the drunken husband spends with a former girl friend, returning to his bride in a battered state after a brawl; the second is about a wealthy, aging-but-still-beautiful woman (baroness? Reixach?) who is using her lover to save her son involved in a drug scandal. The same actor, it is implied, plays the young man in both movies. These fictions germinate and bloom fully from minimal seeds of suggestion. Gaps in the tales as they appear in the text tempt the reader to fill them by extrapolation. If he does so, however, he must recognize that he is going through a mechanical process, one that permits any number of equally legitimate or illegitimate "solutions." The need for continuity has crept in, is constantly creeping in, affecting, of course, the very effort of criticism. This tendency is a mental characteristic that must be taken into account as a force *per se,* acting on any group or ensemble, however heterogeneous. To combat its insidious effects, the writer must show this force to us at work. In *Triptyque* Simon demonstrates our weakness for story telling by getting the process going in the reader and then leaving him to carry on by himself. We do not actually see the fight between the bridegroom and his adversary, we do not observe the adolescent dealing in drugs, nor do we witness the drowning of the child. Indeed, none of these events is ever mentioned. In each case, we are led to finish the story ourselves once the story telling mechanism has been set in motion.

The text itself is, of necessity, continuous, both physically and imaginatively as the product of the mind of its producer (however discontinuous the actual writing may have been). It is subject to another form of continuity in the mind of the reader, the invisible spectator, who not only helps to fill in the apparent lacunae, as we have seen above, but also tends to consider the text as an indivisible whole (however interrupted his reading). To such a reader, Simon proposes that he revise his reading habits, his opinion concerning the function of the text, and the function of the reader himself. Nowhere does Simon so openly challenge the reader-spectator to meditate on these matters as he does in *Triptyque*. By forcing him continually to readjust his focus, to reconsider the elements he takes for granted, to realize how much he creates on his own account, Simon transforms this reader into part of a demonstration. Other writers, notably Robbe-Grillet, have responded to Valéry's strictures about the arbitrariness of fiction, which the captious reader cannot resist rearranging to suit his own fantasy. Few have probed, as Simon does here, into the optics of the viewer subjected by the inventor of the fiction to more rearrangements than he could possibly think up for himself. It is instructive, in the study of fiction that practices rupture of continuity, inversion, imitation, and permutation, to compare with *Triptyque* Robbe-Grillet's *Projet pour une révolution à New York*. Both novels are studies of interference with the fictional development of narration. Whereas in Robbe-Grillet's work the desire for the destruction of the text is mirrored in the narration itself through scenes of torture, rape, and fire, in Simon's novel the attack is more openly directed at the viewer, who is interrupted brutally in his acceptance of the narrative, not only by the destruction of the "story" but by the breakdown of the viewing mechanisms and by violent changes of focus that makes it impossible to "recuperate" the anecdote by way of dreams, imagination, or madness. The "story content" of Simon's novel resists explanation except as a metaphor for its own resistance to explanation.

We may be tempted to liken Simon's procedures to the phenomenological-existentialist effort to define the role of consciousness in its relationship with the world and itself.[3] Can consciousness be conscious of itself as a function? In *Triptyque* we have a long series of scenes that exemplify the watcher being watched. Not only are all the performers in this novel engaged in constant alternation of *voyeurism*— both seeing and being seen in an intimacy normally reserved for the individual consciousness—they are surrounded by the gaze of innumerable undefined spectators, in the theater, circus or boxing ring, themselves re-presented by the chief *vo-*

3. During the first half of this century German thinkers such as Husserl, Heidegger, Jaspers, and their French interpreters, Sartre, Marcel, Merleau-Ponty, became increasingly preoccupied with the problem of man's consciousness as a constituent part of the world which it illumines. Can this consciousness, they asked, being part of what it records, also achieve a transcendental awareness of its own function? Would not this imply a suspension of its involvement with the world? Can consciousness contemplate itself in action? Translations of the works of these thinkers are readily available.

yeur or producer (both in the cinematographic and organic sense) to yet another series of spectators, who are perhaps not the final series since they—the readers—are invited endlessly to contemplate themselves. The language of that re-presentation—painting, photography, text—is carefully defined and perceived as a phenomenon in itself. The interaction between seer and seen—the consciousness of consciousness—is implied in the role each group observed plays in the performance of another group: as soon as the relationship observer observed is established, a recoil places the observer in the field of vision. One could see the whole of *Triptyque* as a metaphor for the transcendental reduction of consciousness to an awareness of itself, as yearned after by Husserl.

One could also see the book as an ironical comment on that attempt. "The most important lesson of reduction is the impossibility of complete reduction," observes Merleau-Ponty.[4] The spectators in this book are not totally engaged in the world of representation; they finally leave the theater and go off into the dark, just as the reader can close the book and dismiss it from his thoughts. But never entirely. "Consciousness is always consciousness of something."[5] The book has become part of the reader's consciousness, just as the reader himself is part of someone else's consciousness, and so on. Something is always left behind, like the wedding car on the deserted street. There is no resolution, no final stopping point, and the novel carefully avoids giving any.

We can never forget, however, that the matter of the novel is written language. The philosopher, who also—sometimes reluctantly—uses language, is obliged by the nature of his calling to restore a certain transparency to that language in

4. *Phénoménologie,* "Avant-propos," p. viii. My translation.
5. Ibid., p. xii.

order that the world—his object—may reappear. The novelist, on the contrary, is free to exploit and even to profit from the obscuring, contradictory, and ambiguous character of the word, since he is not bound to make his text coincide with any universal outside reality. As the exercise of language is different in the two cases, comparing them is often dangerous. More prudent to inquire how the novel itself, as a literary form, is furthered by a production like *Triptyque*. If *La Bataille de Pharsale* deals with the action of the text upon itself and *Les Corps conducteurs* with the variety of interrelated structures it can accumulate, *Triptyque* can be considered as an examination of "text-ure," that is, the use of the "weave" of a text to influence the reading of a novel.

One of the most striking features in *Triptyque* may be the constant variation in material composition of the objects described—the gaudy surface of the postcard, the deeper gloss of the cameo, the transparency of the filmstrips, the pattern of dust and smoke in the spotlights and projectors, the rough, unfinished painting, the flatness of the puzzle, the surface shine and deeper luminosity of water and storewindows—all of which contribute to give a different "feel" to the text, as though the actual substance were present to the senses.

Yet the substance also varies, not only from object to object, but from one representation to the next of the same object, which alters in texture and appearance according to the accompanying qualifications. Sometimes these qualifications make us immediately aware of distortion ("too blue"), or lack of variety (use of identical colors for unrelated areas). Sometimes the feeling of reality is so strong that the discovery that we are looking at a film or a painting comes as a shock. In both cases, however, we are soon made aware that we are not to forget the question of representation. We can compare the effect to one produced by a collection of works executed in different media on a common theme. Such a collection suggests first that no particular medium is "truer" in its representation than another, and second, that each type of representation is a statement in its own right and is not necessarily related to reality.

All the material collected in *Triptyque* passes through metamorphoses that continually alter its shape and texture. How are we to interpret these mutations in the context of the novel?

A text by definition is a "weave" or fabric composed of language and thematic structures. In the traditional novel the reader is usually more aware of the book's themes than of its author's use of language. Excessive emphasis or abrupt alterations in the language structures can, however, surprise the reader into a more careful consideration of the process of textual fabrication. An excellent example of such a surprise would be the famous chapter in *Ulysses* in which Joyce describes a simple happening in a number of different blendings of the English language. The effect here is one of exuberant comedy and enormous disproportion between the means and the end.

Sudden changes in thematic structure are very often less surprising, or more easily accepted. The reader is inclined to postulate one representation as being the point of reference—"anchor" or "truth"—with respect to all the others that then become falsifications, dreams, imagination, that is, fictions within fictions. The author himself is usually responsible for this attitude, claiming one part of his discourse as authentic and the given norm for all the rest. In the well-known passage from Proust's novel that Simon recalls in *La Bataille de Pharsale*, Swann visits the Marquise de Sainte-Euverte; as he enters the splendid stairway, he perceives all the footmen as paintings by Mantegna, then later, the male guests as projections of their monocles. At no time, however, do the footmen become the substance of paintings, nor the guests glassy-eyed fish. The distance between what Swann "really" sees and what his fancy conjures up is carefully maintained. We know that Swann is still in Madame de Sainte-Euverte's salon, that the footmen are footmen, and that the guests are bores. The reader is never invited to consider that the bores themselves are ornamental creatures produced by the text, authenticated only by another part of the text, that is, Swann himself. Some writers, Robbe-Grillet for example in his later novels, prefer to attach an equal value, or non-value, to all the variations of theme in their text, so that not one of these variations authenticates the others. In *La Maison de rendezvous* or *Projet pour une révolution à New York* no "correct" version of events could possibly be discovered.

Simon avoids the comic or exaggerated effects of Joyce and goes perhaps one step further than Robbe-Grillet in dispossessing his themes of all authenticity. In a text of uniform weave (simple expository sequences) he displays a thematic content cut off by continual radical changes of form from any possible relationship with reality. The contrast between the smooth flat surface of the text and the variegated forms of representation described by it creates a tension that can only be resolved by recalling that the text is indeed a text, and the forms it presents are all of equal thematic value. In the "normal" text, taken as a projection of reality, homogeneity of texture has the paradoxical result of effacing the idea of work and distance; only the introduction of reflection, repetition, the *mise en abyme* breaks up the illusion and allows separation of the written world from the real world. In a text like *Triptyque,* in which the illusion is constantly held up to the spectator for what it is, a new homogeneity—the equivalence of all themes and motifs—and a new continuity—a text physically unbroken into paragraphs or other needless divisions—re-establish the one reality of writing. As a result, through a work that is both rigorously constructed and impossible to consider as "finished," that is, as containing a final solution to its thematic content, the reader is forced into awareness of the writer's act.

Three recurrent images in this work impress Simon's lessons on us. The first is a familiar one, a photograph marred by the sudden movement of the person photographed. We remember this procedure from *Histoire* where the trace of the photographer's movement as he tries to include himself in the photo leaves a blurred mark across the shot, like a printing of the sudden passage of time. In *Triptyque,* an anonymous "bird-headed" man is caught, Janus-like, in the act of turning his head from one side to the other, as though surprised in the midst of conversation or action. The resulting image is of two man—or bird—heads on one body. Here a figuration shows the flight of the text from its own meaning, a total turning-away of the head (the interpreting mechanism) at an 180-degree angle from the original direction. The body of the text, which remains static, is topped by the swiveling glance, which encompasses also the wide angle between writing and reading, production and reproduction, signifier and signified.

The second image, confirming the first, is the burning paper or film. The paper catches fire when the light is concentrated upon it through the magnifying glass held by the boy and then is consumed in a widening circle. The film burns when caught in the projector and subjected to overheating from the lamp. In each case, an excess of light (attention) causes destruction of the text and the image. We may read this both as a warning against fixation at any given point of consciousness and as a metaphor for the consumption of the text by the reader-viewer, the image of this consumption being itself consumed through its own effect. The point is reinforced by the association of both scenes with intensely erotic moments. The images of the two-headed man and of the burning matter illustrate the opposition mobility-immobility and the price that it exacts from the reader. If this reader does not recognize the constant movement among the novel's various elements, his pleasure in any one part of the text will be self-consuming.

The third image, developed at greater length is the familiar one of masks: overemphasized, grotesque masks on the clowns, more subtle masks on the actors, finally masks which are faces themselves. The absurd mask of the public entertainer, who by definition is a clown running blindly under the whip of his master (perhaps the "popular" writer is the target here), becomes the delicate make-up on the faces of the movie actors who portray real life situations. Suddenly, however, these actors are seen with the final mask removed, and only the anonymous mass of flesh, blood, nerves, and bones which lie under the protective skin remains. So Simon strips the novel from its public, entertaining figure down to the bare mechanisms that govern its production.

Because this text is constantly being transformed, and its mechanisms continually being dismantled, we cannot make a static picture out of the separate parts of the triptych—they will no longer "fit." Simon's intention is not, however, destructive, but dynamic. By insisting on the number of ways in which signs can be assembled, the variety of materials that can enter into their constitution, the different levels on which they can function, Simon is pointing out the inexhaustible richness of even the most banal theme, once we realize that it can be converted by con*text* and *text*ure into something always new. In such a concept of art, since each version of the real is inserted into a unique system of nonrepeatable relationships, no such thing as a stereotype can exist. The banal thus recovers its value as a usable and reusable part of innumerable possible structures. Ordinary objects are therefore totally rehabilitated, just as the rocks, trees, bottles, and fruit painted by Cézanne are rehabilitated "through ceaseless osmosis from their near and distant neighbors," to reveal "the multiple infinity of realities, all equally possible, all equally true, driving upwards, their presence an erection" (*La Corde raide*, p. 122). *Triptyque* celebrates a true act of generation, the production out of existing matter of completely new forms.

10 ❧ Reflections

Having reached this stage in our investigation, we must recognize that we have come a very long way from the starting point of this study. A backward glance at Simon's production shows us that, after the first tentative efforts, his work separates into two parts. The novels from *Le Vent* to *Histoire* are—in spite of their sumptuousness—generally de-constructive, in that they dismiss, one by one, the established criteria for creating fiction. The anecdote, linear development, the treatment of causality and time, psychological "depth" and character study, true-to-life description, the art of climax and resolution are all tested in these works and found inadequate.

The last three novels, on the contrary, are constructive, in that they are attempts to replace these discredited traditional elements with authentic new ones. The "story" they offer no longer relates to the fortuitous adventures of arbitrary characters. It concerns the one personage who is undeniably true and present and verifiable: the text. Its adventures are the metamorphoses that we see taking place on the page before our eyes. Space, Time, Causality become characteristics of the language that reveals them. This text has no beginning, middle, or end, since all of the elements it employs are focal points for potentials of sense and sound that may develop independently. No crisis and resolution exist in such a text, because it is infinitely rereadable (and thus, for some, unreadable) and endlessly renewable. With every new work, Simon illustrates more and more decisively his own rule of constant interaction: "The novel makes itself, I make it, it makes me."[1]

These works are therefore a provocation. By challenging the reader to examine carefully what is signified by a text, they lead him further and further down a path along which it is difficult for him to retrace his steps. He may indeed, if he follows the arguments scrupulously, be led from a study of the text to a reconsideration of his relationship with the world.

A text is compounded of written language, generally accepted in the Saussurian sense as a system of communication by means of verbal signs. Whereas at one time the sign was thought to have a total exchange value for the object designated, today even the most superficial reader is aware of a flexibility in this arrangement, which can be expressed in the term "via"—"by the way of": between the matter selected for communication and the elements of the system used to communicate, there occurs an interval, a hesitancy (interpreters of Joyce like to speak of the HeCitEncy, from the H. C. Earwicker of *Finnegans Wake*), a slipping not only between the world and the signs intended to represent it, but between the signs themselves and their composites. This slipping, however, is often attributed to the weakness of the sign system, its failure to match the complexity and mutability of the real. At the same time, since nothing remains without formulation, users of language harbor a desire to crystallize and harden apparently successful sign groups, to retain some hold on the shifting patterns of existence. Underlying this attitude is the naive or "natural" belief that the real world is there, more or less as perceived, and hence subject to formulation.

Texts such as *La Bataille de Pharsale, Les Corps conduc-*

1. *Les Lettres françaises* (April 13–19, 1967), p. 4. My translation.

teurs, and *Triptyque* force re-examination of these attitudes. They propose, first of all, a review of our habits of perceiving and recording reality. *Les Corps conducteurs* demonstrates that the recording consciousness is continuously fitting perceptions into pre-existing systems or texts: social, medical, mechanical, mythical, emotional, historical, geographical. Nothing comes to the observer that is not immediately structured, that is, situated in relation to established concepts. All of these systems overlap and interlock into one reality that is the observer's relationship with the world—a reality that is in no way guaranteed to be "true" or universal and is no more than a series of identifiable structures. In *Triptyque,* the way we judge these systems—our categorization—is brought under fire, as we identify and bestow values on groups that subsequently turn out to belong to other systems and adjust differently—and unsatisfactorily—to the totality of the work. In *La Bataille de Pharsale* the narrator, who has been reading Elie Faure's *Histoire de l'Art,* comments on the process of imposing categories upon the world, of deciding what is significant and what is not:

O. is reading in a History of Art the chapter on the German painters of the Renaissance: "They never take the shortest road to the essential and to the most logical goal. The detail always conceals the whole, their universe is not continuous but consists of juxtaposed fragments. We see them in their pictures giving as much importance to a halberd as to a human face, to an inert stone as to a moving body, constructing a landscape like a geographical map, in the decoration lavishing as much care on a cuckoo clock as on the statue of Hope or Faith, treating this statue with the same methods as that clock and when ..." O. takes an automatic pencil out of his pocket and writes in the margin: Incurable French stupidity. [p. 165]

The many systems that make up reality are not necessarily composed of verbal signs. But it seems that only when they enter the written language are they subject to evaluation. Once they are constituted in writing, they accede to a second reality, that of the writing itself. Like fragments broken off from the great puzzle, to which they are linked by multiple connections, statements belonging to such systems stand as newly-created systems themselves, polyvalent at every point of sound and significance. In *Pharsale* we have seen how such verbal systems can "take off" and engender new semantic and phonic clusters. *Les Corps conducteurs* and *Triptyque* show, in a remarkable fashion, how signs in other media—painting, advertising, architecture, film—transmute into verbal signs and renew their valences by means of this exchange.

All of these systems, both internal and external, maintain their distinction through their relationships, not to any static norm, but to one another. We can see how each group of signs in *Pharsale* or *Les Corps conducteurs* is illuminated differently according to the proximity of other groups—the field of battle, for example, or the anatomical diagram. In *Triptyque,* this transformation of one group by its neighbors is put forward aggressively as the very substance of the novel. We have here, particularly in this last case, a refusal of *origin,* a determined referral of any and every sign to other signs only.

The interdependence of all systems suggests also their liberation from their previous dependence on "human" intervention. They are no longer guided or disposed according to the sovereign will of either author or characters in the plot. The human element is one of the factors in the design, not the overriding consideration. Hence, the individual protagonist, who partakes more and more of the pattern of things and is allowed less and less predominance among them, disappears into the text of the last three novels. As he merges with his surroundings, the text no longer reflects the long struggle for disengagement, as it does in the novels from *Le Vent* to *Histoire* where, in the effort to distinguish *who* and *what* speaks and acts, the phrase continuously circles and writhes uneasily about itself. In the last novels a lightening and aeration of the text takes place, reflecting its emancipation from the need to explain and support the individual *against* the world.

At this point, the relationship between Simon's work and many current schools of thought—concerning consciousness and the world, reality, humanism, and the role of language in writing—is difficult to determine. As we have seen, *Triptyque* sometimes appears to be almost a parable of the phenomenological attempt at a "reduction" of consciousness. We have mentioned that Maurice Merleau-Ponty, the French interpreter and developer of Husserl, recognized aspects of his own thought in Simon's work. The few notes that Merleau-Ponty left provide commentary on Simon's vision, his creation of "intermediary" persons, and his use of the "archaic structure" of memory.[2] The philosopher would no doubt have been even more interested in Simon's later work, where his own remark seems to be confirmed: "At each instant we are in the presence of that miracle which is the connection (*connexion*) of experience, and no one knows better than ourselves how this is done, since we are this cluster (*noeud*) of relationships."[3] The basic features of phenomenology, its insistence on consciousness in and of the world, the struggle to take part in and simultaneously transcend experience, the continual incompleteness and renewal ("the inchoative aspect," as Merleau-Ponty says[4]) of all meanings, the *Sinngenesis* of which Husserl speaks,[5] could find illustration in a number of Simon's texts. We should be wary, however, of discovering an endorse-

2. "Cinq Notes," *Médiations,* p. 9; *Entretiens,* p. 46. My translation.
3. *Phénoménologie,* "Avant-propos," p. xvi. My translation.
4. Ibid.
5. Ibid., p. xv.

ment for any philosophical standpoint in the separate elements of a novel.

Interesting, but equally inconclusive comparisons could be made between some aspects of Simon's writing and the work of innovative thinkers in France, for obviously Simon is no stranger to advanced intellectual movements in his own country. We may think of the psychoanalyst Jacques Lacan, who has made studies of the Ego and the Other and the dispersion of the subject within the consciousness, or of the anthropologist Claude Lévi-Strauss who discovers human society as a *montage* of systems of thought. Critics of language and writing are likely to be closer to Simon's immediate preoccupations. Jacques Derrida, for example, creator of the discipline of "Grammatology," which offers a Heideggerian, phenomenological approach to the problem of language, asserts that writing is a network of signs referring, not to any previous unchanging reality, but to an unending series of other signs that surround and differentiate one another and lie in a perpetual immanence making all statements about the world continuously interdependent. On the basis of his definition of *différance*, "that which makes the movement of meaning possible only if each element said to be 'present,' appearing in the theater of presence, refers to something other than itself, preserving in itself the mark of the past element, the trace referring no less to what we call the future than to what we call the past, and constituting what we call the present by this very relationship with what is not itself; absolutely not itself, that is not even a past or a future as modified present," Derrida builds up a complex theory of language and being.[6] Simon often appears to provide examples for this theory. The refusal of "origin" in *Triptyque* ("There is no longer any

6. *Théorie d'ensemble* (Paris, Editions du Seuil, 1968), p. 51. My translation.

simple origin," Derrida says)[7] suggests a visual commentary on the "infinite referral" of signs, just as *La Bataille de Pharsale* and *Les Corps conducteurs* offer verbal and structural connections that seem to illustrate Derrida's ideas about relationships between past and future elements in a text.

The eminent critic Michel Foucault has discussed other problems that come to mind when we read Simon's novels: the distortion and curvature of time and space, the creation of new kinds of interior distance, the dehumanization of the text and the dislodging of the human protagonist, and, in contrast with Derrida, the notion that origin can be found in the brief moment of writing. "And yet," Foucault says, "there is in this language of fiction an instant of pure origin: it is the moment of writing, the moment of words themselves, of ink barely dry, the moment when we see the outline of what, by definition, and in its most material being, can only be a trace."[8]

Many other critics and theoreticians might be mentioned. Claude Simon, however, who claims to be "peu philosophe," maintains privately that he has little acquaintance with most of these writers and even less with their differences of opinion.[9] What he knows of them is through the critics Roland

7. *De la grammatologie* (Paris, Editions de Minuit, 1967), p. 55. My translation.

8. *Théorie d'ensemble*, p. 20. My translation.

9. A detailed discussion of the work of these authors is beyond the scope of this study. Interested readers can consult Derrida, *L'Ecriture et la différence* (Paris, Editions du Seuil, 1967), *De la grammatologie* (Paris, Editions de Minuit, 1967), *La Voix et le phénomène: Introduction au problème du signe dans la phénoménologie de Husserl* (Paris, Presses Universitaires de France, 1967), translated by David B. Allison as *Speech and Phenomena and Other Essays on Husserl's Theory of Signs* (Evanston, Northwestern University Press, 1973); Foucault, *Les Mots et les choses* (Paris, Gallimard, 1966), translated as *The Order of Things*, ed. R. D. Laing (London, Tavistock, 1971), and

Barthes and Jean Ricardou. Ricardou, who has written a number of studies of the New Novel, who also is a novelist and a member of the *Tel Quel* group, has produced detailed and ingenious criticisms of Edgar Poe (see "Le Scarabée d'or" in *Tel Quel*, No. 34), of his fellow writers, and particularly of Simon himself, whose work, as we have seen earlier, is deconstructed and evaluated by Ricardou according to norms greatly influenced by the critics already mentioned. Ricardou's contributions have no doubt determined, to a large extent, the evolution of Simon's thought.

The ideas of Barthes, who treats writing as research, as a way of surprising language at its source before it can be perverted from *"écriture"*—language concerned with its own function—to *"écrivance"* or language subverted towards other ends, are of great importance to Simon. The preface to *Orion aveugle* in which Simon exposes his essential thoughts on writing refers to the well-known "Avant-propos" of Barthes' *Sur Racine*. Barthes is not mainly interested in renovating Literature in its official sense, but in discovering what happens when writing takes place, both in the experience of the writer and in that of the reader who becomes his homologue at different points in space and time. Barthes thus reveals the different "codes" that function on various levels of interpretation and dictate our approach to the text. In a narrative such as Balzac's *Sarrasine* Barthes shows, for example, that the text—beginning with the title and including the smallest detail in the organization of the "story"—is infinitely richer in significant combinations of such codes than the superficial reader cares to suspect. In Barthes' analyses of Racine, we dis-

---

L'Archéologie du savoir (Paris, Gallimard, 1969); Lacan, *Ecrits* (Paris, Editions du Seuil, 1966). The numerous anthropological works of Claude Lévi-Strauss are published in Paris by the Presses Universitaires de France or by Plon.

cover how profoundly we are affected by the alternation of light and darkness, imprisonment and freedom, action and passivity, masculinity and femininity; these oppositions are present but never openly formulated within the poetic and dramatic structures of the plays. The "pleasure of the text" lies, according to Barthes, in discovering its sources of appeal and their relation to, as well as their violation of our customary methods of appreciation. This pleasure can culminate at one extreme in *"jouissance"* a kind of burning consummation of the reader's desire for the text. Barthes boldly calls for a text that, instead of being merely "readable," is "writable" (*"scriptible"*), and for a reader who is "no longer a consumer but a producer."[10] Such a text will be "apart from [other] languages" (*"hors des langages"*), refusing all complicity with other voices, intent on being "language and not *a* language" (*"du langage et non un langage"*).[11]

The similarity between these views and Simon's practice is evident. The patient investigation of the novel that Claude Simon has carried on over a period of thirty years provides above all a precious sum of practical observations which permit a step by step approach to some of the most difficult themes of modern criticism. In following the novelist's research, the reader who might be wary or disturbed because of the abstract nature of certain theoretical speculations can see what lies at their source, that is, the intense interrogation of writer who must discover his own function and what products may result from the questions he asks himself. Simon's works are themselves theory constantly put into practice and contributing to its own evolution. The novelist's productions, therefore, are not to be considered as attempts to shape the

10. *S/Z* (Paris, Editions du Seuil, 1970), p. 10.
11. *Le Plaisir du texte* (Paris, Editions du Seuil, 1973), p. 51. My translation.

text to correspond with preconceived structures, since, on the contrary, the text creates the questions to which it provides the answers. The act of writing, as Simon makes clear in the preface to *Orion aveugle,* is an uncovering of connections among the various systems of the mind by means of the systems of language. Until the uncovering takes place, no one can guarantee what those connections will be.

It would consequently be erroneous, in the case of Simon, to identify any one thinker as playing the role of, say, Saint-Hilaire to Balzac or Claude Bernard to Zola. It would be equally risky to expect in Simon's work a complete exposition of this or that system, since all systems are themselves reduced by the form of the novel, as Simon writes it, to an interplay of structures. Even though we have noted before the rapport between design and structure (in *Les Corps conducteurs,* for example), to refer back from the system of the novel in question to this or that specific external system would be to suspend the very movement we are attempting to describe.

We must admit, however, that the texts opening on questions of so great a range can only stimulate further inquiry. Through study of the exercise of language, we penetrate into a necessary interrogation of the role that writing plays in man's relationship with the world and his hold on reality. In no way, in fact—as modern philosophy fully recognizes—can man begin to define his situation, until he has defined the articulation of language and the systems by which he lives. In this sense, exploration of the modes of writing is a revolutionary act, and Simon conceives it in this way:

Any work that implies thought, whether it be a Dogon or an Eskimo mask, a Gothic cathedral, a Bach concerto, a theory in physics, a page by Proust or a Paul Klee painting, is an attempt to exorcize, to grasp and to transform nature and the world by recreating them in language. The work is both an affirmation and an interrogation, within a vast horizon of answers concerning the meaning, the wherefore of history, of the universe, of being: in other words, of finiteness, a problem which, contrary to what has been claimed, does not concern only those who are free from material worries, but also those who are driven by poverty, hunger, exhausting work, a joyless existence to ask with unassuageable anguish the question: why is there man, why is there life, why is there death?

Schematically, we can say that all languages (verbal, mathematical, musical, pictural) consist essentially in the establishment of relationships, of connections: connections between sounds, colors, volumes, concepts, words, signs, just like those, elsewhere, between masses, coefficients of expansion, temperatures, etc.

"In order to transform life, we must first begin by knowing what it is," wrote Leon Trotsky in *Literature and Revolution,* a remark that is complemented by Proust's phrase: "We only really know what we are forced to recreate through thought." To know life better is therefore *already* to transform it. . . .

Language, writing, do not "express" anything: they create. They have their own dynamism that carries the original impulse of the writer in unexpected directions, and it is through the vast network of relationships, unsuspected before he began writing, that he will progress. From the choice that he will make between them, "consciously" yet obedient to a norm which is greater than himself, and which is that of language itself, from this choice (by keeping some, rejecting or not even perceiving others) will, unknown to him, emerge certain meanings. As he writes—and only as he writes—he discovers a world—and discovers himself.

If the novel consists in telling a story, instead of the tale of heroes exemplary for good and evil—who are inevitably conventional—is it not rather by *being* himself the adventure of a mind searching and searching for itself in language, that he can hope to discover new forms and, as a result, a new substance that will then be, in the world of literature—*the only one in which he can operate*—revolutionary? . . .

I can only tell about my own reality—which, naturally, includes without distinction both what is "true" and what is "imaginary" for me. Yet, a man among men, with my human needs and desires, my reality, although personal, is a fragment of the universal. But it is only in obeying exclusively its own god, in other words, language, that my *telling*, then, will concern all men and thus, perhaps, become a part of the ever-recommencing world revolution.[12]

The argument is that, by understanding the role language plays in the structuralization of our lives and in our attempts to deal with reality through representation, we shall eventually come to learn about the world, and, through this learning, to change it.

Such conclusions may arouse diverse reactions. Those of traditionalist writers are obvious. Those of a traditionalist public also. As Robert Sabatier puts it: "After the appearance of the New Novel . . . the public found itself face to face with a difficult literature, discouraging for people who up to now had considered the novel an entertainment, what Bishop Huet in the seventeenth century called the honest diversion of idle good folk. Since then, many have abandoned the novel, which seemed often to offer them only hard reading, or else they have restricted themselves to popular authors, part of an easy tradition, a naturalist tradition."[13]

Certainly the reader of Claude Simon's works must abandon the idea of the novel as easy entertainment. On the contrary, he is asked to become the active reader required by Paul Valéry, one who makes experiments on books. He must be the "aggressive participator" demanded by the philosopher Julia Kristeva.[14] Yet how can the serious reader, prepared to

12. "Littérature: Tradition et révolution," *La Quinzaine littéraire* (May 1–15, 1967), pp. 12–13. My translation.

13. *Positions et oppositions sur le roman contemporain,* Actes et Colloques 8, Actes du Colloque de Strasbourg (Paris, Editions Klincksieck, 1971), pp. 38–39. My translation.

14. See *Semiotiké: Recherches pour une sémanalyse* (Paris, Editions du Seuil, 1969), p. 181.

work with the author on the text provided for him, be sure that he is carrying out his own experiments correctly?

It is, of course, unfair to suppose that the "adventure" of the writer has been ignored before the arrival of the New Novelists. Poets understood early that this adventure is the generating principle of all great works. The twentieth century nevertheless has the honor of bringing this fact to light very clearly by distinguishing it from the other circumstances of composition. The generation of Valéry and Gide was more interested in the mind that produced literature than in literature itself. And this generation was closely followed, in various ways, by Proust, Faulkner, Roussel, the Surrealists, and other experimenters who all helped to turn attention to the very act of writing, the degree of participation of the reader, and the complex role of language on the conscious and subconscious levels.

Claude Simon has followed only one path in this direction, but, like a good disciple of Valéry, to the end. The new "story" he proposes replaces almost completely the anecdote that provides a series of easy semantic links between different points in the reading. The human mind is, or seems to be, a natural story teller, spinning tales as easily as the spider its web, combining the signs it receives from the outside world into ensembles that help both to satisfy a need for order and organization and to stimulate a thirst for fantasy. The traditional writer who draws attention to this activity may seek to make the reader believe that his work has a philosophical, epistemological, or documentary value. The New Novelist prefers to label story telling as a multifaceted activity, capable of providing the artist with variable, self-perpetuating structures, and the reader with pleasures on various levels. Instead of exploiting this particular structural resource, Claude Simon, unlike some of his contemporaries, is content to eliminate it, little by little. Declining to keep the latent pathos and romantic suggestions of his earlier novels, he closes all escape routes for the mind anxious to invent "explanations," "logical connections," and "meanings." He ceases here to be the true descendant of Faulkner and parts company with many experimental novelists belonging to that tradition.

In reading Faulkner, whatever the dislocation of the temporal structure, however many the vacillations in point of view, and however deep the obscurity of the language, we are led steadily to the finally decipherable, and therefore intelligible, violence at the heart of the novel that stirs the whole mass into convulsive movement. The same is true with most American novelists of the sixties, for example, who still build their experiments around the fable that supports the text. Nearly all represent the disturbance in traditional values by means of violent or fantastic action portrayed in recognizable sequences. Their innovations, therefore, depend to a large extent on fabulation, and this is where they differ greatly from Simon. (Compare, for example, the episodes in John Hawkes's *The Lime Twig* where a bird appears at moments of impending disaster with the pigeon passages in Simon; in one case the image is separable from the text, in the other it *is* the text.) If novelists such as John Barth, Ken Kesey, Fred Chappell, or Kurt Vonnegut "assert the artificiality of [their] fiction in blatant and extreme ways, thus demonstrating that fact and fiction can be distinguished only through the radical use of fictional form,"[15] this, in fact, encourages them toward wild and wonderful fictional constructions that seek to surpass reality. "The form of the fable is vital to our times," asserts Olderman, "it is the perfect form for the two dominant

15. Raymond M. Olderman, *Beyond the Waste Land: A Study of the American Novel in the Nineteen-Sixties* (New Haven & London, Yale University Press, 1972), p. 25.

characteristics of the novelist's vision—the confusion of fact and fiction and the fear of some mystery within fact itself that holds power over us."[16] Simon, on the contrary, while paying homage to violence in its traditional forms—war, sex, death—deliberately banalizes fiction, retains only the most stereotyped structures, and keeps a tight control over the urge toward fabulation. In this respect, he may remind us of a writer such as Cortázar, who relates an absurd or fantastic tale but, at the same time, destroys it (*Rayuela,* for example) by analytical reflections superimposed on the narrative. But Cortázar is more successful in demonstrating from the outside the arbitrary character of the traditional narrative than in forging from the inside, as Simon does, a completely new kind of text.[17]

The later novels clearly demonstrate that Simon moves in the same paths as Joyce. One can see a remarkable coincidence of thematic material and some examples of such encounters have already been noted—the blasphemous Mass in *Histoire* and the divine dove in *Pharsale,* for instance, recall the early chapters of *Ulysses.* A long list of others could easily be compiled. The tramcars in *Le Palace* crisscross the city like those in Joyce's Dublin. A constant preoccupation with cuckoldry, journeys, puzzles, chamberpots or chalices, plumbing, the zodiac, the significance of certain letters or numbers, appears in both authors. In *Finnegans Wake* the twin boys do their history and geometry lessons (in which the basic triangle is present) and spy on their parents making love. Anna Livia Plurabelle is O. or Omega. Battles and a game of football take place in Chapter I. But the visible themes form only the surface structure of these writings. Like Joyce, Simon works—and

16. Ibid., p. 23.
17. In a note to this author, Simon disclaims any acquaintance other than superficial with the recent novel of both North and South America.

plays—on various levels of sense and sound, reality and myth, rhythm and structure, granting to no one element precedence over the rest, but constantly establishing new ties between all the details, however minute, that go to make up a continually renewable text. Like Joyce, Simon brings us along Vico's circular road from the end to the beginning. *Finnegans Wake,* we are told by the noted critic of Joyce, William York Tindall, is a book about itself.[18] Simon's writing is about writing. He lacks, it is true, the Gargantuan fantasy of Joyce and relies far more extensively on the literary, Proustian mechanisms of the memory. His protagonists have little by little dropped their earthy contacts with individual lives (although not completely denuded, like those of Philippe Sollers), instead of acquiring, as Joyce's do, an increasingly bewildering number of these contacts. Nevertheless, Joyce is the Master of the Games from which derive so many of the maneuvers in the texts we are now considering.

Joyce is apt to stifle his reader with the richness of his material. Simon, by excluding the resources of anecdote and of "character"—the picturesque, unusual, or iconoclastic personage—and by the substitution of the text as "hero," rouses in his reader a preliminary sense of deprivation that is no doubt one of the reasons why his works appear difficult to the newcomer. Finding out "what happened" is no longer important, caring about "who" is involved in the action is also irrelevant. In the later Simon novels, the anonymous O. is present, more or less, and that is all. Of his feelings, his reasons, his motivations, we lose little by little all trace. Nothing in the discourse authorizes us to guess at them or to substitute for them our own imaginings. The character with no "story" and no "personality" is the meeting place of all the percep-

18. *A Reader's Guide to James Joyce* (New York, Noonday Press, 1959), p. 237.

tions coming from the outside world and all the interior relationships formed from their stimulus. Visible objects, precisely described, are not for that reason objectively "true" or "real." At no moment, even when these objects are on a page from the encyclopedia, do they leave the field of vision of a particular anonymous individual, or escape from the network of his thoughts. The apparent absence of psychological coloration does not mean that perception has a general or an abstract value. On the contrary, the web of relationships that is revealed indicates a presence. The reader, conscious of this presence, and yet forbidden to recognize it as "someone," is once more disturbed in his habits and forced to reflect on the objective nature of "facts."

Such disturbance must satisfy those who for years have been trying to shake out of his lethargy the lazy reader, sunk in the expectation of purely passive pleasures. What is required, however, is not just a shaking, but a complete earthquake. From now on, the public must provide the text with an effort equal to, and perhaps greater than, that furnished by the writer. The prospect has not always been received with enthusiasm. Some critics will be ready to charge that if we are not going to investigate the mysteries of human nature, or the realities of life itself, but only those of writing—which is an activity as futile as one cares to make it—then all we have in these novels are social games, interesting only to members of private circles and literary snobs, writers of poetic garlands, acrostics, and riddles, games demanding a broad culture and a deeply refined intelligence, but merely games. Others will answer that nothing in man's life is as serious as his games, and that no other game is as serious as that inspired by his efforts to resolve the problem of representation, on which his relationship with the world and with others depends.

The reader, whose role we were questioning at the beginning of this study, now appears as an essential part of the development of the text. However, his function is not interpretation in the usual sense of the word. If he sticks to the traditional norms, he can argue that Simon's work still provides a view of "human nature" and "psychological realism." The sentiments in Simon's earlier novels concerning the omnipresence of death and destruction, the fragility and interchangeability of life, and the heartlessness of fate that "sends all underground and back into the game" have led to this conclusion: that man, the happenings of his existence, his suffering and questioning are parts of a whole made up of elements incessantly composing new and inexhaustible series of combinations, of which no one will ever be definitive or final. Fixing our attention on the writing that tells us this is a way of recognizing that all man's efforts can lead only to the recording—that is, the immobilization through representation —of variable phenomena, of which one is the act itself of recording.

The seekers after "psychology" may be tempted to add that the absence of distinctive traits in Simon's protagonists is compensated by the cumulative effect of the details perceived by the anonymous spectator; the memories and the internal connections that they illuminate form "the patient labyrinth of lines" that trace the image of the human face (as Jorge Luis Borges puts it),[19] most probably that of the author himself. Each perception and each group of images it attracts serve to define the perceiving consciousness. The reader can see only what this consciousness allows him to see and can feel only the effects of combinations formed by these chosen images. Thus, objects and series of images are a mask for character, a

19. *A Personal Anthology,* trans. Anthony Kerrigan (New York, Grove Press, 1967), p. 203.

mask that, in the long run, reveals as much as it hides and suggests the existence of "someone" behind the "something."

This attempt to return to traditional forms of criticism fails, however, to recognize the central question. What is there "new" in these novels that justifies the disturbance of our reading habits? If Simon has been led to a theory of the novel exemplified in *Les Corps conducteurs* and *Triptyque,* it is the result of a series of experiments that provide him with the proof that any other way of writing is, for him, impossible. Is not this proof itself founded on an initial presumption? That is, the novel must be based on a search for the verifiable fact and motivated by a Cartesian determination not to accept as true that which is not demonstrably so. We may suspect that the demands that Simon makes on himself and his readers betray a need for some "truth" that drives him to reject every-thing—stories, characters, happenings—that depends for its effect on outside evidence. The organization of the images appearing on the blank paper under the writer's pen can be called an act of invention, but invention recognized at every instant for what it is—a true activity of the writer, controlled, verified, documented, therefore genuinely experimental. We can see now why the author claims descent from Flaubert and energetically opposes Stendhalian "psychology."

A new step has been taken, however. The transfer of the written "truth" to the living "truth," the historical truth, can take place only at the very moment of the writer's action with-out any other extension. *"Madame Bovary, c'est moi,"* while I am writing. Beyond that act, no other truth exists. The reader learns then that the search for "truths" of a human, scientific, mystical, or political nature must be subordinate to this initial process. What may seem to be "error," judged by the standards of other disciplines, is often, on the contrary, one more truth, possibly fertile, revealed in the process of writing. For the formations crystallized during this process cannot, in themselves, as formations, be false. The words that attempt to capture them are conclusive evidence of their passage. Moreover the passage, or trace in writing, of these formations can be false only if compared to something that is not themselves, that is, some external reality.

One could object that this process could lead to total subjectivity. A continuous relationship with the world and with the consciousness of others is implied, however, by the use in a conventional form of an already constituted language. At no point in Simon's work, even in his most unorthodox experiments, is there rupture with that language, nor does his anonymous protagonist ever lose contact with common experience. (So far, Simon has never relied on ultra-subjective or exotic means—dreams, madness, drugs—to attract readers). The bridge between the outer and the inner worlds remains firm, supported on the one hand by recognizable verbal structures, and on the other by familiar blocks of experience.

Simon declares, in fact, that he "discovers the world gropingly in and through writing."[20] Does this mean that he nevertheless believes that he will eventually reach the ultimate truth about this world? If we judge from *Les Corps conducteurs* the world *in* writing and the world *through* writing are, for the writer, one and the same. The object perceived with meticulous precision generates the written world; this world is filled, through writing, with newly situated images. The composite and changing universe is thus made up of unique discoveries arising from continual rearrangement. For the discoverer, it is the only possible universe, and its reality is as distant as one can imagine from the reality called objective and scientific.

20. See note 34 of the Introduction.

The readers of the nineteenth-century realist novel were offered views of reality that had perhaps not occurred to them before. The readers of Simon's novels now have a similar experience. They cannot expect to see the world portrayed in print as it was a hundred years ago. The time has come for a change in vision and for a critical examination of ways of recording that vision. Simon's reader must be prepared to deal with the preliminary reality of change, to appreciate the traces it leaves through the written language, and then to follow these traces as far and as faithfully as he can. By incorporating the work of art into his own experience, he will then arrive at a further reality, one that does not exclude semantic links but that makes him responsible for them. Interpretation is always shortlived; every act, every transition, every movement is an *inter*-pretation between two or more groups, and we take a metaphorical step every time we pass from one group of images to another.

Claude Simon has claimed this area of passage as his own. In it he has situated the images that make up his mental exisence, and untiringly he traces the varying paths leading from one to the other. Since the path, not the nature of the stopping points, is what matters, the "originality" of the latter is of small import. These points are easily recognizable, whether attributable to Simon or to others, and this fact makes the study of the paths and their variations even easier, for we are not distracted by extraneous questions of truth or reality. Nor is it a matter of the shortest distance, or the most "logical" way, but rather of a distance conceived according to the pictorial and structural needs of the artist, which often impose strange detours. The paths, however, all lead to the discovery of their true nature as paths.

Such a view of the novel is bound to raise considerable opposition. The lines are fairly clearly drawn between those who accept this view and those who deny it any validity at all. The former group includes readers who conceive the novel as having a vital part to play in man's constantly revised apprehension of reality, those who think that the myth has collected into a few essential patterns all possible accounts of the motive forces of the universe and that it is pointless to renew incessantly the individual details of such accounts, those who recognize in the use of language one of humanity's strangest adventures, those who demand an unprecedented effort on the part of the reader.

In opposition are readers who prefer to emphasize the subject matter of a novel organized according to man's more satisfactory dreams—knowledge, causality, teleology, transcendental truth—critics who believe that the well-established techniques of the realist and psychological novel are still adequate for the needs of fiction today, others who fear a decline of the novel into empty formalism, some who care only for the anecdote, some who measure the success of the story teller by the surrender of the reader to the illusion that has been created.

The writers of the new novel demand far more of the reader than acquiescence, or passive enjoyment of the novelist's skill. They require, on the contrary, a reader willing to transform himself into the co-operator of the text, by willingly infusing it with his own dynamism, in the same way that today's artists ask their public to set their work in motion by animating a mobile, turning on an electric current, or simply walking before a mirror. The public can no longer be regarded as a mere receiving apparatus. The participation of the reader is absolutely necessary, if texts like *La Bataille de Pharsale, Les Corps conducteurs, Triptyque* are to take on their multiple dimensions and grow continually with the inquiry that generates them. The reader must be prepared to follow this inquiry on as many levels and in as many directions as he can discover; yet he must remain always ready to return once more to the text in search of more paths, never sure he has exhausted their number. At a time when the audience for the novel appears restricted, Claude Simon is determined to increase his demands for collaboration from his public. The reader with equal determination will be rewarded with a creation whose richness and variety is due, in a large part, to his own efforts.

How can we summarize the contribution of Simon to the present state of the novel and its relationship to the world? Briefly, we can contend that he provides us with a means of relating all the variegated details of existence in original verbal structures valid on the planes of art, common experience, and thought.

The acuteness of Simon's perceptions is amply exemplified in any passage selected at random. To his artist's eye, the object stands out as something spatially and temporally unique. Our appreciation of Simon's description, however, does not depend on the individual features of the object, but on the arrangement in which it is found. The insistence on geometric patterns and collage does more than reveal the influence of Cubist art on Simon's writing. For the characteristic of the collage is that it destroys the artificial boundaries between the *objet d'art* and the real world. If we accept that everything in our minds—real, artifical, imaginary—is juxtaposed in much the same manner as objects in a collage, then the mass of images at our disposal can be considered as a collage too great to recognize in its totality. Through a selection, in which all varieties of elements are mixed, the artist makes us aware that all things are viewed according to their reference to other things and that this reference is not fixed. A piece of newspaper next to an imaginary sandwich forces us to re-examine our way of perceiving both and hence to think about art and the artist's intention. The objects in Simon's texts may be real or imaginary and are sometimes both, alternately, or at one and the same time. We are compelled by this insistent vacillation to put aside our preconceptions, to remain conscious of the function of representation in art, and also to be constantly aware of the milieu in which representation finally recognizes itself   the mind.

In Simon's novels a number of constantly recurring objects have also a second function: they serve as precipitators, in the chemical sense, of thought and feeling. The bird or plumed arrow evokes war, destruction, the passage of time; the horse refers not only to war, death, and time, but also to nature and its metamorphoses; cars, trains, subways, streetcars are the images of movement, repetition, and the hallucination of speed, while postcards, paintings, cross-sections, comic strips show that same speed frozen in immobility; newspapers and notebooks register the passing of time and the detachment of the word from the moment; the cigar box offers stylized images of the exotic and the unknown; the bank, its currency and buildings are the everlasting principle of encounter and exchange; machines, particularly agricultural combines, have both an erotic and a destructive connotation, while the moving cloud, the blowing curtain, the subway entrance, and the arched vault have links with eroticism and war. The people— boxers, soldiers, football players, women—are almost always shown in poses connected with combat or sexual encounter.

Each object is in itself a collage of several significant relationships. Grouped and repeated over and over again, these relationships are endlessly productive, they become more and more numerous and concentrate all of their force around three great themes: Time (including change, movement, repetition)', Combat (war, love, reproduction, play)', Exchange (money, mutation, rebirth). These are the Invariables of human life, which hold us prisoner in the center of an infernal triangle composed of our desires, our efforts, and our mortal fate. The obsessive repetition of these motifs makes us feel the weight of our material and metaphysical preoccupations. These may be as illusory as one pleases, but, as preoccupations, they are there, and Claude Simon reminds us of them relentlessly.

A geometrically formed crystallization of images, then, is irresistibly drawn together by the magnetism of our thoughts and feelings and builds up into designs both abstract and organic, like the stars in the night sky. As we are made conscious of the situation of the object in the design, we are forced to comprehend that nothing in this world, however insignificant it may appear, escapes the patterning process of the restless mind—nothing, unless it be the dissolvent, Death.

Without metaphysical asides, Simon follows the paths leading from one representation to the next and maps the territory where perception and reflection meet, where the real prompts the imaginary, and where questions are asked that have no answer. Unlike some of his contemporaries, he admits that such questions may be asked—or rather, that we ask them—whether they are valid or not. Behind the mask of anonymous humanity he constantly perceives the anxious face of the being who, aware of the uselessness of his cares and suppositions, nevertheless continues to be tormented by them.

Is this face in the process of being eliminated? The anonymous figure of *Les Corps conducteurs*, without physiognomy or history, surrounded by equally anonymous and indifferent objects, may seem very far from the living, individual, differentiated man. Yet he is surely as near to the ordinary mortal as the assassin, the obsessed or alienated being who appears in so many novels. This anonymous figure, although suffering, lucid, eager to make unrealizable contacts and communications, yet perceives the stars and the unchanging aspects of the earth. We may miss the richness of detail of novels like *L'Herbe* and *La Route des Flandres*. But we must recognize that these details, instead of revealing, often obscure the clear view of the weave that binds man to his surroundings, of the fundamental design that shows the work of the mind in the universe.

The difficulty for those who abandon knowledge of reality for the words that record our variable relationships with the real, lies in the fact that, if a certain residual knowledge is not preserved, the word loses its power of evocation and association. When Simon decides to leave the interpretation of the world to the Word, he is aware that the Word, before creating, was created, not by him but by millions of unknown voices, and that it carries with it an indefinable weight of knowledge and interpretation. He himself receives this charge before transmitting it to us and filters it through his own experience. As we in turn receive this interpretation, we find it bears the stamp of Zeno and the *Cimetière marin*, an overwhelming feeling of the mortality of man and the majestic and mechanical indifference of nature. Simon profits from this emotional reaction, a visceral reaction in most of us, and he pursues this advantage by insisting on the repetition and monotony of cyclical movements, by emphasizing the transforming power of nature, and by demonstrating the futility and evanescence of human plans.

The suggestion of man's insufficiency and impermanence appears veiled behind the curtain of words and images like a dimly lit, fading perspective. By placing before it the screen of language and thematic relationships, Simon manages to combine in a delicate equilibrium two designs that, in the history of art, have often been complementary: one builds around a certain sense—or non-sense—of tragic human destiny, the other distinguishes in this destiny a linguistic and artistic activity that surpasses it. As he continually reworks the patterns of the visible world, Simon shows us that, so far from being superficial, they correspond to the most secret constructs of our inner space and are, in fact, the language of these constructs. It has often been said that art transforms life. Simon's activity suggests that for such a transformation to take place, the artist must work constantly through this inner correspondence so that he can first transform art.

In *Les Corps conducteurs* we discern an ascent from the image of the explorer hacking his way with diminishing strength through the unconquerable jungle, up to the passenger seated comfortably in the airplane flying over earthly obstacles, and higher still to the unchanging mythological patterns in the stars. A desire for increasing detachment from the human condition is perhaps suggested here. And indeed, as our distance from the earth and its events increases, the outlines of possible designs become correspondingly clearer. Yet it is not at all certain that Simon is seeking merely to liberate himself through distance. His art depends also on the onrushing forces of disorder that the brave explorer is constantly called upon to repel; without them, the basic movement of Simon's novels would be meaningless. Without the forest, there are no paths; without the darkness, no light, without death, no life. Simon's work exists because of the dichotomy it denounces; this dichotomy is as basic as breathing, yet is distinguished from the simple business of living by the overwhelming need to *tell* about it and to tell with all the skill, variety, and persistence that his own gifts and his god—language—will allow.

Merely to tell is not sufficient: the telling must begin for the reader the process of transformation, enabling him to perceive the "something else"[21] that takes place during the act of writing. Toward this "something else" Claude Simon moves along continually new pathways. We have no reason to suppose that he is ready to eliminate the role of explorer on the pretext that the cartographer has fixed, once and for all, the map of all inner connections. The jungle grows back rapidly. No one knows this better than Claude Simon, for whom the adventure is always beginning. His companion in this adventure is the reader who, discovering through Simon's work fresh links between art, language, and his own perceptions of the world, is transformed to the extent that, coinciding with the desire of the author to make him "lose his time in mine, seek out my themes—my theme,"[22] he will never again read as simply or as idly as before.

21. *Entretiens,* p. 29. "While the writing proceeds, one perceives 'something else' creating itself (not that this happens all alone, of course) and the fact that this 'something else' is, finally, at least as far as I am concerned, much better than the original project, has never ceased to astound me." My translation.

22. Claude Simon in an interview with Claude Sarraute, quoted by Pierre Descaves in "Réalités du roman," *La Table Ronde* 157 (Jan. 1961), 165. My translation. The interview appeared in *Le Monde* (Oct. 8, 1960) and is reprinted in the Collection 10/18 edition of *La Route des Flandres.*

Selected Bibliography

Works by Claude Simon
Novels and Essays

Le Tricheur. Paris, Editions du Sagittaire, 1945.

La Corde raide. Paris, Editions du Sagittaire, 1947.

Gulliver, Paris, Calmann-Lévy, 1952.

Le Sacre du printemps. Paris, Calmann-Lévy, 1954.

Le Vent: Tentative de restitution d'un retable baroque. Paris, Editions de Minuit, 1957.

L'Herbe. Paris. Editions de Minuit, 1958.

La Route des Flandres Paris, Editions de Minuit, 1960. Reprinted in Collection 10/18, 1963.

Le Palace. Paris, Editions de Minuit, 1962. Reprinted in Collection 10/18, 1970.

Femmes (sur vingt-trois peintures de Joan Miró). Paris, Editions maeght, 1966. Reprinted in *Entretiens,* No. 31 (1972).

Histoire. Paris, Editions de Minuit, 1967. Reprinted in the Editions "Folio," 1973.

La Bataille de Pharsale. Paris, Editions de Minuit, 1969.

Orion aveugle. Geneva, Editions Albert Skira, 1970.

Les Corps conducteurs. Paris, Editions de Minuit, 1971.

Triptyque. Paris, Editions de Minuit, 1973.

A number of short texts by Claude Simon, printed in various periodicals, are not listed here, since most have been reprinted in the works noted above.

Articles and Interviews

"Claude Simon: Instantané." (G. D. Aubarède) *Les Nouvelles littéraires,* Nov. 7, 1957.

"Qu'est-ce que l'avant-garde en 1958? Réponse à une enquête." *Les Lettres françaises,* April 24–30, 1958.

"Un Bloc indivisible: Réponse à la question: Pourquoi des romans?" *Les Lettres françaises,* Dec. 4–10, 1958.

"Réponse à une enquête: Pensez-vous avoir un don d'écrivain?" *Tel Quel,* Spring 1960, pp. 38–43.

"Les Secrets d'un romancier." (H. Juin) *Les Lettres françaises,* Oct. 6–12, 1960.

"Techniciens du roman: Claude Simon." *Les Nouvelles littéraires,* Dec. 29, 1960.

"Images de Paris: Claude Simon." (C. Bourdet) *Revue de Paris,* Jan. 1961.

"Débat sur le roman." (A. Bourin) *Les Nouvelles littéraires,* June 22, 29, 1961.

"Entretien: Claude Simon parle." (M. Chapsal) *L'Express,* April 5, 1962.

"Je ne peux parler que de moi." *Les Nouvelles littéraires,* May 3, 1962.

"Débat: Le Romancier et la politique. Et si les écrivains jouaient le rôle de la presse du coeur? demande Claude Simon." *L'Express,* July 25, 1963.

"Pour qui écrit Sartre?" *L'Express,* May 28, 1964.

"Réponse à une enquête: Film et roman: problèmes du récit." Special number of *Cahiers du Cinéma,* Christmas 1966.

"Claude Simon: 'Le roman se fait, je le fais et il me fait.' " *Les Lettres françaises,* April 13–19, 1967.

"Rendre la perception confuse, multiple et simultanée du monde." *Le Monde,* April 26, 1967.

"Littérature: Tradition et révolution." *La Quinzaine litteraire,* May 1–15, 1967.

"Déclaration." *Nouvel Observateur,* May 15, 1967.

"Remarques sur le livre de J. Ricardou, sous le titre *Problèmes du Nouveau Roman:* Trois avis autorisés (Claude Ollier, Philippe Sollers, Claude Simon)." *Les Lettres françaises,* Oct. 11–17, 1967.

"Entretien avec Claude Simon. 'Il n'y a pas d'art réaliste.' " *La Quinzaine littéraire,* Dec. 15–30, 1967.

"Le Roman par les romanciers." *Europe,* Oct. 1968.

"Claude Simon sur les sentiers de la création." (K. Biro-Thierback) *Gazette littéraire,* June 27, 1970.

"Interview avec Claude Simon." (B. Knapp) *Kentucky Romance Quarterly,* No. 2 (1970).

"L'Opinion des nouveaux romanciers: Commentaire de Claude Simon . . . sur le livre de Jean Ricardou (*Pour une théorie du Nouveau Roman*)." *La Quinzaine littéraire,* July 1–15, 1971.

"Réponses de Claude Simon à quelques questions écrites de Ludovic Janvier." *Entretiens,* No. 31 (1972).

"Interview with Claude Simon." (C. DuVerlie.) *Sub-stance,* Feb.–March 1974.

Translations of Simon's Works into English

Translated by Richard Howard:

The Wind. New York, George Braziller, 1959.

The Grass. New York, George Braziller; London, Jonathan Cape, 1960.

The Flanders Road. New York, George Braziller; London, Jonathan Cape, 1961.

The Palace. New York, George Braziller; London, Jonathan Cape, 1963.

Histoire. New York, George Braziller; London, Jonathan Cape, 1967.

The Battle of Pharsalus. New York, George Braziller; London, Jonathan Cape, 1971.

Translated by Helen R. Lane:

Conducting Bodies. New York, Viking; London, Calder & Boyars; Canada, The Macmillan Company of Canada, 1974.

Studies of Claude Simon's Work

Berger, Yves. "L'Enfer, Le Temps." *La nouvelle revue française,* No. 97 (Jan. 1961), 95–109.

Bishop, Thomas. "Fusion of Then and Now." *Saturday Review,* March 30, 1968, p. 28.

——. "La Vue d'Orion ou le processus de la création." *Entretiens,* No. 31 (1972), 35–39.

——. "L'Image de la création chez Claude Simon." In *Nouveau Roman: Hier, aujourd'hui.* Paris, Collection 10/18, 1972, 2 vols., II, 61–71.

Bjurström, C.-G. "Dimensions du temps chez Claude Simon." *Entretiens,* No. 31 (1972), 141–158.

Caminade, Pierre. "Déjeuner avec l'herbe." *Entretiens,* No. 31 (1972), 117–119.

Chapsal, Madeleine. *Quinze Écrivains.* Paris, René Julliard, 1963, pp. 163–171.

Deguy, Michel. "Claude Simon et la représentation." *Critique* 187 (Dec. 1962), 1009–1032.

Descaves, Pierre. "Réalités du roman." *La Table Ronde* 157, (Jan. 1961), 163–172.

Doubrovsky, Serge. "Notes sur la genèse d'une écriture." *Entretiens,* No. 31 (1972), 51–64.

DuVerlie, Claud. "Pour un *Comment j'ai écrit certains de mes livres* de Claude Simon." *Romance Notes* 14 (1972), 217–222.

——. "Sur deux oeuvres récentes de Claude Simon." *Die neueren Sprachen* 21 (1972), 543–549.

Fitch, Brian. "Participe présent et procédés narratifs chez Claude Simon." *Revue des lettres modernes* 94–99 (1964), 199–216.

Fletcher, John. "Claude Simon and the Memory Enigma." In *New Directions in Literature.* London, Calder & Boyars, 1968, pp. 116–128.

——. "Erotisme et création ou la mort en sursis." *Entretiens,* No. 31 (1972), 131–140.

Frohock, W. M. "Continuities in the New Novel." In *Style and*

Temper. Cambridge, Mass., Harvard University Press, 1967, pp. 122–127.

Guicharnaud, Jacques. "Remembrance of Things Passing: Claude Simon." *Yale French Studies* 24 (Summer 1959), 101–108.

Heath, Stephen. *The Nouveau Roman: A Study in the Practice of Writing.* Philadelphia, Temple University Press, 1972.

Howlett, J. "La Route des Flandres." *Les Lettres nouvelles,* Dec. 1960, pp. 178–181.

Janvier, Ludovic. *Une Parole exigeante: Le Nouveau Roman.* Paris, Editions de Minuit, 1964.

———. "Sur le trajet de ces corps." *Entretiens,* No. 31 (1972), 69–80.

Jean, Raymond. "Pour saluer *La Route des Flandres,*" in *La Littérature et le réel: De Diderot au Nouveau Roman.* Paris, Albin Michel, 1965, 214–218.

———. "Commencements romanesques." In *Positions et oppositions sur le roman contemporain,* ed. M. Mansuy. Actes et Colloques 8, Actes du Colloque de Strasbourg; Paris, Klincksieck, 1971, pp. 129–136.

———. "Les Signes de l'éros." *Entretiens,* No. 31 (1972), 121–129.

Lancereaux, D. "Modalités de la narration dans *La Route des Flandres.*" *Poétique* 14 (1973), 235–249.

Lesage, Laurent. "Claude Simon et l'Ecclésiaste." *Revue des lettres modernes* 94–99 (1964), 217–223.

Levitt, Morton P. "The Burden of History." *Kenyon Review* 31 (1969), 128–134.

———. "Disillusionments and Epiphany: The Novels of Claude Simon." *Critique: Studies in Modern Fiction* 12 (1970), 43–71.

Mauriac, Claude. *L'alittérature contemporaine.* Paris, Albin Michel, 1969, pp. 292–305.

Mercier, Vivian. "Claude Simon: Order and Disorder." *Shenandoah* 17, 4 (Summer 1966), 79–92.

———. "James Joyce and the French New Novel." *TriQuarterly* 8 (1967), 205–219.

Merleau-Ponty, Maurice. "Cinq Notes sur Claude Simon." *Médiations* 4 (Winter 1961–1962), 5–9. Reprinted in *Entretiens,* No. 31 (1972), 41–46.

Morrissette, Bruce. "The New Novel in France." *Chicago Review,* 15, 3 (1962), 1–19.

Pellegrin, Jean. "Du mouvement et de l'immobilité de Reixach." *Revue d'esthétique* 25 (1972), 335–349.

Pingaud, Bernard. "Sur la Route des Flandres." *Les Temps modernes* 178 (Feb. 1961), 1026–1037.

———. *Ecrivains d'aujourd'hui.* Paris, Grasset, 1961, pp. 471–477.

Pugh, Anthony. "Simon: The Narrator and His Double." In *Direction in the Nouveau Roman.* Canterbury, University of Kent Press, 1971, pp. 30–40.

Raillard, G. *"Triptyque." Les Cahiers du chemin* 18 (April 15, 1973), 96–106.

Ricardou, Jean. *Problèmes du Nouveau Roman.* Paris, Editions du Seuil, 1967.

———. "La Bataille de la phrase." *Critique* 26 (March 9, 1970), 226–256. Reprinted in *Pour une théorie du Nouveau Roman,* Paris, Editions du Seuil, 1971, pp. 118–158. From this same study the chapter "L'Essence et les sens," pp. 200–210, is reprinted in *Entretiens,* No. 31 (1972), 104–112.

———. *Le Nouveau Roman.* Paris, Editions du Seuil, 1973.

———. "Un Tour d'écrou textuel" (sur *Triptyque*). *Magazine littéraire* 74 (March 1973).

Rossum-Guyon, Françoise van. "De Claude Simon à Proust: Un Exemple d'intertextualité." *Les Lettres nouvelles,* Sept. 1972, pp. 107–137.

———. "Ut pictura poesis: Une Lecture de *La Bataille de Pharsale." Degrés* 3 (July 1973), k–k15.

Roudiez, L. S. *French Fiction Today: A New Direction.* New Brunswick, Rutgers University Press, 1972, pp. 152–182.

Rousset, Jean. "Trois Romans de la mémoire: Butor, Pinget, Simon." In *Formalisme et Signification. Cahiers Internationaux de Symbolisme* 9–10 (1965–1966), 79–81.

Séguier, Marcel. "Proposition en lieu et place d'un avant-propos à une réflexion collective." *Entretiens*, No. 31 (1972), 9–13.

————. Le Langage à la casse." *Entretiens*, No. 31 (1972), 81–95.

Seylaz, Jean-Luc. "Du *Vent* à *La Route des Flandres:* La Conquête d'une forme romanesque." *Revue des lettres modernes* 94–99 (1964), 225–240.

Simon, Claude. "La Fiction mot à mot." In *Nouveau Roman: Hier, aujourd'hui*. Paris, Collection 10/18, 1972, II, 73–97.

Simon, John K. "Perception and Metaphor in the 'New Novel': Notes on Robbe-Grillet, Claude Simon and Butor." *Tri-Quarterly* No. 4 (1965), 153–182.

Sturrock, John. *The French New Novel: Claude Simon, Michel Butor, Alain Robbe-Grillet*. London, Oxford University Press, 1969.

Wilhelm, Kurt. "Claude Simon als 'nouveau romancier.' " *Zeitschrift für französische Sprache und Literatur* 75 (1965), 309–352. Reprinted in *Der "Nouveau Roman": Ein Experiment der französischen Gegenwartsliteratur*, Berlin, E. Schmidt Verlag, 1969, pp. 43–103.

Books on the Novel and the "New Novel"

Only a few indications can be given here. One could start with the bibliography of the *Encyclopédie du Nouveau Roman* by Pierre Astier (Paris, Debresse, 1969) and with Astier's *La Crise du roman francais et le nouveau réalisme* (Paris, Nouvelles Editions Debresse, 1968). Some periodicals have published special numbers on this subject, for example, *Esprit* (July 1958 and July 1964) *Yale French Studies* 24 (Summer 1959), *Revue des lettres modernes* 94–99 (1964), *Marche Romane* 21, 1–2 (1971). Of great importance is the collective work of the Centre Culturel de Cerisy-la-Salle, *Nouveau Roman: Hier, aujourd'hui* (Paris, Collection 10/18, 1972), 2 vols.

Index

The Novels of Claude Simon

Designed by R. E. Rosenbaum.
Composed by York Composition Company, Inc.,
in 11 point Intertype Baskerville, 2 points leaded,
with display lines in monotype Deepdene.
Printed letterpress from type by York Composition Company
on P & S Offset Vellum, 60 pound basis.
Bound by Vail-Ballou Press
and stamped in All Purpose foil.